# Dark Nights, Deadly Waters

# DARK NIGHTS, DEADLY WATERS

*American PT Boats at Guadalcanal*

## KEITH WARREN LLOYD

LYONS
PRESS

*Essex, Connecticut*

An imprint of The Globe Pequot Publishing Group, Inc.
64 South Main Street
Essex, CT 06426
www.globepequot.com

Distributed by NATIONAL BOOK NETWORK

British Library Cataloguing in Publication Information available

**Library of Congress Cataloging-in-Publication Data**
Names: Lloyd, Keith Warren, author.
Title: Dark nights, deadly waters: American PT boats at Guadalcanal / Keith Warren Lloyd.
Other titles: American PT boats at Guadalcanal
Description: Essex, Connecticut: Lyons Press, 2023. | Includes bibliographical references and index.
Identifiers: LCCN 2023007959 (print) | LCCN 2023007960 (ebook) | ISBN 9781493072064 (cloth) | ISBN 9781493072071 (epub)
Subjects: LCSH: Guadalcanal, Battle of, Solomon Islands, 1942–1943. | Torpedo-boats—United States—History—20th century. | World War, 1939-1945—Pacific Area. | World War, 1939–1945—Naval operations, American.
Classification: LCC D767.98 .L569 2023 (print) | LCC D767.98 (ebook) | DDC 940.54/265933—dc23/eng/20230413
LC record available at https://lccn.loc.gov/2023007959
LC ebook record available at https://lccn.loc.gov/2023007960

*To fellow sailors—past, present, and future.*

*"Any man who may be asked in this century what he did to make his life worthwhile, I think can respond with a good deal of pride and satisfaction: I served in the United States Navy."*

—President John F. Kennedy
August 1963

# Contents

# PROLOGUE

## *Solomon's Gold*

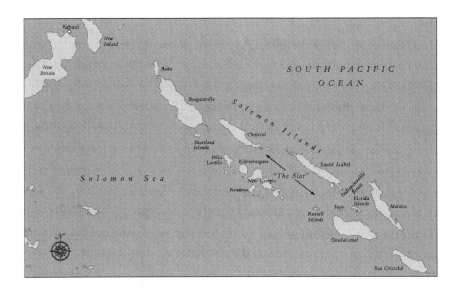

"It is scarcely believable that I can remember it with pleasure, and affection and a sense of beauty," the soldier-turned-author James Jones would write. "One can hardly credit that a place so full of personal misery and terror, which was perfectly capable of taking your life and on a couple of occasions very nearly did, could be remembered with such kindly feelings, but I do. The pervasive mud, jungle gloom and tropical sun, when they are not all around you smothering you, have a haunting beauty at a far remove. When you are not straining and gasping to save your life, the act of doing so can seem adventurous and exciting from a distance. The greater the distance the greater the adventure. But, God help me, it was beautiful."

Rising in dramatic relief from the floor of the sea, the island's verdant peaks soar to a height of 7,000 feet, their rugged purple crests clear and sharp against the backdrop of a brilliantly blue tropical sky. Upon approaching the leeward coast, the mariner's eye will take in the sparkling turquoise water and foaming white surf lapping onto gently sloping beaches of golden sand, backed by swaying coconut palms. The eye is then drawn irresistibly into the dense hinterland beyond, a dark mass of tangled rainforest and green plains of kunai grass rippling in the ever-present sea breeze.

But a tropical paradise it is not, the island's seemingly idyllic features belying the many and varied perils to be found within. The softly waving fields of kunai grass serve as a fitting example. Appearing lush and pleasing from a distance, kunai grass will grow taller than the height of a man and is as sharp as a bayonet along its edge. The grassy plains themselves are flanked by many acres of mangrove swamps, the miasmic breeding grounds for millions upon millions of malaria-bearing mosquitoes. The blazing equatorial sun maintains the temperature of the dank air at a near-constant 85 degrees Fahrenheit. Frequent tropical rains, often exceeding 100 inches in a year, keep the dark volcanic soil a soft, fetid, and disease-ridden quagmire and the surrounding jungle a miserable, dripping steambath. The landscape is vigorously defended against all trespassers by intrusive clouds of biting insects, scorpions, venomous coral snakes, leeches, huge scuttling land crabs, and giant creeping centipedes. In the numerous coastal estuaries, saltwater crocodiles doze beneath the nearly stagnant, scum-covered surface.

It was not until 1568 that the existence of the island was even known to Europeans. In the summer of that year a 150-man expedition of sailors, soldiers, cartographers, and priests, led by the Spanish explorer Álvaro de Mendaña de Neira, departed the shores of Peru aboard the sister galleons *Los Reyes* and *Todos Santos*, sailing westward into the vast reaches of the South Pacific. Several weeks later, in dire need of food and fresh water and their numbers thinned by scurvy, the explorers landed on the island's northern coast.

Discovering flecks of alluvial gold along the muddy banks of one of the island's many rivers, Mendaña would conclude, with the sort of sixteenth-century conquistadorian logic that boggles the twenty-first-century mind, that he had found the source of Solomon's gold, nearly 9,000 miles from that ancient Hebrew king's Levantine stomping ground. Mendaña therefore declared that the surrounding archipelago should be called the Solomon Islands, while granting permission for one of his subalterns, Pedro de Ortega Valencia, to name this particular island after his Andalusian hometown: Guadalcanal.

"The Terrible Solomons," as a visiting Jack London would eventually call them, lie approximately 400 miles to the east of New Guinea's tail and about 1,300 miles to the northeast across the Coral Sea from Brisbane, Australia. The chain consists of 6 rather large and 900 smaller islands and islets, arranged in two roughly parallel columns stretching northwest to southeast for nearly a thousand miles, the columns separated by a long and narrow sound that plunges to a depth of over 20,000 feet.

Beginning with Mendaña, the explorers of rival European empires would call upon the Solomons at varying intervals over the next three centuries, seeking gold, spices, slaves, or whatever else they could find to pillage or exploit for the glory of their respective kings under the justifying banner of Christendom. Ignoring centuries-old place names given to the different islands by their Melanesian tribal natives, the explorers would rename several in honor of sponsoring nobles or beloved homelands.

After the Spanish had their turn christening Guadalcanal, San Cristobal, Malaita, Florida, and Santa Isabel, the French would arrive to name one of the larger islands Choiseul, in honor of the foreign minister that served Louis XV. The leader of the French expedition, Louis Antoine de Bougainville, bestowed his own name upon the largest of the Solomons, located on the northwestern end of the chain. Then came the British, who established a crown protectorate over the Solomons and dubbed four of the lesser island groups within the archipelago the Treasuries, the Shortlands, the Russells, and the New Georgias.

The transecting channel, which ran from the Shortlands on the northwestern end to Savo Island on the southeast, would thereafter be labeled as New Georgia Sound on Admiralty charts. A few of the islands would remain relatively unbothered by Europeans and retain their exotic-sounding Melanesian names: Buka, Vella Lavella, Kolombangara, Savo, Gavutu, Tonambogo.

Aside from the local Melanesian population largely forsaking the practice of head hunting and cannibalism, by the year 1941 the Solomons were hardly more civilized than they had been in Mendaña's time. As their ancestors had done for literally thousands of years, most native islanders lived and worked contentedly in their primitive coastal villages, eking out a modest existence by fishing, hunting wild pigs, and subsistence farming local root vegetables like taro and sweet potatoes. Modern amenities such as electricity and clean running water were virtually nonexistent, and the primary means of transportation remained the dugout canoe.

A far-flung and mostly forgotten backwater of the British Empire, the Solomons were home to fewer than a thousand whites, most of whom were British, Australians, and New Zealanders employed as foreign service officers, interisland steamship captains, missionaries, oil prospectors, or plantation managers. The chief export was copra, the dried kernels of coconut meat used in the manufacture of vegetable oils, and copra plantations were by far the largest employers in the islands. A handful of District and Patrol Officers of His Majesty's Colonial Service, along with their cadre of native policemen, maintained law and order, collected taxes, performed customs inspections, mediated disputes between native tribes, and managed a host of other governmental affairs.

The sheltered anchorage of Tulagi Harbor, seat of the British Solomon Islands Protectorate 20 miles north of Guadalcanal, was the only modern settlement of any appreciable size. There a small collection of government offices, the Resident Commissioner's house, an obsolescent wireless station, an executive golf course, a cricket pitch, a ten-room hotel, a small government-run hospital, and a Chinese mercantile district were situated along the waterfront. The Tulagi Club, an exclusive, private clubroom of the type found in every British overseas holding from Kingston to Calcutta to Hong Kong, featured a bar with billiard tables, tennis courts, and a swimming pool. The only military presence in the archipelago was a detachment of two dozen commandoes of the Australian Army's 1st Independent Company stationed on Tulagi and a like number of Royal Australian Air Force (RAAF) personnel operating a seaplane base on the nearby conjoined islets of Gavutu-Tanambogo.

The residents of the Solomons would probably have continued to live in peaceful isolation and obscurity for many years, and perhaps would still be doing so even today, had it not been the desire of the militant Empire of Japan to bring the islands into their proclaimed "Greater East Asia Co-Prosperity Sphere." In 1931, Japan subjugated neighboring Manchuria, and since 1937 had been executing a brutal and protracted war of conquest on the Chinese mainland. On September 27, 1940, the Japanese signed the Tripartite Agreement to form a military alliance with Nazi Germany and Fascist Italy, two nations already at war with Great Britain. That same week, Japanese troops forcibly occupied Vietnam in French Indochina, a move that was seen as a direct threat to British-controlled Malaya and Singapore.

A near-total dependency on foreign oil, however, served as the Achilles' heel of the Japanese military juggernaut. Over 80 percent of Japan's oil was imported from the United States, with the remainder coming mostly from British Borneo and the Dutch East Indies. In an effort to curb further Japanese aggression in the Far East, in July 1941 the government of the United States imposed a full-scale oil embargo against Japan. This was accompanied by the closure of the Panama Canal to Japanese shipping, the freezing of Japanese financial assets in the United States, and a ban on further shipments to Japan of high-octane aviation gasoline and scrap metal used in the manufacture of war material. The British and Dutch were quick to follow with painful sanctions of their own, completely cutting off Japan's access to foreign oil.

On December 7, 1941, the Japanese suddenly attacked the American naval base at Pearl Harbor, Hawaii, with over 300 carrier-based aircraft, killing 2,400 Americans and destroying or heavily damaging eighteen ships of the US Pacific Fleet, including eight battleships. The attack represented the first objective outlined in the Imperial Japanese Navy's

"Operation Order Number 1," which had been signed into action by the Commander-in-Chief of the Combined Fleet, Admiral Isoroku Yamamoto, aboard his flagship *Nagato* in Saeki Bay on November 5.

"In the east, the United States Fleet will be destroyed and United States lines of operation and supply lines extending toward the Far East will be cut," the order stated. "In the west, British Malaya will be invaded and the Burma route, British lines of operations and supply lines extending toward the east will be cut. The enemy forces in the Orient will be destroyed and enemy bases of operations and areas rich in natural resources will be captured."

American, British, and Commonwealth forces in the Far East, which had long considered themselves militarily superior to the Japanese in nearly every category, were caught completely off-guard by an Asian rendition of *blitzkrieg* warfare that swept rapidly across the Pacific Basin with stunning efficiency. The strategic and tactical coordination of Japanese naval units along with their seamanship, gunnery, skilled use of torpedoes, and proficiency in night combat far exceeded their supposed capabilities. Japanese naval aviators proved among the best in the world, and in their hands new combat aircraft such as the Mitsubishi A6M Zero fighter easily outperformed their British and American opponents. The Japanese soldier, thought to be comically doltish, nearsighted, physically weak, and no serious threat to the armies of the west, instead displayed remarkable endurance, skill, and tenacity on the field of battle. In short, the Japanese were performing what was thought to be the impossible, and at a frightening pace.

Within hours of the attack on Pearl Harbor, Japanese bombers flying from airfields in Formosa swiftly neutralized American air power in the Philippines. Japanese forces then seized the American territory of Guam and invaded Burma, Thailand, the Philippines, and Malaya. By Christmas, the exhausted and surrounded American and Filipino troops of General Douglas MacArthur were withdrawing to defensive positions on Luzon's Bataan Peninsula. The British had surrendered Hong Kong. The stubborn defenders of Wake Island, an American base 2,300 miles west of Hawaii, had likewise been forced to capitulate. The Japanese then landed on British Borneo to begin seizing the coveted oil fields.

Singapore would fall next, an utter debacle that resulted in the surrender of 80,000 British and Commonwealth troops.

"When I reflect on how I have longed and prayed for the entry of the United States into the war," British Prime Minister Winston S. Churchill stated in a personal cable to US President Franklin D. Roosevelt, "I find it difficult to realize how gravely our British affairs have deteriorated by what has happened since December 7. We have suffered the greatest disaster in our history at Singapore, and other misfortunes will come thick and fast upon us. Your great power will only become effective gradually because of vast distances and the shortage of ships. It is not easy to assign limits to the Japanese aggression."

The ultimate goal of Japan's campaign of destruction against Allied forces in the Far East and the near-simultaneous capture of their overseas military installations was "to establish a policy of autonomous self-sufficiency and economic independence." Known as the "Southern Plan," the capture and consolidation of British and Dutch possessions in Southeast Asia would secure vast reserves of crude oil, rubber, rice, metal ores, and other strategic resources vital to the continued expansion of the Japanese Empire.

In the days following their invasion of the Dutch East Indies, Japanese forces would push even farther into the southern hemisphere. Following an intense bombardment by carrier-based planes on January 23, 1942, the Imperial Japanese Army's South Seas Detachment, a brigade of 5,000 rigorously trained and disciplined light infantry seconded to the navy's 4th Fleet, stormed ashore on the island of New Britain in the Bismarck Archipelago. The invasion force quickly routed the garrison of Australian troops based in and around the port city of Rabaul, just 175 miles from Buka, the northernmost of the Solomon Islands. Almost immediately the Japanese began transforming Rabaul and its excellent anchorage, Simpson Harbor, into a major air and naval base complex to support further conquests.

That was quite enough for the European inhabitants of the Solomons, most of whom fled for Australia or New Zealand after the Japanese landed at Buka in early March. For the duration of the war, the majority of native tribes dispersed throughout the islands would remain steadfastly loyal to the British Crown, while the allegiance of a few swayed with the wind like indigenous coconut palms—and the prevailing wind was coming from Tokyo. As the Japanese closed in, several British and Commonwealth planters, mission teachers, prospectors, and colonial administrators living in the Solomons gathered caches of weapons, ammunition, and supplies. Then, equipped with government-issued wireless radio sets and accompanied by their most devoted native scouts, they melted into the jungle highlands.

As commissioned officers in the volunteer reserve of the Royal Australian Navy or the British Solomon Island Protectorate Defence Force, they were to serve as "coastwatchers," setting up observation posts and clandestine radio stations, gathering intelligence, and reporting on the strength and disposition of Japanese forces operating in the Solomons. The early warning and human intelligence they would relay to friendly forces over the course of the next two years would prove invaluable, and is credited with saving the lives of countless Allied soldiers, sailors, and airmen. The coastwatcher organization would be code-named "Ferdinand" by its officer-in-charge, Commander Eric Feldt of the Naval Intelligence Center in Townsville, Australia. The name had been taken from Munroe Leaf's character of the pacifistic bull, made popular by a 1938 Walt Disney animated film.

"It was a reminder to them that it was not their duty to fight, and thus draw attention to themselves," Feldt would later record. "Like Disney's bull, who just sat under a tree and smelled the flowers, it was their duty to sit, circumspectly and unobtrusively, and gather information. Of course, like Ferdinand, they could fight if they were stung."

The Imperial Japanese General Staff would begin planning two more southward thrusts immediately following the capture of Rabaul, each spearheaded by the 4th Fleet under Vice Admiral Shigeyoshi Inouye. Two ports on the Papuan Peninsula, Lae and Salamaua, were to be seized during the second week of March 1942. In early April, the South Seas Detachment would launch an amphibious invasion against the Allied base of Port Moresby, while elements of the Special Naval Landing Force would assault Tulagi in the Solomons and begin developing the island as a seaplane base and naval anchorage.

Should this come to pass, the result would be an even more isolated Australia, with Japanese forces dominating the continent's northern and eastern approaches. Long-range reconnaissance aircraft and seaplanes fanning out from these newly acquired Japanese bases would ensure that no Allied convoy steaming westward from the United States would be safe. Troop transports, cargo ships and their escorts would be forced to run a deadly gauntlet of Japanese land-based bombers and submarines, or perhaps even cruisers and destroyers, undoubtedly sustaining heavy losses while fighting their way to Australia.

If the Allies yielded the Solomons, the idea of consolidating Australia into a base for future offensive operations in the western Pacific would most likely have to be abandoned. Where the next Japanese hammer blow would then land was anyone's guess: The New Hebrides, New Caledonia, Fiji, American Samoa, New Zealand, or even Australia itself would be laid bare to invasion.

# CHAPTER ONE

# The Mosquito Fleet

"This young man has run away from home. He's underage and not entitled to enlistment. I want you to cancel it and send him home."

Senator Francis E. Warren of Wyoming lifted his eyes from the telegram on his desk and fixed his gaze upon the man sitting before him. The youngster was rather short and slight of build, with light-colored hair and eyes, high cheekbones and a pair of protruding ears that seemed much too large for his head. But he also carried himself with a certain quiet confidence and possessed the rough hands, sunbrowned face, and well-worn, practical clothing of a seasoned ranch hand. Something wasn't adding up.

As it turned out, the message had been a lie, the desperate act of an anxious father. Emory Scott Land was, in fact, nineteen years of age and therefore quite old enough to enlist in the army. It was the spring of 1898, and the United States of America had just declared war on Spain. Without bothering to notify his parents, "Jerry" Land had left home and caught a ride on an eastbound freight train for Cheyenne with the intention of joining the Rough Riders, a regiment of volunteer cavalry being raised by Theodore Roosevelt. Land's father, a prominent cattleman from Laramie, was seeking Senator Warren's help in foiling the plan, most likely at the urging of the young man's panic-stricken mother.

"Do you want to serve your country?" Warren asked sympathetically.

"Yes, sir," the deeply embarrassed Land replied.

"Well, why don't you take the examination for the Naval Academy?" Warren suggested. "You're supposed to be a bright young man. The examination will be held next week here in Cheyenne."

After returning to Laramie "with his tail between his legs," as Land himself would later admit, he thought the matter over and decided to return the following week to sit for the exam. Three months later, and having never before seen an ocean, Land found himself boarding another eastbound train for Annapolis, Maryland. He would finish fourth among the Naval Academy Class of 1902 with the rank of cadet lieutenant commander. Sick with fever on the day of graduation, Land was astonished when his exalted hero, Theodore Roosevelt, who by then had become president of the United States, appeared suddenly at his bedside to present his diploma.

The day would mark the beginning of a distinguished career of naval service that would span the next four decades. After two years of sea duty with the Asiatic Fleet aboard the battleship *Oregon*, Land was sent to the Massachusetts Institute of Technology to obtain a post-graduate degree in naval architecture. Becoming a specialist in submarine construction, he was a chief designer for the navy's pioneering *S*-class of submarines in the 1920s. Brilliant, innovative, and a tireless worker—he would continue working as a consultant for General Dynamics right up until his death at the age of ninety-two—Land collected many decorations and accolades as he moved steadily up the ranks of the officer corps.

After being selected for flag rank in 1932, Rear Admiral Land became chief of the Bureau of Construction and Repair, the forerunner of the Bureau of Ships. An outspoken proponent of standardization with regard to naval construction, Land believed the navy should invest in ships of simple, efficient, and functional design that, in time of war, could be produced on a massive scale by many different shipyards. As the navy's construction chief, and later as chairman of the US Maritime Commission during World War II, Land would champion a long list of highly successful ship design projects, which included the *Gato*-class fleet submarine, the *Fletcher*-class destroyer, the Liberty cargo ship, and the Patrol Torpedo (PT) boat.

The motor torpedo boat, a small, speedy craft capable of launching self-propelled torpedoes, had been in use by the navies of many foreign nations since the late nineteenth century. Knowing that they could never hope to match the tremendous power of the Royal Navy on the high seas, the French developed the *Jeune École*, or "young school" concept of naval warfare, which called for high-speed torpedo boats and submarines to diminish the strength of a larger enemy battle fleet with aggressive hit-and-run attacks.

In the initial stages of its development, the Imperial Japanese Navy embraced the *Jeune École* strategy, purchasing two dozen torpedo boats laid down in French and British shipyards. At the Battle of Tsushima in May 1905, after a Russian armada of fifty ships had been utterly decimated in a daylight surface action by the superior gunnery of Japanese battleships, surviving Russian vessels were then subjected to relentless nocturnal attacks by Japanese torpedo boats, which led to the total capitulation of the Russian fleet the following morning.

The *Motoscafo Armato Silurante*, or MAS torpedo boat, was used with deadly effectiveness by the Italian Navy during the First World War, performing many daring raids against the Austro-Hungarian battle fleet in the Adriatic Sea. In December 1917, two MAS boats roared into the port of Trieste and launched two torpedoes that sank the coastal defense ship *Wien* at her berth. The Italians would score again in spectacular fashion on June 10, 1918, when the *MAS-15* sent two torpedoes crashing into the Austro-Hungarian dreadnought battleship *Szent István* off the coast of Croatia. After losing propulsion and developing a heavy list, the *Szent István* capsized and sank with the loss of eighty-nine lives, a visually dramatic event famously captured on film from the decks of a nearby escort ship.

In the years following the First World War, the *Regia Marina* continued to produce faster and more deadly classes of MAS boats. The Coastal Forces of the Royal Navy also made extensive use of what they classified as MTBs, the most ubiquitous being the Vosper 70-footer, while the Germans developed the *schnellboot* fast attack craft, later known to Allied forces as the E-boat.

Historically, the US Navy had shown very little interest in the development of small combatant craft like the motor torpedo boat. The reason for this was quite simple. After suffering through many decades of neglect and decline, the navy enjoyed an invigorating renaissance beginning in the 1890s. Spurred on by the work of visionary navalists such as Alfred Thayer Mahan, Benjamin Tracy, and Theodore Roosevelt, the United States amassed a robust fleet of modern steel-clad, steam-driven battleships and cruisers. The navy's mandate was to ensure the safe and unfettered communication of seaborne commerce, protect American interests abroad by the forward projection of seapower, and in time of war, concentrate its forces to destroy the enemy fleet with the use of overwhelming firepower. It was—and still is—a "blue water navy."

American naval strategists tended to view the motor torpedo boat as a purely defensive weapon, more suitable for protecting shorelines and harbors against attacks by marauding enemy warships. The French, Japanese, Italians, and British may have previously employed motor torpedo boats in the littoral environment with marked success, but these were nations geographically positioned in close proximity to their enemies. The tremendously long coastline of the United States might be unfortified and exposed, but any potential attacker would be required to steam across one of two vast oceans in order to reach it. The mission of the US Navy, by design an offensive force, was to locate and sink a hostile fleet long before it came within sight of American shores.

A period of rapid overseas expansion occurred with the coming of the twentieth century, however, and for the first time the United States began acquiring territory abroad. After the brief but vicious war with Spain in 1898, the Philippines, Puerto Rico, and Guam were ceded to the United States. The following year, the Stars and Stripes was raised over the Hawaiian Islands. By 1914, a transisthmus canal had been completed in Panama and was being operated under American control. It had been deemed necessary to garrison all of these new acquisitions with American troops, and to establish a network of "advanced bases" for the US battle fleet.

The advanced base provided for the fueling, repair, and replenishment of naval vessels, along with facilities for the rest and recuperation of their crews. This allowed warships to remain forward-deployed for longer periods, patrolling vital commercial shipping lanes, extending American naval power and hegemony into a selected region, and returning to the mainland United States only periodically for major repairs, reconditioning, and the rotation of personnel. Units of the fleet frequently called upon advanced bases at Cuba's Guantanamo Bay, Panama's Galeta Island, Cavite in the Philippines, or Pearl Harbor in Hawaii. After only a few day's respite, they were back at sea and underway to continue their mission. It was therefore necessary for the advanced base to be capable of defending itself, using military units stationed at or near the installation for that purpose. These were usually the composite defense battalions of the US Marine Corps, the US Army's Coastal Artillery Corps units, and the land-based fighter and bomber squadrons of the US Army Air Corps.

In 1920, Major Earl H. "Pete" Ellis, an intelligence officer on the staff of Marine Corps Commandant John A. Lejeune, completed an exhaustive reconnaissance of the islands of the Central Pacific and reported his findings in the landmark *Operation Plan 712, Advanced Base Operations in Micronesia.* Rife as it was with the sort of ill-considered rhetoric that helped perpetuate a widespread perception of Japanese mental and physical inferiority, and thus a gross underestimation of a future enemy's military prowess, Ellis's work otherwise reads like an oracle's prophesy with regard to the coming Pacific War. It would serve as a guidebook for the development of amphibious warfare doctrine and the defense of advanced bases for both the Fleet Marine Force and the US Navy.

"The defense must be such as to leave the greatest possible mobile sea and air force free for its legitimate work: the destruction of enemy sea and air power," Ellis wrote. "When the advanced base fixed and mobile air defense does not effect the degree of security desired on account of natural harbor characteristics or other reasons, a mobile sea defense as needed must be assigned to supplement them . . . the defense would normally consist of the following types: patrol boats with light guns, antiaircraft guns and depth bombs; mine sweepers; destroyers, submarines and aircraft assigned for counterattack."

Rear Admiral Land, himself a naval visionary, viewed the motor torpedo boat as just the sort of "mobile sea defense" platform the navy required for the security of its overseas bases, as advocated by planning officers like Pete Ellis. On December 5, 1936, Land wrote a memorandum on the subject for the Chief of Naval Operations, Admiral William H. Standley.

"Developments since the war of the motor torpedo boat type, then known as Coastal Motor Boats, have been continuous and marked in most European navies," Land wrote. "There has been considerable interest in the fundamentals of the type among the small boat designers and builders in this country, out of a patriotic desire to develop pleasure boats which may be of value for naval use in the event of mobilization."

"The results being obtained in the foreign services are such as to indicate that vessels of considerable military effectiveness for the defense of local areas are being built, the possibilities of which should not be allowed to go unexplored in our service," Land continued. "It is, of course, recognized that the general strategic situation in this country is entirely different from that in Europe, so that motor torpedo boats could not in all probability be used offensively by us. It appears very probable, however, that the type might very well be used to release for offensive service ships otherwise unavoidably assigned to guard important geographic points such as an advanced base itself."

"If the department concurs," Land offered, "this bureau suggests the inauguration of an experimental program of such boats and will endeavor to have included in its appropriations for experimental work, funds for the construction of two boats each year, preferably one by contract on designs of private naval architects and one from departmental designs."

Land first had the memorandum reviewed by Rear Admiral Harold Bowen, who pledged the support of his Bureau of Engineering, before forwarding the proposal to the office of the CNO. There it was reviewed by Rear Admiral William S. Pye, Assistant Chief of Naval Operations, who agreed with Land's assessment that a well-designed motor torpedo boat, given satisfactory speed and armament and with a properly trained crew, could provide a formidable mobile defense for an advanced naval base. Pye was also aware that General Douglas MacArthur, in his capacity as military advisor to the Commonwealth government of the Philippines, had been vigorously petitioning the Navy Department for assistance in developing a fleet of motor torpedo boats for patrolling the many thousands of miles of vulnerable coastline in that expansive and strategically important archipelago.

After receiving Admiral Pye's willing endorsement, Land's memo was sent on to Secretary of the Navy Claude A. Swanson. The Secretary then referred the matter to the General Board of the Navy, an advisory panel of nine senior naval officers, most of whom were in the process of winding down their long careers and looking forward to retirement. The board served to coordinate the efforts of the navy's eight material bureaus and deliberated on a broad scope of topics ranging from the technical to the philosophical, everything from global strategy and fleet tactics to the desired specifications for a particular ship or weapons system.

Emory Land's proposal would be returned to the SECNAV "in" basket after receiving the lukewarm approval of the General Board. The reason for the board's acquiescence seems to have been an overriding fear that the failure to explore the merits of the modern motor torpedo boat might leave a foreign aggressor in possession of a potent tactical capability that the US Navy itself did not possess. Such a failure could not be allowed to occur on their watch, especially at a time when war in the Pacific seemed likely. On May 7, 1937, Swanson signed his approval to Admiral Land's recommendation—and the experimental program that would produce the US Navy PT boat was born.

***

The Shore Establishment Division of the Secretary of the Navy's office, listed as SOSED on the navy's interminable roster of bewildering acronyms, was designated as the point agency for the new PT boat project. Within SOSED's purview was a small craft program, which concerned itself with awarding contracts for the design and construction of various harbor launches and lighters. Since the PT boat was to be used in the defense of shore installations, it made sense, at least in the short term, to assign the responsibility of its development to SOSED's small craft specialists. Commander Robert "Mick" Carney, a future Chief of Naval Operations who would serve as Admiral William F. "Bull" Halsey Jr.'s trusted chief-of-staff during much of the Pacific War, was named project officer. According to his daughter, Betty Taussig, Carney so thoroughly enjoyed the hands-on work of evaluating new PT boat designs that "he was like a little boy loose in an electric train shop."

The PT boat initiative also attracted the keen interest of the sitting president of the United States. Franklin Delano Roosevelt simply couldn't help himself; a passionate and unapologetic navalist, as a young man he had idolized his distant cousin Theodore, following in his footsteps to become Assistant Secretary of the Navy. Later, as commander-in-chief, FDR took no special pains to conceal the fact that the navy was his favorite among the armed forces, and often referred to the sea service as "my navy." Naval vessels were his preferred mode of transport when traveling abroad, his most beloved being the heavy cruiser USS *Houston*. Two of Roosevelt's sons had been commissioned into the Naval Reserve while a third had joined the Marine Corps, and the president kept the close confidence of many senior naval officers whom he considered dear friends. Like Winston Churchill, who would use the self-styled sobriquet of "former naval person" in their personal correspondence, Roosevelt would find the temptation to involve himself in naval matters far beneath his station quite impossible to resist.

During Roosevelt's tenure in the Navy Department, the acquisition of small combatant vessels for antisubmarine patrol and coastal defense had been something of a pet project for the young Assistant Secretary. Over the objections of the General Board, who insisted that the money could be better spent elsewhere, Roosevelt managed to win congressional approval for the construction of 440 Submarine Chaser (SC) patrol boats. Of these, 120 were operated by American forces while the balance were transferred to Allied navies during the First World War.

The effectiveness of Roosevelt's SC boats in combatting the German U-boat menace, and the question of whether or not the navy received an adequate return on its investment, was the subject of some debate within naval circles both during and after the war. There is little conclusive evidence to confirm that American SC boats were responsible for the sinking of a single enemy submarine during World War I. Proponents of the SC would tout their deterrent effect, claiming that their mere presence had caused German U-boat commanders to shy away from the American coast, while their detractors agreed that the type had been appropriately named "submarine chaser," rather than "submarine destroyer."

Despite this past experience, or perhaps vainly because of it, President Roosevelt would lend his enthusiastic support to the new PT boat program. He would closely monitor its progress through his naval aide, Rear Admiral Daniel J. Callaghan, and also through Charles Edison, a son of the late Thomas Alva Edison then serving as Assistant Secretary of the Navy. Roosevelt charged Edison with securing from Congress the necessary funds for the project. Following a conference at the White House on June 9, 1938, Edison would tell reporters that the president "had decided to call upon the skill of American speedboat designers to create a mosquito fleet of superlative speed." One wonders if even FDR picked up on Edison's rather obscure historical reference, for the term "mosquito fleet" dates back to the Second Seminole War of 1835–1842, when the US Navy employed a number of flat-bottomed boats to transport soldiers and marines throughout the Florida Everglades.

In July 1938, the House Appropriations Committee passed a measure providing $15 million for "the construction of experimental vessels." Over the course of the next two years, eight PT boat prototypes would be developed, based off designs by the yacht builders Henry B. Nevins of New York; Sparkman and Stephens of Newport, Rhode Island; and by the navy's own Bureau of Construction and Repair. Designated *PT-1* through *PT-8*, they were laid down in the yards of the Fisher Boat Works of Detroit, Higgins Industries in New Orleans, Fogel Boatyard of Miami, and in the Philadelphia Navy Yard.

Ranging in length from 56 to 81 feet, the first seven models featured hulls fashioned from mahogany, spruce, or oak, while the navy-designed *PT-8* was of aluminum construction. In accordance with the navy's performance demands, each boat was designed to achieve a top speed of at least 40 knots, with a range of 275 miles at top speed and 550 miles at cruising speed. The specified armament included at least two .50-caliber heavy machine guns, two 21-inch torpedoes, and four depth charges.

The Electric Launch Company, or Elco, a subsidiary of the submarine manufacturing firm Electric Boat Company of Bayonne, New Jersey, had in the meantime obtained a 70-foot Scott Paine motor torpedo boat from Great Britain at the company's own expense, which was then designated *PT-9*. During trials conducted in rough winter seas off the coast of Rhode Island, the performance of the *PT-9* so impressed Commander Mick Carney that on December 7, 1939, exactly two years before the attack on Pearl Harbor, Elco was awarded a contract to produce eleven PT boats based on the Scott Paine design.

The Chief of Naval Operations at that time was Admiral Harold R. "Betty" Stark, a former commander of the Asiatic Fleet's torpedo flotilla, which included several of the navy's first steam-driven torpedo boats. In April 1940, Admiral Stark issued orders for the formation of the first two motor torpedo boat squadrons. Rather than PT boats being individually commissioned as United States Ships, Stark decided that the boats would be referred to only by their hull numbers and would not be christened. Instead the *squadron* would receive a commission with the boats assigned to the parent unit, much like aircraft were assigned to carrier-based fighter or bomber squadrons. This provided a streamlined command organization for administration, training, maintenance, and logistics, and allowed for a degree of interchangeability between boat crews.

Motor Torpedo Boat Squadron One, known as MTBRON 1 in the truncated verbiage of the navy, was activated on July 24, 1940, at the sprawling Norfolk Navy Yard in Virginia's Hampton Roads. Lieutenant Earl Caldwell, a tough and exacting destroyer officer who had been serving as an instructor at the navy's torpedo school in Newport, Rhode Island, was selected as commanding officer. Since Charles Edison's announcement, the catchy phrase "mosquito fleet" had gained traction with the popular press. Shortly after taking command, Caldwell wrote to Walt Disney in California, asking the cartoon maker's help in designing a unit insignia for MTBRON 1 featuring a mosquito. Disney, himself a veteran of naval service, turned the job over to one of his staff artists, Hank Porter.

Within days, Caldwell received Porter's drawing of a scowling mosquito wearing a white sailor's hat, riding a speeding torpedo over the crest of a breaking wave. When wire service photographs of Caldwell's new flagship *PT-9* appeared in newspapers sporting the clever mosquito-on-a-torpedo emblem, requests for Disney-designed unit insignia began flooding into the company's Burbank studio from American military units stationed around the world. There were so many, in fact, that Disney had to assign Porter and another cartoonist, Roy Williams, to perform the work full time. Over 1,200 were produced before the end of World War II, all free of charge.

MTBRON 2 was established on November 8, 1940, with Caldwell overseeing both units until another destroyer officer, Lieutenant William Specht, arrived in February to assume command. Like Caldwell and Specht, several "plank owners" of the original PT boat squadrons were officers and petty officers of the regular navy, men with considerable seagoing experience. Most of these were "tin can sailors," veteran destroyer men chosen for their knowledge of torpedo warfare and night combat tactics as well as their expert seamanship. As more names were added to the squadron muster rolls, however, an increasing number of PT crewmen were drawn from the ranks of the Naval Reserve.

Dark clouds of war were gathering on the horizon, and the US Navy was laboring mightily to build up its strength in terms of both manpower and ships. The United States had been a signatory to the Five Power Treaty of 1922 and the London Naval Treaty of 1930, both of which stringently curtailed future naval construction. In just nineteen months of involvement in the First World War, the United States suffered 53,000 combat deaths, leading to a strong isolationist sentiment among many Americans and leaving their elected officials reluctant to attach their names to any proposed defense spending legislation. Austerity measures imposed by three consecutive Republican administrations had resulted in only a handful of naval vessels being laid down in American shipyards during the 1920s. On his inauguration day of March 4, 1933, President Roosevelt inherited a navy that was pitifully understrength in terms of both ships and sailors.

"To maintain a navy which is not strong enough to win in battle is the worst form of extravagance," Representative Carl Vinson of Georgia would proclaim on the floor of the House in 1934. At the urging of President Roosevelt and with the technical assistance of naval officers like Emory Land, Vinson introduced a series of naval appropriations bills that led to a revitalization of the American shipbuilding industry, created thousands of jobs in the midst of the Great Depression, and ultimately allowed the US Navy to fight and win the Second World War.

In June 1933, the US naval register would list just 311 commissioned vessels, including aircraft carriers, battleships, cruisers, destroyers, submarines, minecraft, and auxiliaries. That number would swell to some 790 ships of all types by December 1941. Correspondingly, the number of US naval personnel on active duty would more than quadruple during the same period, from 9,481 officers and 79,727 enlisted men in 1933 to 38,601 officers and 332,274 enlisted men by December 1941.

Only a fraction of the new officers came from Annapolis—the Naval Academy Class of 1940, for example, consisted of just 456 graduating midshipmen. The majority were Naval Reserve officers recalled to active duty or ROTC students who upon graduating from college received the gold bars of a navy ensign. Still others were young college graduates with little to no military training who completed a three-month Direct Commissioning Program and were known throughout the navy as "Ninety Day Wonders."

For patriotic young men who joined the navy seeking adventure, and who had grown up watching the likes of Douglas Fairbanks and Errol Flynn on the silver screen, the notion of tearing across the water at the wheel of a sleek powerboat bristling with machine guns and torpedoes held a deliciously dangerous and romantic appeal. Duty aboard a PT boat would therefore become a highly sought-after assignment. Among the graduates of one V-7 Direct Commissioning Course held on the East Coast in 1941, over 200 newly minted ensigns applied for just thirty available slots in the new PT squadrons.

Many of these coveted billets would be filled by Naval Reserve officers graduated from Ivy League institutions. In selecting officers for PT duty, navy detailers were instructed to seek out those with previous sailing experience who were adept in the handling of small boats. At the time, pleasure craft ownership and the pursuits of yachting and powerboating were for the most part reserved for the affluent. Many of these young men already held membership in the exclusive yacht clubs of the Eastern Seaboard, and the summers of their teenage and college years had been spent sailing Sparkman and Stephens yawls or racing Chris-Craft speedboats through the waters of Cape Cod, Ipswich Bay, or Nantucket Sound.

These well-heeled sons of New England and the Mid-Atlantic region shared a rich nautical heritage—perhaps even a few were descended from those who had sailed, or at least financed, the swift and well-armed privateers that preyed upon British merchantmen during the American Revolution. Future PT boat skippers would include reserve officers like Henry S. Taylor, a Yale man from Long Island, New York; the brothers John and Robert Searles of Englewood, New Jersey, both graduates of Princeton; and a Harvard alumnus from Brookline, Massachusetts, by the name of John F. Kennedy.

Dick Keresey was from Delawanna, New Jersey, and had graduated from Dartmouth College and Columbia Law School before joining the navy under the V-7 program in 1941. Hoping for a billet in naval intelligence, he was instead assigned to the torpedo school in Rhode Island. Keresey would jump at the chance to join the PT squadrons then being formed, though he later admitted that he "would have volunteered for bomb disposal" in order to be released from his dreadfully boring assignment.

"I remember very clearly the first time seeing a PT boat," Keresey said. "I tell you, I fell in love with that PT boat the minute I saw it, and what really finished me off was when they leveled off the engines. The sound of those engines starting, it's a sound I'll remember all my life. They started up with a whine, and then a cough, and then that rumble. It was a beautiful sound."

"I fell in love with the boats," said former Boatswain's Mate First Class Robert Lenehan, who served aboard *PTs 114* and *120.* "When I first got on PTs, I thought that there was nothing in the world that ever rode any slicker, or better, or faster, or more exciting."

Initially, two officers and eight enlisted sailors were assigned to each boat crew. As the boats evolved into more complex vessels with additional weapons and radar, the crews grew in size, ranging from twelve to seventeen officers and men. Generally, the boat captain held the rank of lieutenant or lieutenant junior grade (jg), while the executive officer (XO) was usually a lieutenant (jg) or an ensign. The complement of enlisted personnel would often vary, but usually included a boatswain's mate or a deck sailor to supervise the care and maintenance of the boat, a quartermaster specializing in navigation, a cook, a radioman, two or three gunner's mates to maintain and man the deck guns, two or three motor machinist's mates watching over the engines, and at least one torpedoman to care for the steel "fish" that delivered the PT boat's lethal striking power. Quite often a cook, motor machinist or boatswain would man one of the gun positions when the crew went to battle stations.

After graduating from boot camp in either Great Lakes, Illinois, or San Diego, California, enlisted personnel qualified for their occupational rating and ascended to the rank of petty officer by attending one of the navy's service schools, or by "striking" for a rating as an apprentice seaman aboard ship. Like the majority of their officers, the enlisted men detailed to the PT squadrons were for the most part recently mobilized reservists, and despite having an average age of only twenty-one years old, many were already qualified petty officers. From the outset, each man was required to not only be thoroughly proficient in performing his primary job, but also possess a working knowledge of his shipmate's job functions in case that man were to become incapacitated.

"On a naval vessel, generally you always had one particular job that you did," Lenehan explained. "But on a PT boat, there was the constant possibility in action that somebody would be killed. So everybody had to have a certain amount of understanding of everybody else's job. That was one of the unique things about PTs."

"You had to learn everything on the boat—navigation, radio, torpedoes, everything that performed," said John O'Keefe, a motor machinist's mate on the *PT-107*. "You had to be able to step up and take over as skipper of the boat if you had to. Everybody had to do it. When I went in, at the first of the war, it was necessary for you to be single to get into the PTs. You couldn't ride a boat and be married. You had to be an honor student at your service school. You had to volunteer for PT service."

\*\*\*

To Caldwell and his men fell the task of "shaking down" the new PT boat prototypes and determining their strengths and weaknesses. A preliminary series of exercises along the East Coast was conducted to allow the crews to become accustomed to the handling characteristics of the experimental craft and to give the newly installed engines a critical "breaking-in" period. After MTBRON 2 took possession of the first batch of ten Elco 70-footers, both squadrons were ordered to migrate south for the winter of 1940, cruising from Norfolk to Miami and thence to Key West and Cienfuegos, Cuba, all the while putting the boats through their paces and evaluating their seakeeping properties.

As the formation motored southward along the Atlantic coast amid the crisp winds and rolling groundswells of autumn, the men with little blue water experience—and even those who had previously served aboard destroyers—would quickly learn the value of the small craft sailor's adage "one hand for you, one hand for the boat." The novelist Robb White, a naval officer who fought in the South Pacific, once sketched a telling description of what it was like to ride across the open sea aboard a PT boat.

"It took you only once to find out why they told you not to fall down on a PT boat," White wrote. "Standing up, holding on, your bent, loose knees absorbed the pounding of the hull against the sea, your body balanced with the astounding roll and pitch. If you fell down, when you tried to push yourself up, the deck dropped out from under you, then the boat came up as you came down."

By the time the flotilla arrived in Miami, the experimental boats of MTBRON 1 were suffering from a multitude of structural and mechanical problems, and the decision was made to send the ten Elcos ahead to complete the shakedown cruise to Cienfuegos.

"We got 'shaken down' all right," recalled Jack Searles. "Coming back, a heavy storm hit us halfway between Cuba and Key West. One of our PT boats had her bow demolished and was almost swamped." At one point during the passage from Cuba, Searles's commander ordered him below to the chart room to plot their position by dead reckoning.

"There was no quick solution," Searles would explain. "For the past twenty-four hours, there had been many changes in course and speed. Allowance had to be made for heavy seas, changes in direction, and the velocity of the winds. Suddenly, the skipper was at my elbow, asking if I had his position yet. I replied, 'Yes, sir. But, excuse me.' I reached down, grabbed a large wastebasket, and filled it half full of upchuck. The exhaustion, heat, motion, and smell of gas was more than I could stand. 'We are right here,' I said, turning to the chart and marking it with our DR position.'"

Fundamental flaws in design, questionable seaworthiness, temperamental marine engines that failed to endure the rigors of sea trials, and production delays eventually led to the first seven PT designs being rejected by the navy. The Elco boats of MTBRON 2 performed reasonably well during the shakedown cruise, but after the decision was made to arm the navy's PT boats with four 21-inch torpedoes instead of two, the 70-foot Elco was also deemed inadequate. Their hulls were simply too short to accommodate all four torpedoes. Elco's naval architects then went to work on a 77-foot version of the Scott Paine design, which was readily accepted, and two dozen were ordered. After spending the winter in south Florida, both squadrons proceeded to New York Harbor, where the 70-foot Elcos were transferred to the Royal Navy under the Lend Lease Act.

In an effort to settle upon a standard PT boat design, the navy invited competing firms to participate in what would come to be known as the "Plywood Derbies," a series of grueling, 190-mile high-speed endurance tests held on the waters of Long Island Sound in July and August of 1941. The "derbies" pitted the Philadelphia Navy Yard's *PT-8* against nine other prototypes manufactured by Elco, Higgins, and the Huckins Yacht Company of Florida, boats that ranged from 70 to 81 feet in length. Under the watchful eyes of officers from the Board of Inspection and Survey, the boats raced eastward at full throttle from the mouth of New Haven Harbor, rounded the north light of Block Island, and sprinted for the finish line on Long Island's Montauk Point.

The boats were evaluated not only for their speed, but also for their maneuverability and durability while running the punishing course. The first of the Elco 77-foot boats, *PT-20*, turned in the most impressive performance, followed by the Higgins *PT-70* and the Huckins *PT-69*. In the end, Huckins received a government contract to build eighteen boats, which were used for training and coastal patrol duties and never saw combat. The Elco design, further refined to a length of 80 feet, and the Higgins 78-footer would become the standard PT boats of the US Navy.

***

Contrary to popular legend, PT boats were not made entirely of engineered plywood. Their hulls were actually made of solid mahogany, harvested from the Gold Coast of Africa or the forests of British Honduras, milled into six-inch-wide planks, and fastened to a skeleton of wooden frames using thousands of brass screws. A tightly stretched layer of aircraft fabric impregnated with a phenol resin glue was then applied with hot irons to make the hull watertight, followed by a second, outer layer of mahogany planks. Each layer was three-eighths of an inch thick. The main deck was also mahogany, with strongback timbers supporting the gun and torpedo mounts. The boat's low-profile charthouse, machine gun turrets, and the interior bulkheads that separated the hull into watertight compartments were, in fact, fashioned from marine-grade fir plywood.

The hull of a PT boat, as written in navy specifications, was designed to be "of the lightest weight, consistent with adequate strength, stiffness and durability for the service intended, and with an eye to simplicity for mass production." A 77-foot Elco, 20 feet wide at the beam and drawing 4 feet of draft, would displace around 46 tons. A "hard chine," or steep V-shaped angle to the hull, allowed the boat to "plane," or skim smoothly across the surface of the water. This lightweight "planing hull" design, along with a muscular power plant, was responsible for giving the PT boats their impressive speed.

The Elco, Higgins, and Huckins PT boats were powered by three monstrous Packard 4M-2500 marine engines. These were liquid-cooled, 2,490-cubic-inch (40.8-liter) V12 motors capable of generating up to 1,500 horsepower, each driving its own independent propeller shaft and fueled by 100-octane aviation gasoline. The Packard was equipped with a Holley aircraft carburetor and centrifugal supercharger. Designed specifically for use in PT boats, the Packard motor was derived from the First World War–era Liberty aircraft engine. Ironically, the first adaptation of the Liberty engine to a maritime environment occurred during the Prohibition period of the 1920s, when they were installed into "rum runner" speedboats by enterprising smugglers. After the repeal of Prohibition, a few of these resourceful artisans actually found employment with the Elco and Higgins boatworks. According to one PT officer, when discussing solutions to a daunting technical problem, it was not uncommon for an Elco or Higgins employee to preface his remarks with the phrase: "Well, back when I was a rummy, we used to . . ."

It can therefore be said that criminal ingenuity helped win the war.

Speed was essential, not only to the PT boat's potency in combat but for its very survival. When all three engines were properly tuned and running smoothly, a PT boat with a clean hull was capable of achieving speeds in excess of 40 knots. Since any increase in the overall weight of the boat often resulted in a corresponding decrease in speed, armor protection for the boats was kept to a minimum. Initially, only the cockpit was protected by armor plating. Many boat skippers had the armor removed, feeling an obligation to share in the same hazards faced by their gunners and torpedomen, who were required to perform their duties while exposed to enemy fire.

A widely circulated sea story told of one young bluejacket, newly assigned to duty aboard PT boats, who ducked into his machine gun turret to avoid an incoming volley of enemy bullets. When the sailor was later informed that the turrets were made of nothing more than 3/4-inch plywood and contained no armor, he fainted on the spot. Later it became common practice while in the combat theater for PT crews to scavenge the remains of crashed airplanes for armor plating, which they would then install around the more vulnerable topside positions of their craft.

The PT boats had a decidedly low-slung and streamlined topside profile, both for the purposes of improved aerodynamics and to help avoid detection by limiting the height of the boat's silhouette against the horizon.* The clean forecastle had storage for a 50-pound anchor, ready service boxes of ammunition, and vertical hatches leading to stowage and crew spaces below. On some of the earlier PT models, a pair of First World War–vintage .30-caliber Lewis machine guns, dubbed

_____
*Author's note: What follows is a general description of the Elco PT boat, the first deployed to the Solomon Islands and therefore featured prominently in succeeding chapters. This is in no way intended to diminish the contribution made by Higgins PT boats in World War II.

"peashooters" by the boat crews, were mounted on pedestals just forward of the charthouse. Later a Swiss-designed 20-millimeter Oerlikon automatic cannon was swivel-mounted on the foredeck.

The charthouse amidships enclosed the open-air cockpit, where the helm, engine throttle controls, instrument panel, compass, searchlight, radio whip antennae, and torpedo director were located, and where the boat's skipper, XO, and quartermaster usually stationed themselves. The cockpit was flanked fore and aft by two hydraulically operated gun turrets, each mounting a pair of hard-hitting and reliable Browning M2 Basic Aircraft .50-caliber machine guns capable of firing 800 rounds per minute with an effective range of 2,000 yards. On either side of the boat, two torpedo tubes were mounted in tandem, each containing a 21-inch by 21-foot Bliss–Leavitt Mark 8 torpedo. Another low-profile structure, the canopy for the day room cabin, stood just abaft the cockpit, upon which a life raft was stored and the boat's signal mast erected. On later-arriving models a larger mast was installed, topped by a football-shaped SO-type radar dome.

The after portion of the boat contained dispensing racks for up to eight Mark 6 depth charges. Many boats carried only two, since each depth charge weighed 325 pounds. A large access hatch and ventilating shafts for the engine room were between the depth charge racks. Another gun station was usually—but not always—centered on the fantail. This would evolve from a battery of Lewis guns to a 20-millimeter Oerlikon and eventually a single Swedish-designed 40-millimeter Bofors automatic cannon. Secured to the stern transom was the smoke generator, a pressurized cylinder containing 32 gallons of titanium tetrachloride. When released into ambient air, the liquid chemical immediately transformed into a dense screen of white smoke. This was intended to conceal a darting PT boat from view and hopefully spoil the aim of enemy gunners.

Belowdecks, the PT boats were deceptively spacious and well appointed. A saltwater head was located in the bow. Just aft of the head were the crew's living quarters, where tiered bunks were built into the port and starboard bulkheads along with a mess table and gear lockers. The captain and his XO each had a small stateroom connected by a shared head. Lying to starboard was an officer's wardroom, which was roughly the size of a seating booth one might find in a roadside diner. A gunnery locker on the starboard side amidships stored ammunition and spare parts as well as a complement of small arms, which included Colt .45-caliber pistols, 1903 Springfield and M1 Garand rifles, M1 carbines, Thompson submachine guns, Mark 8 Eureka signal flare pistols, and often a 12-gauge Winchester pump shotgun.

Between the officer's quarters and the engine room was the crew's day room, a place of refuge for the boat's "moto-macs" from the intense heat and incessant noise generated by the three rumbling Packards. The day room also provided additional berthing space. Beneath the day room were three fuel tanks, each holding 1,000 gallons of aviation gasoline when filled to capacity. In the engine room the three Packard motors were positioned side by side, along with the auxiliary generator, heat exchanger, and electrical panels. Just abaft the engine room was a shallow compartment known as a lazarette, which included a workbench and storage for tools.

The chartroom, as the name suggests, contained a chart table along with navigation and radio equipment. A small but functional galley included stowage for canned foodstuffs and utensils, and an electric stove, freezer, and refrigerator. Armor plating would often be found mounted to the galley bulkhead behind the refrigerator, a testimony to the high value placed on the appliances by the boat crews. For the boats that didn't have a trained cook on board, the job of preparing the communal meal often fell to a sailor who might display a certain flair for the culinary arts. A rather lighthearted pamphlet produced by the Bureau of Ships, titled *Know Your PT Boat*, offered some valuable wisdom for those assigned to the shared duty of "mess cranking," the navy's term for assisting with meal preparation and the washing of dishes.

"A bit of advice about the cook," it read. "He's likely to be temperamental and have his moods. He needs help at meal time. So keep him in good humor by mess cranking without griping and helping him get supplies. He may serve you breakfast in bed some morning. Generally, he's a good gunner, too. You'll learn to count on 'cookie.'"

"'The galley stove with all its attachments and source of power must be known by everyone," *Know Your PT Boat* further advised. "Above all, remember to have your generator running and galley switch 'on' when the stove is operated. Also bear in mind that finding and destroying the enemy is more important than a hot pot of Joe. So don't gripe if the galley must be secured to give the needed juice to the radio equipment."

*\*\*\**

In September 1941, the armies of Nazi Germany were preparing to lay siege to the Soviet cities of Kyiv and Leningrad. In all German-occupied territories, Jewish citizens were ordered to display a yellow Star of David prominently on their outer clothing. In London, Charles De Gaulle announced the formation of the Free French government-in-exile. While on Neutrality Patrol in the North Atlantic, the destroyer USS *Greer* fired upon the submarine *U-652*, an incident denounced as an "act of piracy" by the German government. President Roosevelt responded by issuing orders for the US Navy to "shoot on sight" any German U-boats found within American territorial waters.

In the United States that September, the Brooklyn Dodgers clinched the National League pennant for the first time in twenty-one years, while the New York Yankees defeated the Boston Red Sox to finish first in the American League. In a defense of his heavyweight boxing title held at New York City's Polo Grounds, Joe Louis defeated Lou Nova by technical knockout in the sixth round. Movie audiences flocked to see Gary Cooper's portrayal of *Sergeant York* and the Bob Hope comedy *Caught in the Draft.*

The first of 2,700 Liberty cargo ships, the SS *Patrick Henry*, was launched at the Bethlehem Shipyard in Baltimore. Construction began on the Pentagon building in Arlington, Virginia. Across the Potomac, in an ornate conference room on the second floor of the Old Executive Office Building on Pennsylvania Avenue, Japanese ambassador Kichisaburo Nomura would continue to negotiate with American Secretary of State Cordell Hull for the purpose, ostensibly, of averting an all-out war in the Pacific.

That same month of September 1941 would see the first overseas deployment of motor torpedo boat squadrons to the US Navy's advanced bases. The reorganized MTBRON 1, now under the command of Lieutenant William Specht and equipped with a dozen new Elco boats, was on its way to Pearl Harbor. This was in response to a request from Admiral Husband E. Kimmel, Commander-in-Chief Pacific Fleet, for "small craft in the 14th Naval District for patrol purposes, to relieve the load on our limited number of destroyers." Preparations were also underway to send MTBRON 2 to defend the Panama Canal Zone. Eighty-three officers and enlisted men of the newly established MTBRON 3, commanded by Lieutenant John Bulkeley and equipped with six Elco 77-footers, would embark upon their fateful journey to the Philippine Islands.

As diplomatic negotiations between the United States and Japan neared an impasse and tensions between the two nations were strained to the breaking point, an aggressive move by the Japanese somewhere in the Pacific seemed inevitable. The prevailing opinion among American military and civilian leaders was that Guam, Wake, or the Philippines would be the most likely targets of a Japanese first strike. For men like twenty-four-year-old Ed Hoagland, a Ninety Day Wonder from East Hampton, New York, who would later command a squadron of PT boats, going to war wasn't a matter of *if*, but *when*.

"There was no doubt in my mind," Hoagland would later write, "that with all that was going on in Europe and Japan, the United States would soon be at war."

# Nobody Gives a Damn

LIKE ANY OTHER TRANQUIL SUNDAY MORNING ON THE ISLAND OF Oahu, the day had dawned pleasantly warm, with light easterly trade winds and billowing white cumulus topping the deep green mountain peaks. Along the eastern shore of Ford Island in the center of Pearl Harbor were seven of the huge steel leviathans that formed the powerful core of the US Pacific Fleet, moored in column along what had come to be known as Battleship Row. An eighth battleship rested in dry dock in the Navy Yard across the channel. The pealing of church bells in nearby Pearl City announced that it was time to gather for eight o'clock services, and aboard the many ships of the fleet, buglers prepared to sound Morning Colors.

At the submarine base in Pearl Harbor's southeast loch, six of the 77-foot Elco PT boats belonging to MTBRON 1 were tied alongside the repair barge *YR-20*, which was serving as a makeshift tender for the squadron. The other six boats were in the process of being craned aboard the fleet oiler *Ramapo* for transfer to Bulkeley's squadron in the Philippines. Most of the PT sailors were at breakfast aboard the *YR-20* when a large formation of aircraft suddenly appeared over the harbor. Gazing skyward, Ensign Nile Ball, the twenty-eight-year-old skipper of the *21* boat who had the duty as Officer of the Deck, noted that the planes had red circles emblazoned on their wingtips.

"They look like Japs," a nearby chief petty officer observed, as if to read Ball's thoughts. As the men watched, each plane tipped over into a steep dive and dropped a 500-pound bomb on the seaplane base at the southern end of Ford Island. Ball turned and sprinted for the *YR-20*'s mess deck.

"Man the guns!" the young officer shouted to the men at the breakfast tables. Spilling outside into the bright sunlight, the sailors found tightly formed, three-plane echelons of Nakajima B5N "Kate" torpedo bombers zooming past on their way to attack Battleship Row. Soon every PT boat in the anchorage was blazing away at the Japanese planes with automatic weapons—even those that had already been hoisted onto the main deck of the *Ramapo*.

"I had my Tommy gun and I took a few shots at them, but anybody that had a gun was shooting it, no matter what kind it was," recalled Radioman Second Class Alphonse Stockdale. "They were that close. They were coming over our head and going for the big stuff and not paying any attention to us, so we got to shoot at them at pretty close range."

The sailors of 'RON 1 would account for at least two of the twenty-nine Japanese planes shot down during the attack on Pearl Harbor, a score from which they could derive little satisfaction. By the time the last Japanese raiders made good their escape at around 10:00 a.m. Hawaiian time, reams of deep orange flame and turbulent columns of dense black smoke were rising high into the blue tropical sky from the utterly decimated battleships of the Pacific Fleet. Over 2,400 Americans lay dead.

As the light of dawn moved across the Pacific, General Douglas MacArthur, commander of US Army Forces Far East, was gripped by an uncharacteristic and confounding paralysis. Even after hearing the news of Pearl Harbor, MacArthur failed to issue orders for his air chief, Major General Louis Brereton, to conduct offensive strikes against Japanese airfields within range of the Philippines, or to disperse his planes from the major air bases of Luzon to smaller, satellite airfields throughout the islands.

At 12:35 p.m. Philippine time, over one hundred Japanese bombers and eighty fighter planes bombed and strafed Clark and Iba airfields, destroying nearly half of MacArthur's modern combat aircraft on the ground along with their hangars, repair shops, and fuel and ammunition stores. When it was over, Brereton was forced to evacuate the surviving

Boeing B-17 Flying Fortresses to airfields in Mindanao on the southern end of the archipelago, and had only a handful of Curtiss P-40 Warhawk fighters remaining to oppose a Japanese invasion that was sure to come. Total Japanese air supremacy over the Philippines had been achieved in a single afternoon. For this MacArthur was somehow spared the condemnation heaped upon Admiral Kimmel in Pearl Harbor and the commander of the army's Hawaiian Department, General Walter Short, even though he had nine hours' notice that hostilities had begun.

Two days later, on the afternoon of December 10, the desperate clanging of church bells and wailing of air raid sirens sounded over the city of Manila and the Cavite Navy Yard, sending the crews of MTBRON 3 scrambling to get their half-dozen boats underway. Soon a flight of twenty-seven twin-engined Mitsubishi G3M "Nell" medium bombers appeared over Corregidor, the fortified island that guarded the entrance to Manila Bay. The bombers were cruising serenely in a large V formation at 20,000 feet, and the V was pointing directly at Cavite. American fighter interceptors were nowhere to be seen. John Bulkeley knew that his PT boats stood their best chance of survival on the waters of Manila Bay, maneuvering at high speed.

With the Japanese at too high an altitude to reach with their deck guns, the PT sailors could only watch as the formation of Nells continued east before making a smart turn to line themselves up with Sangley Point, the promontory that jutted into the bay just south of the city of Manila where the Navy Yard was located. Soon came the sickening *crump* of explosions from across the water, followed by rising columns of black smoke. Then five Aichi D3A "Val" dive bombers, easily identified by their fixed landing gear and tapered elliptical wings, suddenly appeared out of nowhere.

Spotting the six PT boats, each Val rolled into a plunging dive. During their training, PT officers had been advised to watch and wait for an enemy dive bomber to release its deadly payload before putting the helm hard over, a tip passed on by British MTB crews after doing battle with German Stukas. Every man knew that it would take a sharp-eyed XO and a skipper with quick reflexes to pull off such a maneuver. Upon hearing their XO's harrowing cries of *"bombs away,"* the skippers made wrenching evasive turns at full throttle, their wooden hulls slamming through the heaving waters of the bay. Machine gunners braced themselves within their cylindrical turrets and hammered away at the zooming Vals, while every other man aboard grabbed onto something solid and held on for dear life. The trick worked; all the bombs fell wide, and three of the five Japanese attackers were sent spiraling into Manila Bay.

Cavite Navy Yard had been left a blazing wreck.

"It was truly an aviator's dream of a perfect target for fragmentation and incendiary bombs," wrote Rear Admiral Francis Rockwell, commander of the 16th Naval District of the Philippines.

The headquarters buildings, naval hospital, barracks, powerhouse, docks, warehouses, repair shops, fuel oil tanks, and—worst of all for the PT crews—the aviation gasoline and torpedo storage facilities were all flattened by Japanese bombs. Practically every structure on the base was on fire. Water mains that had been shallowly buried in the sandy soil of the promontory were uprooted by the bombing, leaving little to no water pressure for fighting the flames. Unable to put to sea before the attack came, the submarine *Sealion* received two direct hits while sitting at her berth, and was so badly damaged that she would later be scuttled. Alongside her was the burning minesweeper *Bittern*, which would suffer the same fate. Five hundred naval personnel and Filipino civilian employees had been killed or seriously wounded. The boats of 'RON 3 soon returned to the burning dockyard where they found Admiral Rockwell helping gather the wounded, his khaki shirt stained dark with blood. The admiral ordered the PT boats pressed into service as waterborne ambulances, evacuating the worst of the casualties to hospitals in nearby Manila.

Lacking effective air cover and his fleet base now a total loss, Admiral Thomas C. Hart, commander of the US Asiatic Fleet, had little choice but to order his cruisers, destroyers, and submarines to withdraw to British Malay and the Dutch East Indies. Bulkeley and the men of MTBRON 3, however, were ordered to remain behind in Manila Bay. The reason for this decision may be found in the title of a book that tells the tale of the squadron's plight, written by the war correspondent William Lindsay White and later adapted into a film starring Robert Montgomery and John Wayne: *They Were Expendable*.

Immediately following the air raid on Cavite, the squadron was relocated to Sisiman Cove in Mariveles Bay, a horseshoe-shaped inlet on the southern tip of the Bataan Peninsula just across a narrow channel from Corregidor. Facilities there were spartan, few torpedoes were left, and there was an inadequate supply of aviation gasoline. Over one hundred barrels of gas had gone up in flames when the Japanese bombed the Cavite Navy Yard, forcing the PT sailors to scrounge from various sources around Manila Bay. One batch of gasoline was found to be tainted with wax, the work of saboteurs.

"This foreign substance clogged gas strainers and carburetor jets to such extent as to cause most unreliable operating, necessitating the cleaning of carburetors and strainers hourly," Bulkeley wrote in an after-action report. "It was never known when a boat engine would stop. It eventually became necessary to open the gas tanks and thoroughly clean with the limited means available. The lubricating oil contained sand."

The PT boats required near-constant maintenance, and their performance would suffer further due to a lack of spare parts. At anchor in Mariveles Bay was the elderly submarine tender *Canopus*, which had received two direct hits from Japanese dive bombers during two separate raids and was so badly damaged that she had to be left behind when the Asiatic Fleet withdrew to southern waters. Some of her onboard repair and fabrication shops, however, were still intact. During daylight hours, the crew of the *Canopus* deployed smoke pots around the ship to leave the impression that she was a smoldering, abandoned derelict. At night the ship bustled with activity, with her mechanics and technicians working alongside the PT moto-macs to keep the boats running.

Despite these formidable challenges, the PTs still managed to continue their nightly patrols, often chasing after sightings of Japanese vessels that proved to be false. On December 17, they would rescue nearly 300 survivors from the SS *Corregidor* after the interisland steamer struck a floating mine at the mouth of Manila Bay. On Christmas Eve, three days after Japanese troops landed in force on the shores of Lingayen Gulf, the *PT-33* ran hard aground while investigating some lights thought to be coming from a Japanese submarine near Cape Santiago. In order to keep the boat from falling into enemy hands, the *PT-33* was set afire and destroyed.

On the final day of 1941, with Japanese pincers closing in from north and south, 80,000 Filipino and American troops completed their fighting withdrawal to the Bataan Peninsula, a complex retrograde maneuver often cited as an example of MacArthur's remarkable skill as a field commander. There his troops dug into defensive positions and waited in vain for the arrival of the Pacific Fleet to bring supplies and reinforcements. As their stocks of food and medicine steadily dwindled, tropical diseases and malnutrition began to take an even heavier toll on the Bataan garrison than Japanese shells. MacArthur continued to issue communiqués from his underground headquarters on Corregidor, promising that "thousands of troops and hundreds of planes" were on the way—assurances that MacArthur himself had received.

In time, it would become apparent to the American soldiers fighting on Bataan, and to their brothers-in-arms in MTBRON 3, that they had been written off by the generals and admirals in Washington. Those who spent their days in War and Navy Department conference rooms, shuffling unit symbols across map tables like so many chess pieces, had decreed that they were to be sacrificed. It was obvious that the brass was counting on their continued resistance to tie down large numbers of Japanese troops, airplanes, and ships, buying time for reeling Allied forces in the Pacific to regroup. Still the men held, for weeks upon weeks, throwing back one ferocious Japanese assault after another, during which time one of them composed a weary and bitter poem of defiance.

> *We're the battling bastards of Bataan;*
> *No mama, no papa, no Uncle Sam.*
> *No aunts, no uncles, no nephews, no nieces,*
> *No pills, no planes, no artillery pieces.*
> *And nobody gives a damn.*
> *Nobody gives a damn.*

The PT crews continued to soldier on, conducting frequent patrols along the coast of Bataan and into Subic Bay, strafing enemy troops on the beaches, attacking enemy transports and landing barges, evacuating casualties, and carrying dispatches to and from Corregidor. The *PT-31* would be lost on January 19, after contaminated fuel clogged the carburetors of two engines and her third motor overheated. The drifting *31* boat then became hopelessly grounded on the eastern shore of Subic Bay behind enemy lines, forcing the crew to set her ablaze before making the perilous overland journey down the Bataan Peninsula to Mariveles. By the end of the month the *PT-32* was falling apart, with her hull in need of extensive repair and one engine out of commission. Her three sisters were in only slightly better condition.

Bulkeley began laying plans for the squadron's escape to mainland China, after their last torpedoes were expended and the boats neared the end of their combat effectiveness. His plans would never come to fruition. Despite a determination to "share the fate of the garrison," on February 23, 1942, General MacArthur was issued a direct order by President Roosevelt to leave the Philippines. Once safely ensconced in Australia, MacArthur was to assume command of all Allied forces in the Southwest Pacific.

"MacArthur was the only Allied general who had proved that he knew how to fight the Japanese, and in whom the public therefore had confidence," the historian William Manchester wrote of the decision. "He was the best-informed US officer in the Far East, America's one hero in the war thus far, an irreplaceable man who could provide leadership and example in the Pacific campaigns that lay ahead. In addition, if he were captured or killed, the Japanese would have scored a tremendous psychological victory."

The initial plan called for MacArthur to slip through the Japanese blockade aboard the submarine *Permit*, which had already been dispatched from its base in Java for that purpose. Being somewhat claustrophobic, the general was not keen on the idea. Then stateside radio news programs began broadcasting appeals for MacArthur, whose stirring press releases had electrified the American home front, to be evacuated from the Philippines in order to take command of all American forces in the Pacific.

Whether this was merely coincidence or the result of a leak from the White House or War Department, MacArthur and his staff had no choice but to assume the Japanese had heard the broadcasts as well. Sure enough, reports were soon received of Japanese air and naval forces stepping up their patrols around Subic Bay and Corregidor, and that additional Japanese warships were steaming toward Manila Bay.

MacArthur decided not to wait for the arrival of the *Permit*; instead the general and his entourage would be spirited away by Bulkeley's four remaining PT boats to Mindanao, where a trio of B-17 Flying Fortresses would be waiting to fly them to Australia. MacArthur himself had asked Bulkeley if his PT boats were capable of undertaking such a mission, to which the lieutenant responded confidently that the trip would be "a piece of cake."

The PT crews then set to work, performing as extensive an overhaul of their by-now worn-out Packard motors as their meager supply of spare parts and lubricants would allow, and lashed twenty extra 55-gallon drums of gasoline to the deck of each boat. Even after their engine tune-ups, with the addition of this extra weight the boats were barely capable of making 30 knots, and the *32* boat, now running on two engines, would struggle to reach even that.

MacArthur had been authorized to take with him only his family and his chief-of-staff, Major General Richard K. Sutherland, but insisted on bringing along several key members of the "Bataan Gang," all of whom he considered critical for establishing his new command in Australia. This led to Lieutenant Bulkeley having to make the most agonizing decision a commander must face: which of his men to leave behind. Thirty-two members of MTBRON 3 would be ordered to remain on Bataan, where they would fight as infantry alongside other stranded sailors and earthbound members of the Army Air Corps.

Accompanied by his wife Jean and four-year-old son Arthur, General MacArthur boarded Bulkeley's *PT-41* at Corregidor's north dock and departed at 7:45 p.m. on March 11. Also on board were General Sutherland, three additional staff officers, and Arthur's Chinese nanny. Dispersed throughout the three other PTs were a dozen members of the Bataan Gang, including five brigadier generals and army physician

Major Charles H. Morhouse, along with Admiral Rockwell and his chief-of-staff, Captain Herbert Ray. Once past the entrance to Manila Bay, the boats assumed a diamond-shaped formation with *PT-41* in the lead. In the event they were attacked by the Japanese, Bulkeley had issued orders for the three other boats to engage the enemy while the *41* boat ran away at full throttle.

"The weather deteriorated steadily, and towering waves buffeted our tiny, war-weary, blacked-out vessels. The spray drove against our skin like stinging pellets of birdshot," MacArthur would record in his memoir *Reminiscences*. "We would fall into a trough, then climb up the steep water peak, only to slide down the other side. The boat would toss crazily back and forth, seeming to hang free in space as though about to breach, and would then break away and go forward with a rush. I recall describing the experience afterward as what it must be like to take a trip in a concrete mixer."

Aboard the *PT-34*, Admiral Rockwell watched in horror as the boat's skipper, Lieutenant Robert Kelly, sighted along his outstretched arm and pointed index finger to obtain a bearing on a nearby island.

"My God, don't you have a pelorus?" the admiral wanted to know. "How the hell do you navigate?"

"By guess and by God, sir," Kelly replied with a grin.

In the foul weather and pitch darkness, the boats easily lost contact with one another, a problem worsened by the fact that the *PT-32* was incapable of keeping pace with her sisters. As dawn approached, the captain of the *32* boat, Lieutenant (jg) Vincent Schumacher, spotted another vessel closing fast. Ordering his crew to their battle stations, he cranked the *PT-32* into a sharp turn to bring her torpedo tubes to bear. The ropes securing the gasoline drums were slashed and the drums pushed overboard. Just before the order to open fire was given, Brigadier General Hugh Casey suddenly shouted, "It's one of our boats!"

It was, in fact, the *PT-41*. Lieutenant Bulkeley was still at the helm, with a grim-faced General MacArthur towering over him in the cockpit. By then Bulkeley had become well known for his personal courage, and also for his temper. In an angry voice, he ordered the flustered Schumacher to fish the bobbing gasoline drums from the sea. When this proved too time-consuming and difficult, Bulkeley had his machine gunners sink them. The light of dawn was now streaking the eastern horizon, and before they were spotted by Japanese search planes it was imperative for the boats to press on to their planned rendezvous. This was a secluded cove on the leeward coast of Tagauayan, a small island in the northern reaches of the Sulu Sea roughly halfway between Manila Bay and Mindanao. As a precaution, the *Permit* had been instructed to make the rendezvous at Tagauayan as well.

It wasn't until 4:00 p.m. that the two PT boats entered the welcoming shelter of the cove, where overhanging trees would help conceal them from aerial observation. There they found the crew of the *PT-34* waiting along with their rather anxious complement of passengers. The *35* boat and the *Permit* had not yet arrived. At the insistence of both Sutherland and Rockwell, MacArthur reluctantly gave his consent to continuing the journey on the surface, rather than wait for the submarine to arrive. The general expressed concern about the possibility of even rougher seas ahead and the effect it might have on the passengers. Rockwell informed MacArthur that he was far more worried about being discovered by the Japanese while lingering at Tagauayan than running into foul weather on the journey south.

MacArthur turned to his chief-of-staff.

"Dick, I can't do anything to Rockwell," he said in a somber voice, "but if it's rough tonight, I'll boil you in oil."

It was obvious that the *PT-32* was finished; Schumacher and his crew were ordered to remain at Tagauayan and await the arrival of the *PT-35* and *Permit*. Schumacher's passengers were then transferred to the *41* and *34* boats, which were laboriously refueled from the spare drums with the use of hand pumps. By 6:00 p.m. they were underway once again, on a southeasterly course for the port of Cagayan de Oro on the northern coast of Mindanao.

An hour later they encountered the spine-chilling sight of a Japanese cruiser on the horizon, but the PT boats managed to avoid detection by pointing their bows into the setting sun. Just as MacArthur had feared, that night the boats were tossed by angry waves peaking at 15 to 20 feet, relentlessly tormenting their already seasick passengers. But the foul weather also provided concealment from snooping Japanese planes.

"I've sailed every type of ship in the navy except one of these MTBs," Rockwell shouted to Kelly above the roar of the wind and sea, "and this is the worst bridge I've ever been on. I wouldn't do duty on one of these for anything in the world—you can have them!"

At long last, the mountains of Mindanao hove into view through the dawn haze of March 13, 1942.

"Good navigation, Kelly," a grateful Admiral Rockwell commented. "I wouldn't have believed it possible." Disembarking at the Cagayan landing, MacArthur told Bulkeley, "Lieutenant, I'm recommending a Silver Star for all members of your crew. You've taken me out of the jaws of death and I won't forget it."

Later that same day, Ensign Anthony Akers's missing *PT-35* finally arrived at the Cagayan harbor, carrying MacArthur's intelligence officer, Colonel Charles Willoughby, and three other tempest-tossed army passengers, all of whom were elated to once again feel solid ground beneath their feet. The trip might not have been the "piece of cake" Bulkeley had promised, but the general, his family, and his staff were all safe, delivered through 560 miles of enemy territory by the battered Elcos. On the morning of March 17, MacArthur and his party landed safely in Australia, where the general famously announced to reporters: "I came through and I shall return."

After two days of waiting at Tagauayan, Lieutenant Schumacher and his crew were finally taken off by the *Permit*, which then sank the dilapidated *PT-32* with her deck guns. The three remaining boats of MTBRON 3 would continue the fight against the Japanese in the waters of the southern Philippines until battle damage and mechanical deterioration made it no longer possible. On March 19, they evacuated Philippine president Manuel Quezon and his family to Mindanao from the island of Negros. In the early morning hours of April 9, the *41* and *34* boats engaged the Japanese heavy cruiser *Kuma* off the coast of Cebu Island, striking her hull with a torpedo that failed to explode.

The following day, Kelly was forced to beach the *PT-34* on the shores of Cauit Island, after the boat was seriously damaged in an attack by strafing Japanese planes, which killed one man and injured three others. While stranded on the beach, the abandoned boat was attacked a second time by enemy aircraft and destroyed. The *PT-35*, under repair at Cebu, was burned by her fleeing crew as Japanese troops entered the city. Bulkeley's flagship *PT-41* would meet a similar fate, set aflame by army troops on Mindanao ahead of the advancing Japanese.

MTBRON 3 had ceased to exist as a fighting unit. Eighteen officers and men had been killed in action. Thirty-eight would become prisoners of war, only twenty-nine of whom would survive the brutality of Japanese detainment camps. Seven men escaped to the island of Leyte, where they joined a band of Filipino and American guerrilla fighters. They were finally relieved in October 1944 when, as promised, MacArthur returned to the Philippines at the head of a 200,000-man army.

Before Mindanao fell to the Japanese in May 1942, John Bulkeley, Anthony Akers, Robert Kelly, and the former XO of *PT-41*, George Cox, were flown to Australia on MacArthur's orders. Bulkeley would continue on to Washington, where on July 1, 1942, he was awarded the Medal of Honor by President Roosevelt.

***

In the immediate aftermath of the surprise attack on Pearl Harbor, Admiral Husband E. Kimmel, Commander-in-Chief Pacific Fleet (CINCPAC) since February 1941, was relieved by Secretary of the Navy Frank Knox. Kimmel was replaced by the calm and confident Chester W. Nimitz, a slender, blue-eyed, sandy-haired Texan of thirty-six years' naval service. Nimitz was heading the Bureau of Navigation at the Navy Department in Washington when he was selected for the CINCPAC post by President Roosevelt, and over a legion of admirals more senior.

"Tell Nimitz to get the hell out to Pearl and stay there till the war is won," Roosevelt grumbled to Knox.

Nimitz would be reporting directly to Admiral Ernest J. King, who had been newly appointed to the post of Commander-in-Chief United States Fleet (COMINCH). On March 12, 1942, an Executive Order merged his position with that of Chief of Naval Operations (CNO), granting King complete operational control over the US Navy and, consequently, making him one of the most powerful admirals in world history. *Incorrigible, autocratic, territorial,* and *uncompromising* are but a few of the adjectives used by his contemporaries to describe Ernest J. King the man; other observations made in private were undoubtedly more colorful. FDR once quipped that King "shaved every morning with a blow torch," while one of the admiral's own daughters would remark, "He's the most even-tempered person in the United States Navy. He's always in a rage."

"King was a sailor's sailor," declared Samuel Eliot Morison, the Harvard professor and Naval Reserve officer who served as the US Navy's official historian during World War II. "He believed what was good for the navy was good for the United States, and indeed the world. In that sense and in that alone he was narrow. But he had a firm grasp of naval strategy and tactics, an encyclopedic knowledge of naval detail, an immense capacity for work, and complete integrity. Endowed with a superior intellect himself, he had no toleration for fools or weaklings."

Landing in Pearl Harbor on Christmas Day, Chester Nimitz barely had time to unpack his valise, meet his new staff, and survey the damage wrought by the Japanese attack before he received a radio message from King, urging him to "undertake some aggressive action for the effect on general morale." An expedient change-of-command ceremony was conducted on the foredeck of the submarine *Grayling* on the final day of 1941, between the passing of persistent tropical rain squalls and amid the sickening stench of rotting flotsam and the thick gobs of spilled fuel oil that still marred the surface of the harbor.

Afterward, Nimitz was asked by Robert Casey of the *Chicago Daily News* what he planned to do next. Putting on an optimistic face, Nimitz replied with the lyrical Hawaiian phrase *ho'omanawanui,* meaning "all things will work out in the fullness of time." That answer, of course, did not satisfy the reporter.

"It means bide your time, keep your powder dry, and take advantage of the opportunity when it's offered," Nimitz further explained, leading Casey to later remark that the admiral "was reasonably frank about saying nothing."

Nimitz knew that King was correct; the fight needed to be taken to the Japanese. The navy had been caught flat-footed on December 7, and further humiliated by their failure to deliver relief to the gallant defenders of Wake Island. Now losses were mounting in the western Pacific as the Japanese steamrolled over the Philippines and Dutch East Indies. Before the war, the US Navy's annual "fleet problems" had envisioned a major sortie in response to a Japanese attack, with battleships at the core of the fleet formation, flanked by cruisers and destroyers and with carriers bringing up the rear to provide air cover, all steaming west to hunt down and destroy the Japanese Combined Fleet. After Pearl Harbor, such an ambitious naval campaign was clearly out of the question. Nimitz would be forced to throw away the playbook and order the deployment of highly mobile task forces centered on an aircraft carrier, screened by fast cruisers and destroyers.

On February 1, Vice Admiral William F. "Bull" Halsey Jr.'s *Enterprise* task force conducted the first of several hit-and-run carrier raids against Japanese advanced bases, a strategy King would famously describe as "Hold what you've got and hit 'em where you can." American carrier planes pounded the airfields and port facilities of Roi, Namur, and Kwajalein in the Marshall Islands and struck at Japanese shipping anchored in Kwajalein's vast lagoon. Japanese installations on the islands of Wotje and Taroa were also bombarded by the heavy cruisers *Northhampton*, *Salt Lake City*, and *Chester*. On that same day, Task Force 17, under the command of Vice Admiral Frank "Jack" Fletcher flying his flag from the carrier *Yorktown*, launched a similar raid against the Japanese advanced bases of Makin, Jaluit, and Milli in the Gilbert Islands.

These "bold and audacious" operations, according to Yamamoto's chief-of-staff, Rear Admiral Matome Ugaki, were "heaven's admonition for our shortcomings." Flouting all conventional wisdom, the American carriers ventured deep into enemy-held waters to strike Japanese installations, closing to well within range of enemy shore-based air power before launching their own planes. The daring and aggressive Bill Halsey would prove ideally suited for the task, playing a hard-charging, seagoing Sherman to the more methodical Nimitz's Grant. Halsey was a briny old sea warrior, whose charisma and profane catchphrases would endear him to the sailors of the fleet and war correspondents alike.

"We had been whipped in the attack that opened the war and had been on the defensive ever since," Halsey would later write. "When our task forces sortied for the Marshalls raid, you could almost smell the defeatism around Pearl. Now the offensive spirit was reestablished; officers and men were bushy-tailed again. So, presently, was the American public. At last we had been able to answer their roweling question, *Where is the Navy?*"

In the meantime, naval cryptanalysts at the Fleet Radio Unit in Melbourne, Australia—FRUMEL—and at the Combat Intelligence Unit of the 14th Naval District in Pearl Harbor—Station HYPO—had begun to suspect that the Japanese were preparing for another major offensive in the South Pacific. The intelligence shops, which were by then able to partially decode messages sent in the Japanese Navy's JN-25B radio cipher, had been tipped off by a marked increase in the volume of enemy radio traffic. An analysis of just which Japanese commands were exchanging these messages indicated that the next target might be northeastern Australia, the New Hebrides, or New Caledonia, and that Rabaul was the likely staging area for the new assault.

Nimitz then dispatched Vice Admiral Wilson Brown's Task Force 11, built around the carrier *Lexington*, to the South Pacific in order to be in a position to counter the next Japanese move. The late morning of February 20 would find the *Lexington*, accompanied by four heavy cruisers and ten destroyers, just 350 miles northeast of New Britain and steaming on a southwesterly course at 20 knots, intent on launching a hit-and-run strike against Rabaul the following morning at first light. Their presence would soon be detected by Japanese search planes, and that afternoon eighteen twin-engined Mitsubishi G4M "Betty" medium bombers were sent to attack the *Lexington* group.

This would prove to be a suicide mission, as the vulnerable Betties had been hastily armed and launched without any fighter escort. Sixteen would be shot down by the *Lexington*'s fighters or by antiaircraft fire from the carrier and her screening vessels. Knowing that the element of surprise had been lost and that evasive maneuvers performed during the

Japanese air attack had caused his ships to consume extra fuel, Brown ordered his force to withdraw. On March 6, Australian Consolidated PBY Catalina flying boats patrolling the straits between New Guinea and New Britain would confirm what the codebreakers at FRUMEL and HYPO already suspected—the Japanese 4th Fleet was on the move.

Reconnaissance aircraft found Rabaul's Simpson Harbor nearly empty, and Japanese warships and transports were spotted heading into Huon Gulf, a large inlet on the northeastern coast of New Guinea. Their obvious intention was to establish beachheads at both Lae and Sala-maua, two small ports 20 miles apart and facing each other across the gulf. Both towns already had first-rate airfields, operated in peacetime by New Guinea Airways for the purpose of providing passenger and cargo service to nearby gold mining operations. Naval intelligence had already determined that Lae and Salamaua were to serve as bases of support for a planned Japanese assault on Port Moresby, which lay on the southern coast of the Papuan Peninsula across the rugged, 15,000-foot spine of the Owen Stanley mountain range.

On the morning of March 10, the deep rumble of aircraft engines echoed across the jungle-covered slopes of New Guinea's mountain passes. Cruising just off Port Moresby on a flat, calm sea were the *Lexington* and *Yorktown*. A strike mission of 104 aircraft was winging south to attack the Japanese amphibious forces off-loading at Lae and Salamaua. In addition to excellent flying weather, the naval aviators also enjoyed the element of surprise, for no Japanese Zero fighters were there to oppose them. Crated supplies, vehicles, and docks were set ablaze, shore parties and infantry units were strafed, and a transport, a minesweeper, and a light cruiser were sunk.

The shock and suddenness of the raid would prompt Vice Admiral Shigeyoshi Inouye to postpone the planned leapfrog movement to Port Moresby until early May. With the wily American flat-tops lurking somewhere in the Coral Sea between New Guinea and Australia, Inouye wanted the carriers of the *Kido Butai* present to provide additional air cover for his invasion fleet. Then the 4th Fleet would have sufficient strength to not only execute the Port Moresby operation, but seize Tulagi in the Solomon Islands at the same time.

\*\*\*

As far back as November 1941, big four-engined Kawanishi H8K flying boats, code-named "Emily" by the Allied forces, had been performing reconnaissance missions over the Solomons. After Pearl Harbor, small flights of Japanese planes began performing somewhat desultory strikes against Tulagi. The raids had little effect other than to hasten the evacuation of British colonists and Chinese merchants, and served to sharpen the skills of coastwatchers in identifying and reporting the strength, course, and speed of Japanese aircraft formations.

That would all change on April 25, 1942, when Japanese planes based on Rabaul pummeled the seaplane base on nearby Gavutu-Tanambogo with a renewed ferocity. Similar air strikes against the Tulagi area continued every day for the next week, growing steadily in their intensity and prompting the RAAF to evacuate its surviving PBY Catalinas from the Solomons. On the second day of May, the Australian coastwatcher Jack Read, assigned to watch over Buka Passage on the northern tip of Bougainville, reported a large formation of Japanese ships steaming southeast down the New Georgia Sound.

This was the Tulagi invasion force, commanded by Rear Admiral Kyohide Shima, consisting of two *Mutsuki*-class destroyers, five minesweepers, two subchaser patrol craft, a 7,600-ton freighter, and two large minelayers that had been converted into troop transports. Embarked were 400 infantrymen, antiaircraft gunners, and construction workers of the Special Naval Landing Force. The invasion group was supported by two naval task forces, which included the light aircraft carrier *Shoho*, six cruisers, a destroyer, and a seaplane tender. Just as Shima's force rounded Savo Island, two small interisland coasters carrying the last holdouts of the Australian military contingent in the Solomons, including RAAF base personnel and commandoes, slipped out of Tulagi Harbor and managed to escape.

Martin Clemens, a District Officer with His Majesty's Colonial Service, had since February been serving as a coastwatcher at Aola Bay on the northeastern shore of Guadalcanal. Clemens was of Scottish blood and Cambridge-educated, a tall and robust young man of considerable endurance and resourcefulness, attributes that would serve him well in the many trying days that lay ahead. When the war broke out, Clemens had petitioned the Colonial Secretary and asked to be released for full-time military service. To his great disappointment the request was denied, the explanation given was that there were too few colonial administrators in the Solomon Islands as it was.

"Little did we know how soon the war would be at our doorstep," Clemens wrote in his memoirs. As a formality, he had been commissioned a captain in the British Solomon Islands Protectorate Defence Force. If captured by the Japanese, it was hoped that his status as a military officer might result in Clemens being detained as a prisoner of war rather than executed as a spy. This was perhaps wishful thinking, for it is highly unlikely that the Japanese, who paid little attention to international law with regard to the humane treatment of prisoners, would have bothered to make such a distinction.

With the help of his nine-man native police force, Clemens developed a rather crude but effective early warning system on Guadalcanal. During daylight hours, a lookout was stationed at the top of a huge banyan tree and would blow into a conch shell to signal the presence of enemy aircraft. In the local patois known as "pidgin," the lookout would then call down to a messenger, reporting the number and type of aircraft seen: "Two fella Kawanishi, come long west." The message was then carried to Clemens at the Aola station, who would broadcast a contact report over the Ferdinand network.

Clemens had passed his twenty-seventh birthday on Guadalcanal that April, but his duties as a colonial officer and coastwatcher kept him so busy that he scarcely noticed. He had overheard Read's sighting report of May 2, and correctly surmised that the Japanese flotilla was headed for Tulagi. Clemens and his men watched the bombing of Tulagi by planes from the *Shoho* just prior to the landing of Japanese troops, and could hear muffled explosions from across the waters of Sealark Channel. Soon afterward one of the two fleeing coasters carrying the haggard and weary members of the Tulagi garrison put into Aola Bay, where the solicitous Clemens took them in and gave them breakfast. On the beach after sunset, the men were able to see the yellow glow of the burning seaplane base on Gavutu-Tanambogo.

"That night, the third of May, was one of the most miserable in my life," Clemens would write. "None of us dared to go to sleep, in case some hostile visitor appeared out of the dark to catch us unawares." Martin Clemens did, in fact, manage to snatch a couple hours of sleep just before dawn, only to be shaken awake by the lookout messenger.

"Sah, altogether Japan'e catch'm trouble!" the messenger said excitedly. As he wiped the sleep from his eyes, Clemens became aware of the sound of aircraft motors, a much heavier bass droning than he was accustomed to hearing from Japanese planes.

"About 0800 the noise of airplanes from the north increased, and we rushed out to witness the magnificent spectacle of twelve dive bombers plunging down out of the clouds over Tulagi," Clemens described. "Another squadron of twelve bombers followed shortly afterward, and we spotted four fighters after 1230. What a sight for sore eyes—it was the largest number of Allied planes that most of us had ever seen."

What the coastwatcher and his guests were witnessing was, in fact, the opening salvo in the Battle of the Coral Sea. The attacking planes were from the *Yorktown*, flagship of Task Force 17 under Jack Fletcher. The minelayer-transport *Okinoshima* and the destroyer *Kikuzuki* were both hit by Douglas SBD Dauntless dive bombers during the attack, leaving the *Kikuzuki* so badly damaged that she had to be beached on the shores of Gavutu to prevent her sinking. Shima managed to put the landing force ashore and get his ships underway to clear the harbor by early afternoon, just as a second strike from the *Yorktown* arrived overhead. Two of the departing minesweepers were sunk by American dive bombers, while Grumman F4F Wildcat fighters shot down a pair of Japanese float planes over Tulagi Harbor. Afterward they strafed the beachhead and the bridge of the destroyer *Yuzuki*, killing her captain and nine of her crew.

Signals intelligence provided by Lieutenant Commander Joseph Rochefort and his team of Japanese linguists and codebreakers at Station HYPO had allowed Admiral Nimitz to stay one step ahead of the Japanese. On April 29, CINCPAC ordered the *Yorktown* group along with the *Lexington* task force, now under the command of Rear Admiral Aubrey Fitch, to intercept the anticipated Japanese moves against Port Moresby and Tulagi. Fletcher would exercise tactical command over the combined force, which consisted of two carriers, six heavy cruisers, and thirteen destroyers. Having just completed the final and most audacious of the early hit-and-run carrier raids, which saw sixteen army B-25 medium bombers under Lieutenant Colonel Jimmy Doolittle launch from the carrier *Hornet* to bomb Tokyo itself, Bill Halsey's Task Force 16 was also racing south to join Fletcher.

Halsey would not arrive in time to join the fight. Over the next four days, Fletcher's task forces slugged it out with Inouye's 4th Fleet in what would be the first of the great carrier duels of the Pacific War, where all the destruction was wrought by carrier-based planes and the opposing fleets never came within sight of one other. For his second attempt at taking Port Moresby, Inouye's fleet had been reinforced by Carrier Division 5, made up of the *Shokaku* and *Zuikaku*, veterans of the attack on Pearl Harbor. Both of their air groups would be badly mauled in the battle, losing nearly one hundred aircraft along with most of their pilots. The *Shokaku* was seriously damaged by three direct hits from Fletcher's SBDs and forced to return to Japan for extensive repairs. The light carrier *Shoho* was sunk.

Wracked by serious internal explosions after being struck by two bombs and two aerial torpedoes, the *Lexington* had to be scuttled. The Americans would also lose sixty-nine aircraft, a destroyer, and a fleet oiler. The *Yorktown* was sent limping back to Pearl Harbor with a gaping hole in her flight deck and a hull pierced by several near misses, a gleaming oil slick trailing in her wake.

Coral Sea would be counted as an American victory by the narrowest of margins. While the naval battle itself had been fought to a near draw, in the end the Japanese were forced to reverse course and cancel their planned invasion of Port Moresby. His days as a seagoing admiral at an end, Shigeyoshi Inouye was subsequently relieved of command of the 4th Fleet and recalled to Japan.

Less than a month later, Joe Rochefort and the staff of Station HYPO would deliver to Admiral Nimitz what was perhaps the greatest intelligence coup of the entire Pacific War. After sifting through hundreds of decrypted radio intercepts and performing many hours of painstaking analysis, Rochefort informed the CINCPAC intelligence officer, Commander Ed Layton, that the Japanese were planning to invade Midway Island, an American advanced base 1,500 nautical miles northwest of Pearl Harbor. Yamamoto had ordered the vast majority of the Japanese Combined Fleet to sortie for the operation, with Vice Admiral Chuichu Nagumo's powerful First Carrier Striking Force in the van. A massive fleet comprised of four heavy and two light carriers, seven battleships, fifteen cruisers, forty-two destroyers, and numerous auxiliaries along with a landing force of 5,000 elite Japanese troops was expected to arrive in the waters off Midway during the first week of June.

Admiral Nimitz hastened to reinforce the Midway garrison with everyone and everything available, including old and new aircraft of all types, shore defense guns, tanks, antiaircraft batteries, a battalion of Marine Raiders, and the PT boats of MTBRON 1, now under the command of Lieutenant Clinton McKellar Jr.

"My boat and another boat were at Wiliwili, Kauai, when we received orders to rendezvous with the balance of our squadron west of Kauai Point," recalled Clark Faulkner, skipper of the *PT-22*. "I ran alongside Clint McKellar's PT and asked, 'Where the hell are we going?' He said, 'Midway.' I said, 'Where's that?' He said, 'Look at the chart.' And he threw a roll of charts over to me. So we ran on our own bottoms 1,500 miles to Midway."

In what would be the longest open water run yet made by PT boats, all twelve of McKellar's boats struck out for Midway on May 25, 1942, and were refueled by seaplane tenders along the route. After the better part of four days at sea, the boats arrived in Midway lagoon only slightly worse for wear, all except for the unfortunate *PT-23*, which had to return to Hawaii after suffering a broken crankshaft.

With Bill Halsey laid up at the naval hospital in Pearl Harbor after an attack of debilitating psoriasis, Nimitz turned command of Task Force 16 over to Halsey's capable subordinate, Rear Admiral Raymond Spruance. Two carriers, six heavy cruisers, and nine destroyers stood out from Pearl Harbor on May 28, with Spruance flying his flag from the

*Enterprise.* Fletcher's Task Force 17 would follow two days later, after the *Yorktown* was hurriedly patched together in just seventy-two hours by the Pearl Harbor Navy Yard. Their destination was the aptly named "Point Luck," a rendezvous point 325 miles north of Midway where they would lie in wait for the approaching Japanese fleet.

What followed was one of the most pivotal battles in the history of naval warfare, an epic David-versus-Goliath struggle that would ultimately turn the tide of the Pacific War. Nagumo's carrier planes bombed and strafed Midway Island on the morning of June 4, 1942, inflicting moderate damage but failing to put the airfield out of action. The sailors of 'RON 1 would once again acquit themselves in battle, their machine guns contributing to the Midway garrison's withering volume of antiaircraft fire that knocked down eleven Japanese planes.

The PT boats also rescued several downed marine aviators who had been forced to ditch their stricken aircraft or parachute into the sea after their obsolete Brewster F2A Buffalo fighters proved no match for the fast and nimble Japanese Zero. During the one-sided dogfight, a few Brewster pilots purposefully dove for the PTs in the lagoon with Zeroes hot on their tails, hoping that the enemy fighters would be driven off by the heavy machine gun fire of the boats. On one occasion, PT sailors witnessed a Japanese Zero pilot firing upon an American who had bailed out of his damaged plane and was drifting downward in a parachute.

"We all opened up on him," Al Stockdale remembered. "He veered off and the [American] pilot was saved. In fact, the pilot came aboard the boat and thanked us for being in the right place at the right time for him."

American carrier-based torpedo planes and the Midway air group suffered greatly while pressing home their attacks on the Japanese fleet, but the redoubtable SBD dive bomber pilots flying from the decks of *Enterprise* and *Yorktown* would send all four Japanese fleet carriers and a heavy cruiser to the bottom. Every one of Nagumo's 248 combat aircraft were either shot down, lost at sea, or went down with their sinking carriers. Over 3,000 Japanese were killed, including many more of their irreplaceable naval aviators, and once again a Japanese invasion armada had been forced into retreat. The Americans would lose the tired *York-town* and a destroyer, along with 150 aircraft and 300 personnel killed in action.

As night fell on June 4, the boats of MTBRON 1 sortied from Midway lagoon and steered northwest through a band of rain squalls on a search for the damaged remnants of Nagumo's strike force. Finding only burning patches of fuel oil and floating debris, the PTs returned to base when the first rays of dawn appeared on the eastern horizon.

# A Helluva Way to Run a War

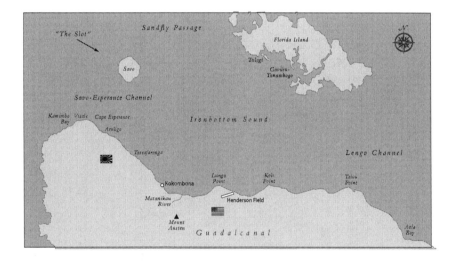

For the men of the First Marine Division, their first glimpse of Guadalcanal was that of a dark, saw-toothed mass jutting from the distant horizon beneath the twinkling Southern Cross, a deeper black shadow against the gloom of the early morning sky. Gathered at the starboard railing of the crowded transport ship *American Legion*, the marines gazed across the intervening expanse of ink-black sea and spoke in low tones, as if they were wary of arousing their sleeping enemy.

A steady tropical breeze tousled their hair—the Corps had yet to develop an obsession with high-and-tight haircuts—and pressed the olive-colored dungarees against their lean and hardened bodies. Weapons, ammunition, and deuce gear had been carefully inspected and re-inspected dozens of times. The smoking lamp was out, causing idle hands to fidget anxiously. Displaying the sort of nascent bravado commonly found among untested young men, some expended their nervous energy by chatting expressively with their buddies, speculating on what they might encounter upon hitting the beach. They had already breakfasted on the hearty Australian staple of steak and eggs, which, for those whose stomachs had permitted them to eat, would be the last square meal they would receive for quite some time.

Drifting among the marines and scribbling into a black gilt-edged notebook was Richard Tregaskis, an affable, bespectacled, and exceptionally tall and lanky reporter for Hearst's International News Service. Tregaskis was a twenty-five-year-old native of Elizabeth, New Jersey, and a graduate of Harvard University, and though of prime military age had been classified 4-F due to poor eyesight and a newly diagnosed case of diabetes. He also stood at 6 feet, 7 inches, a height that the military viewed as too burdensome to accommodate. Airplane cockpits, tank turrets, and shipboard compartments were simply not designed for men that tall. Still determined to contribute to the war effort in some meaningful way, Tregaskis managed to make his way to the Pacific as a war correspondent, where he covered the Doolittle Raid and the Battle of Midway from the flight deck and ready rooms of the carrier *Hornet*. After being tipped off by Admiral Ray Spruance that something big was about to happen in the South Pacific, he asked to be embedded with the marines.

Before shipping out for the Solomons, Tregaskis was issued the longest set of marine dungarees that could be found, which still failed to completely cover his slender wrists and ankles. His extraordinarily large feet posed another problem: Marine Corps boondockers in size 14W were hard to come by. Until a pair could be procured, he would be forced to wear canvas sneakers with his uniform. One marine expressed concern that if the tall and gangly Tregaskis were captured, the enemy might try to use him as an observation post.

Ascending to the bridge of the transport, Tregaskis found the ship's officers "less calm than the marines. Theirs was the worry of getting the ship to anchorage without her being sunk, and they seemed high-strung and incredulous."

The fifty-odd attack transports, cargo vessels, cruisers, and destroyers of Task Force 62, under the command of Rear Admiral Richmond Kelly Turner, had managed to close to within visual range of Guadalcanal without any indication of their being spotted by the Japanese.

"I can't believe it," a navy lieutenant said to Tregaskis. "I wonder if the Japs are that dumb. Either they're dumb, or it's a trick."

There were no tricks at hand. The Japanese had simply been caught unawares, their relaxed vigilance a symptom of what Admiral Matome Ugaki, Yamamoto's chief-of-staff, would later call "victory disease." It hadn't taken long, after their unabated series of triumphs across the Pacific, for an institutional complacency and overconfidence to pervade both the Japanese Army and Navy. Most Japanese—even those serving in the military—remained blissfully ignorant of the heavy losses suffered in the Coral Sea battle and of the shattering defeat at Midway.

Upon their return to mainland Japan, survivors of the Midway operation had been confined to their bases and forbidden to communicate with family or friends. State-controlled media trumpeted the news of yet another smashing Japanese victory while providing wildly exaggerated claims of American losses, leading many to believe that the US Navy was on the verge of total collapse. Ineffective radio intelligence, half-hearted air searches, and now inattentive shore-based lookouts had all aided Turner in achieving complete surprise. For the Japanese based on Guadalcanal and across the Sealark Channel on Tulagi and Gavutu-Tanambogo, their first indication of the presence of an American naval task force was the horrifying shriek of incoming 8-inch high-explosive shells.

"Suddenly, from the bridge, I saw a brilliant yellow-green flash of light coming from the shape of a cruiser on our starboard bow," Tregaskis would describe. "I saw the red pencil lines of the shells arching through the sky, saw flashes on the dark shore of Guadalcanal where they struck. A second later I heard the b-rroom-boom of the cannonading. I should have been ready for that, but was nervous enough, so that I jumped at the sound."

The time was 6:14 a.m. on August 7, 1942.

Ten weeks earlier, Melanesian natives had brought word to Martin Clemens that Japanese scouting parties were landing on Guadalcanal's Lunga Point. Shortly afterward there were reports of Japanese destroyers anchored offshore, of a wharf being constructed, and a tent camp established just inland from the beach. Days later, the Japanese were observed setting fire to the kunai grass on the site of the now-abandoned Lever Brothers copra plantation.

Clemens conferred via teleradio with Don Macfarlan and Ashton "Snowy" Rhoades, two fellow coastwatchers stationed on opposite ends of the 90-mile-long island. Rhoades speculated that the Japanese were burning the grass in order to clear the way for a new airfield. His suspicions would be confirmed on July 6, when a convoy of thirteen Japanese supply ships dropped anchor off Lunga Point and began unloading earth-moving equipment, road rollers, trucks, generators, gasoline drums, tentage, construction materials, provisions, and even an ice-making plant. A force of 2,200 Korean laborers was deposited ashore along with 400 Japanese combat troops. A proclamation was issued to all Guadalcanal natives that able-bodied men between the ages of fourteen and fifty would be required to go to work for the Japanese.

"The Japs appeared to have settled in on Guadalcanal," Clemens wrote.

Their position growing more precarious by the day, the coastwatchers packed up their bulky teleradio sets and took to the surrounding jungle. Accompanied by a small, dedicated band of native policemen and his mongrel dog Suinao, Clemens set up residence in the remote mountaintop village of Vungana. The days that followed were spent gathering intelligence on Japanese activities with the help of native scouts, dodging enemy patrols and low-flying Kawanishis, and struggling to maintain the benzene-fueled generator that charged the batteries of the teleradio. Food and supplies soon began to run short, and the fear of being discovered by the Japanese was looming large. From Ferdinand headquarters came vague and cryptic responses to the coastwatchers' situation reports, encouraging them to "stick it out," and that "it won't be long now."

"Having gone to bed with no dinner on 6 August, I slept pretty solidly, and it was not the dawn that awakened me," Clemens recalled. "Starting about 0610, very heavy detonations, at very short intervals, were heard from Lunga and Tulagi. There was no doubt what they meant. I was up in a flash, tired no longer. I could hardly comprehend that help had finally come, and yet, instinctively, I knew that it had."

From their mountaintop perch, Clemens and his men counted over thirty Allied warships cruising slowly through the Sealark Channel, and saw the gun barrels of cruisers and destroyers spouting bursts of flame and pillars of smoke as they provided covering fire for the schools of tiny landing craft streaming ashore. Twisting the tuning dials of his teleradio, Clemens soon heard voices that were distinctly American, and shortly afterward came an announcement that the US Marines had landed on Tulagi and Guadalcanal.

"I had heard of the marines, but had never met them at close quarters," Clemens recalled.

***

Crouched behind the gunwale of a Higgins landing boat as it churned toward Guadalcanal's northern shore was Private First Class Robert Leckie, a machine gunner assigned to H Company, 2nd Battalion/1st Marines. Leckie and his squad listened to the sound of naval artillery shells tearing through the sky and the steady thrumming of the boat's motor, steeling themselves for the moment they would be forced to trundle through the surf and across the flat, wide-open beach through intense Japanese machine gun and mortar fire.

"The boat struck the shore, lurched, and came to a halt," Leckie remembered. "Instantly I was up and over. The blue sky seemed to swing in a giant arc. I had a glimpse of palm fronds swaying gently above, the most delicate and exquisite sight I have ever seen. There followed a blur. It was a swiftly shifting kaleidoscope of form and color and movement. I lay panting on the sand, among the tall coconut trees, and realized I was wet up to the hips. I had gotten twenty yards inland. But there was no fight. The Japanese had run. We lay there, fanned out in battle array, but there was no one to oppose us. Within moments, the tension had relaxed. We looked at the exotic surroundings. Soon there were grins and wisecracks."

"Hey lieutenant," one of Leckie's buddies called out to their platoon leader. "This is a helluva way to run a war."

\*\*\*

The overall strategy for "running the war" had been devised long before the attack on Pearl Harbor. The most recent "Rainbow" series of war plans, drawn up by the Army-Navy Joint Planning Board between 1938 and 1940, had superseded the "color-coded" plans of the 1920s. The most applicable of these would turn out to be Rainbow Five, which anticipated that the United States would be allied with Great Britain in a two-ocean war against the German-Italian-Japanese Axis. Rainbow Five called for a concentration of Allied forces against what was considered the greater threat, the forces of Nazi Germany, while outlining the mostly defensive measures to be implemented in the Pacific.

This "Germany first" strategy was formally adopted at the Arcadia Conference, held in Washington, DC, just two weeks after America's entry into the war, and attended by Roosevelt and Churchill along with their most senior generals and admirals. The Arcadia talks resulted in the formation of the Combined Chiefs of Staff, an Anglo-American panel that would decide upon matters of global military strategy and resource allocation. It was agreed that the Allied war effort would be organized into geographical theaters of operations, each led by a supreme commander exercising control over all Allied forces in the region. It was further agreed that a joint British and American expeditionary force would invade French Morocco and Algeria in late 1942, opening a second front to the rear of German and Italian forces operating in Libya and Egypt.

Admiral Ernest J. King, however, wanted to recapture Tulagi and Guadalcanal in the Solomon Islands, "Germany first" policies notwithstanding. Moreover, he wanted the US Navy and its marines to do the job.

"From the outset of the war, it had been evident that the protection of our lines of communications to Australia and New Zealand represented a *must*," King wrote in a report to the Secretary of the Navy. "With the advance of the Japanese in that direction, it was therefore necessary to plan and execute operations which would stop them. Early in April, the Japanese had overrun the island of Tulagi, where on 4 May 1942 they were attacked by our carrier-based bombers just before the Battle of the Coral Sea. In July, the enemy landed troops and laborers on Guadalcanal Island and began the construction of an airfield. As the operation of land-based planes from that point would immediately imperil our control of the New Hebrides and New Caledonia areas, the necessity of our ejecting them from those positions became increasingly apparent."

With his usual level of dogged persistence, King pleaded his case for an invasion of Tulagi and Guadalcanal before his fellow members of the US Joint Chiefs of Staff. In addition to invoking the time-honored military aphorism that the best defense was a strong offense, King argued that momentum and timing were also critical factors in the decision. The time to push into the lower Solomons was *now*, while the Americans still held the initiative in the aftermath of their resounding victory at Midway, and before the Japanese could complete the airfield on Guadalcanal and consolidate their positions. King's "offensive-defensive" plan, code-named Operation Watchtower, was approved by the Joint Chiefs on July 2, 1942.

By that time, the vast Pacific theater of operations had been divided into two major areas of responsibility. From his headquarters in Brisbane, General Douglas MacArthur commanded all American, British, Dutch, and Commonwealth troops in the Southwest Pacific Area (SWPA), which included Australia, Papua New Guinea, the Philippines, Borneo, the Dutch East Indies, and the upper Solomon Islands. Admiral Chester Nimitz, while retaining command of the US Pacific Fleet, had assumed the additional role of CINCPOA, or Commander-in-Chief Pacific Ocean Areas. Since this command was responsible for conducting combat operations across the greater portion of the earth's surface, it was subdivided into North, Central, and South Pacific area commands. The latter, known as SOPAC, encompassed the land, sea, and sky south of the equator and east of 160 degrees longitude, and was commanded by Vice Admiral Robert L. Ghormley from his headquarters in Auckland, New Zealand.

On June 24, a full two weeks before his Watchtower plan won the approval of the Joint Chiefs, King transmitted a warning order "to be handled with the utmost secrecy" by Nimitz, instructing COMSOPAC to begin planning for the "seizure of Tulagi and adjacent islands." In Auckland two days later, Admiral Ghormley was paid a courtesy call by Major General Alexander Archer Vandegrift, who had just arrived in the New Zealand port city of Wellington with the vanguard of his First Marine Division.

"Vandegrift, I have some very disconcerting news," Ghormley told the marine.

"I'm sorry to hear that, Admiral," Vandegrift responded.

"You'll be more sorry when you read this," Ghormley replied, handing Vandegrift a copy of the top-secret dispatch.

"Archie" Vandegrift was a seasoned old campaigner who had seen his first combat action in Nicaragua while serving under the legendary Smedley Butler back in 1912. He had led an infantry platoon during the fighting at Veracruz, pursued Charlemagne Peralte and his bloodthirsty throng of bandits through the jungles of Haiti, and commanded Marine Embassy Guards in the tension-filled atmosphere of mainland China in the late 1930s. Every inch a US Marine, Vandegrift was steeped in the sacred traditions of the Old Corps, which had built its storied reputation on being the "First to Fight."

But at this Vandegrift was aghast. His First Marine Division was to serve as the landing force for Operation Watchtower, set to begin in just five weeks time, on August 1, 1942.

"I didn't even know the location of Guadalcanal," Vandegrift would admit. "I knew only that my division was spread over hell's half-acre, one-third in Samoa, one-third in New Zealand, and one-third still at sea. My equipment, much of it new, had to be broken in; my supply had to be sorted and combat-packaged, shortages had to be determined and filled. After explaining all of this to Ghormley, I said, 'I just don't see how we can land anywhere by August first.'"

Convinced that such a premature foray into the Solomons would lead to disaster, Ghormley bitterly replied, "I don't see how we can land at all."

Fortunately, the SOPAC commander was able to postpone the operation for another week, until August 7. While Vandegrift's staff gathered all the crude maps and sketchy intelligence of the islands that could be found in order to begin developing their operations plans, marines and sailors labored on the Wellington docks day and night to offload the division's equipment and supplies. The gear then had to be properly combat-loaded back onto the attack transports and cargo vessels. Ready or not, the First Marine Division shipped out for the Solomon Islands on July 31, after a hastily organized landing exercise was conducted on the beaches of Koro Island in the Fijis, an effort the frustrated Vandegrift would describe as "a complete bust."

The ships of Kelly Turner's South Pacific Amphibious Force—also known as Task Force 62—aboard which Vandegrift's marines were embarked, were being escorted by five American and three Australian heavy cruisers and a squadron of destroyers under the command of Rear Admiral Victor Crutchley of the Royal Navy. Keeping station to the south of Guadalcanal were the aircraft carriers *Saratoga*, *Enterprise*, and *Wasp*, the new fast battleship *North Carolina*, six cruisers, and sixteen destroyers belonging to Jack Fletcher's Task Force 61.

As the invasion fleet rounded the northwestern tip of Guadalcanal at 2:40 a.m. on August 7, a half-dozen transports sheered away from the main column and steamed for Tulagi. Embarked aboard these ships was a landing force under the command of the assistant division commander, Brigadier General William Rupertus, comprising Colonel Merritt Edson's elite First Raider Battalion, the First Parachute Battalion, and two infantry battalions. The remaining ships of Turner's amphibious task force continued on for Guadalcanal's Lunga Point, carrying the First, Fifth, and Eleventh Marine Regiments along with Vandegrift's division headquarters and support units, some 11,000 men.

Taken completely by surprise, the Japanese troops and their Korean laborers on Guadalcanal fled into the surrounding jungle when the first shells of the Allied shore bombardment screamed downward to burst within their encampments. Just after 9:00 a.m., the marines scrambled from their landing craft onto what had been designated as Beach Red, a 2,000-yard section of the island's northern shoreline near Lunga Point.

The marines quickly pushed inland for 500 yards, encountering virtually no resistance. The fleeing Japanese left behind a dozen mangled dead, with much of their clothing, weapons, and ammunition still stashed in their bivouacs. Breakfast fires were found smoldering beneath pots of simmering meat stew and rice, next to wooden mess tables where chopsticks had been propped neatly against porcelain bowls. Inside a newly constructed and well-equipped infirmary, marines encountered a weak and febrile Japanese soldier who had been abandoned by his caregivers, his body wracked by malaria.

Marine riflemen poked cautiously through half-finished barracks and elegantly furnished officer's huts before coming upon great stacks of crated provisions, a find that would later prove quite fortuitous. Japanese trucks, cars, bicycles, and a myriad of tractors and construction equipment were captured intact and would soon be put to good use by marine engineers and navy Seabees. As more assault waves came ashore, the marines continued their advance toward the nearly completed but now deserted Japanese airfield.

The first Japanese counterattack against the Guadalcanal landings would come later that day, in the form of twenty-seven medium bombers, sixteen dive bombers, and escorting Zero fighters from the 25th Air Flotilla based at Rabaul. An early warning of the raid was flashed across the Ferdinand emergency frequency by the Australian coastwatcher Paul Mason on Bougainville, allowing time for Fletcher's Wildcat pilots to prepare a proper reception, and for Turner's crews to secure the boating of troops and supplies and man their battle stations. Just over an hour after receiving Mason's alarm, the V formation of Japanese planes appeared over the roadstead. While none of the transport ships were hit in the attack that followed, the destroyer *Mugford* was slightly damaged. Sixteen of the attackers were splashed by American carrier-based fighters and shipboard antiaircraft fire.

Meanwhile, Marine Raiders and Parachutists were landing on Tulagi and Gavutu-Tanambogo to stiff Japanese resistance. Unlike their comrades on Guadalcanal, the 900 troops of the Special Naval Landing Force and the Yokohama Air Group based on these much smaller islands had nowhere to run. A final message was transmitted from the operators of the Japanese radio station on Tulagi just after eight o'clock that morning, informing their parent command at Rabaul that they were burning their codebooks and preparing to demolish their radio equipment.

```
Enemy troop strength is overwhelming. We will
defend to the last man.
```

Withdrawing to a network of bunkers and tunnels carved into Tulagi's rugged limestone cliffs, the Japanese resisted the advance of the Marine Raiders with great ferocity, sallying forth at intervals to perform head-long charges or nocturnal infiltrations of the marine lines. Refusing to surrender even when faced with utterly hopeless odds, the Tulagi garrison kept their promise to their masters in Rabaul and continued to fight until nearly annihilated, an ominous portent of many bloody Pacific island campaigns to come. Just three Japanese survived the fighting on Tulagi to be taken prisoner, while forty-five marines were killed and seventy-six wounded. The Parachute Marines on Gavutu-Tanambogo had a similarly tough fight on their hands, requiring the reinforcement of infantry and light tanks along with supporting naval gunfire and air strikes to finish the job. Seventy Americans were killed in the battle for the two conjoined islets, while 476 of the 536 Japanese defenders perished.

By the late morning of August 8, the marines on Guadalcanal gained possession of the airstrip, which they would soon name Henderson Field in honor of Major Lofton Henderson, a marine aviator killed in action at the Battle of Midway. Later in the day, as shore parties were struggling to move the voluminous supplies that had been piled on the beach to dumps farther inland, the naval air squadrons of Rabaul paid two more visits to the beachhead. After being riddled by antiaircraft fire, a Japanese plane crashed into the transport *George F. Elliot*, which would burn out of control for the next several hours before being abandoned and scuttled. The destroyer *Jarvis* was struck by a torpedo in her starboard side, which flooded her forward fireroom. She would be attacked by Japanese aircraft a second time while on her way to Australia for repairs, and tragically lost with all hands.

That night aboard his flagship *McCawley*, a visibly upset Admiral Turner shared with Vandegrift the stunning news that Jack Fletcher was intending to withdraw his aircraft carriers. Fletcher cited heavy losses among his fighter squadrons—twenty-one Wildcats had been lost over two days of aerial combat, from an original complement of ninety-nine— and that his ships' fuel bunkers were running critically low, an assertion that both Turner and Vandegrift found highly questionable.

"Terrible" Turner was notoriously ill-tempered, but at this he was furious. Without air cover, the admiral explained, his amphibious fleet would also be forced to withdraw, even though much of Vandegrift's badly needed heavy equipment, food, and supplies were still aboard the cargo ships. Turner promised to have his already exhausted crews work throughout the night to land as much material as they could, but the ships would have to depart at daybreak.

Still numb with shock after hearing the news, Vandegrift had no sooner departed from the *McCawley* when, in the general's own words, "all hell broke loose."

Seven heavy cruisers and a destroyer from the newly established Japanese 8th Fleet, commanded by Vice Admiral Gunichi Mikawa, had slipped past two American radar picket destroyers and set upon Crutchley's screening force arrayed to the north and south of Savo Island. Years of rigorous training in night combat operations would pay the Japanese rich dividends; over the course of thirty murderous minutes, they would hand the Americans their worst naval defeat of the war aside from Pearl Harbor.

"The salvos of firing came with increased intensity, so that the sky was lighted by the quick flashes for minutes on end, and the rumbling of the firing was an almost continuous sound," Richard Tregaskis would record. "We knew then that there was a sea fight going on. Possibly, it was the battle for Guadalcanal. Possibly, if our people out there lost the battle, the Japs would be ashore before morning, and we would have to fight for our lives. The terror and power and magnificence of man-made thunder and lightning made that point real. One had the feeling of being at the mercy of great accumulated forces far more powerful than anything human. We were only pawns in a battle of gods, then, and we knew it."

Four heavy cruisers, *Astoria*, *Quincy*, *Vincennes*, and the HMAS *Canberra* were decimated by Japanese gunfire and torpedoes and sank to the floor of the channel. A fifth cruiser, *Chicago*, and two destroyers were badly damaged. Nearly 1,100 Allied sailors lost their lives, and afterward Sealark Channel would be christened with the blood-chilling nickname of Ironbottom Sound.

Admiral Mikawa, however, fearing attacks by American carrier planes in the coming daylight, ordered his ships to turn about and steam for Rabaul immediately after the initial engagement. Had he pressed his advantage and located Turner's transports, the slaughter of Task Force 62 might have been complete. After the devastating losses suffered by the battleship force at Pearl Harbor, it had been up to the 8-inch heavy cruisers to deliver the hitting power of the Pacific Fleet's surface forces. Now three of these priceless warships had been sunk; a fourth was heavily damaged and would spend the next six months in dry dock.

With no air cover, and with only one heavy and two light cruisers remaining along with a handful of "tin can" destroyers for protection, Turner had no choice but to order his transport group to depart immediately, without completing the job of unloading Vandegrift's gear and supplies. The marines on Guadalcanal were on their own. The morning after the disaster at Savo Island, General Vandegrift summoned his regimental and battalion commanders to his command post, which was set up in a coconut grove a few yards inland from Beach Red.

"Sometimes a commander can withhold bad news, sometimes not," Vandegrift wrote. "I told these officers of the major naval engagement whose outcome we did not yet know. I told them of Fletcher's carriers precipitately retiring, which meant the transports were leaving.... God only knew when we could expect aircraft protection, much less surface craft; with the transports gone the enemy would shift his attacks against us and we could expect surface attacks as well."

Knowing how important it was for every man in the division to understand the predicament they were in, Vandegrift instructed his colonels and majors "to relate these unsavory facts to their junior officers, NCOs and men. But they must also pound home that we anticipated no Bataan, no Wake Island. Since 1775 marines had found themselves in tough spots. They had survived and we would survive—but only if every officer and man on Guadalcanal gave his all to the cause." Vandegrift then issued his threefold orders: The defensive perimeter around the beachhead and Henderson Field needed to be contracted and consolidated, all remaining supplies had to be moved off the beach posthaste, and the airfield made ready to receive aircraft.

Daily rations were cut by a third, with marine cooks using the tinned meat, tinned fish, and white rice left behind by the Japanese to supplement the meager twenty-day supply of food that made it ashore. Despite almost daily air raids, work on the airfield progressed at a steady pace, with marine engineers utilizing Japanese tractors, road rollers, and dump trucks fueled by Japanese gasoline. It was during this low ebb, when the marines were left without air or naval support, using captured equipment, living on short rations, and spread thinly along the perimeter that someone began referring to Watchtower as "Operation Shoestring." The name stuck.

Spirits received a welcome boost on August 15, when four fast destroyer-transports made the dangerous run from Espiritu Santo in the New Hebrides and landed a 120-man detachment from CUB One, a navy advanced base support unit, along with barrels of aviation gasoline, aerial bombs, lubricating oil, and spare parts. Five days later, a dozen SBD dive bombers and nineteen Wildcat fighters of Marine Air Group 23 took off from the escort carrier *Long Island* and landed on the newly finished Henderson Field, to the wild cheers of marine infantrymen and engineers.

These were encouraging developments, but Vandegrift was soon faced with yet another daunting problem: Additional Japanese combat troops had landed on Guadalcanal, several miles to the east of the Henderson Field perimeter. This vital bit of intelligence, gathered from the reports of reconnaissance patrols and CINCPAC cryptanalysts, was confirmed by Martin Clemens, who finally emerged from the jungle to offer his services to the marines.

An advanced detachment of 900 troops from the Imperial Japanese Army's 28th Infantry Regiment under the command of Colonel Kiyonao Ichiki, the same unit that was supposed to have taken Midway Island two months earlier, were landed by a half-dozen Japanese destroyers in the early morning hours of August 19 at Taivu Point, 22 miles east of Lunga Point. Acting on faulty reconnaissance information that grossly underestimated the number of American troops on Guadalcanal, and afflicted by the "victory disease" then running rampant through the Japanese military, Ichiki decided to make a brazen frontal assault against the marine defenses. Ichiki's detachment hit the eastern flank of Vandegrift's line along a tidal lagoon the marines had nicknamed "Alligator Creek" at 1:30 a.m. on August 21, beginning with heavy enfilading machine gun and mortar fire, followed by a series of hell-bent, screaming banzai charges across a sandbar where Alligator Creek met the sea.

But the men dug-in on the opposite bank were United States Marines, not the poorly trained, thinly armed, and terrified Chinese conscripts most Japanese soldiers were accustomed to fighting. They not only steadfastly held their ground, as their fathers had at Belleau Wood and as their sons would two decades later at Khe Sanh, but nearly succeeded in wiping out Ichiki's entire command. Accurate rifle, machine gun, mortar, and canister fire ruthlessly mowed down each successive banzai charge, and a sweeping counterattack supported by tanks enveloped the remaining Japanese before they could escape.

Nearly 800 Japanese soldiers were killed, including Colonel Ichiki himself. Only about 30 survivors managed to stagger back to Taivu Point to rejoin the 100-man rear guard. Rear Admiral Raizo Tanaka, commander of Japanese destroyer units during the Guadalcanal campaign, would later compare Ichiki's reckless assault to "a housefly attacking a giant tortoise. The odds were all against it."

At the same time Ichicki and his men were meeting their fate on the banks of Alligator Creek, Tanaka's flagship *Jintsu* was steering a southerly course for Guadalcanal, having put to sea from the Japanese fleet base at Truk on August 16. His mixed squadron of one light cruiser, eight destroyers, and four patrol boats was escorting three slow transports, laden with the balance of Ichiki's regiment along with 1,000 troops of the Special Naval Landing Force.

Tanaka was in a foul mood, despite the fact that his convoy was being escorted by Nagumo's strong task force of three aircraft carriers, three battleships, and numerous cruisers and destroyers. Orders had been handed down from the Imperial General Staff that the Americans were to be driven from the lower Solomons immediately and at all costs. That kind of pressure resulted in operations being planned in haste, and a lack of shipping would cause the reinforcement of Japanese Army units on Guadalcanal to be conducted in a piecemeal fashion. Furthermore, it was known that the airfield on Guadalcanal was now operational, and American carrier task forces were thought to be returning to the Solomons area.

"With no regard for my opinion, as commander of the Reinforcement Force, this order called for the most difficult operation in war—landing in the face of the enemy—to be carried out by mixed units which had no opportunity for rehearsal or even preliminary study," Tanaka would later state. "It must be clear to anyone with knowledge of military operations that such an undertaking could never succeed. In military strategy expedience sometimes takes precedence over prudence, but this order was utterly unreasonable."

American carriers had, in fact, returned to the waters off Guadalcanal. Admiral Fletcher was once again in overall tactical command, flying his flag from the *Saratoga* and accompanied by the *Enterprise* task force led by Rear Admiral Thomas C. Kinkaid. In the ensuing carrier action of August 24, what would come to be known as the Battle of the Eastern Solomons, the Japanese light carrier *Ryujo* was sunk, and heavy bomb damage was dealt to the *Enterprise*. The following morning, Tanaka's convoy was attacked by eighteen planes of the "Cactus Air Force," the name given to the Henderson-based air group, derived from the Allied code name for Guadalcanal.

Admiral Tanaka, who would later admit that his forces had been "caught napping," would be knocked from his feet when a Marine Corps SBD planted a 500-pound bomb on the forecastle of the *Jintsu*, killing twenty-four of the crew and causing intense fires and flooding. The transport *Kinryu Maru*, which was carrying most of the naval infantry detachment, received several direct hits, caught fire, and began listing heavily. As the destroyer *Mutsuki* pulled alongside the sinking ship to take off survivors, a flight of four Espiritu Santo–based B-17 Flying Fortresses suddenly appeared overhead. Five more 500-pounders rained down upon the hapless *Mutsuki,* which sank like a stone. Shifting his flag to the destroyer *Kagero,* the badly shaken Tanaka ordered his surviving vessels to withdraw to the Shortland Islands via the New Georgia Sound.

Tanaka would later remark that the experience "made it more obvious than ever what sheer recklessness it was to attempt a landing operation against strong resistance without preliminary neutralization of enemy air power. If the present operation plan for Guadalcanal was not altered, we were certain to suffer further humiliating and fruitless casualties."

Orders were then received from 8th Fleet Headquarters in Rabaul to "use destroyers to transport army troops." With American strike aircraft now based at Henderson Field, approaching Guadalcanal in daylight was out of the question. Tanaka's destroyers soon began making nocturnal high-speed runs down the New Georgia Sound, delivering reinforcements and supplies to beleaguered Japanese forces on Guadalcanal.

By departing from their base in the Shortlands Islands off the southern tip of Bougainville just before dusk, the ships of Destroyer Squadron Two were able to land their embarked troops, equipment, and supplies on Guadalcanal's shores and be safely out of range of the Cactus Air Force by sunrise. Under the cover of darkness on August 29 and again on August 30, Tanaka's destroyers landed the 1,100 remaining troops of the Ichiki Regiment on Taivu Point. Using this same method, which the Japanese referred to as "Rat Transportation," another 1,000 soldiers belonging to the Kawaguchi Brigade were landed without incident two nights later.

To marines on "The Canal," the Japanese destroyer captains seemed to grow bolder with each successful reinforcement mission. Once their troops were safely ashore, the destroyers would often linger in the waters of Ironbottom Sound, taking the time to fire starshells over the marine positions and pound Henderson Field with their 5-inch guns. The bombardments not only caused damage and casualties but also succeeded in "murdering sleep," as Robert Leckie would describe it while borrowing a phrase from Shakespeare's *Macbeth.* The Americans, who had already named the long and narrow New Georgia Sound "The Slot," soon began calling Tanaka's nightly destroyer runs, which were being conducted with the regularity of a busy commuter rail line, the "Tokyo Express."

General Vandegrift was not amused by such clever nicknames. Rather, he was greatly alarmed at the impunity with which the Japanese were able to land troops, equipment, and supplies on Guadalcanal. Using this slow-but-steady method of building up their forces, it would be only a matter of time before the Japanese had enough heavy weapons and manpower ashore to mount a serious effort to retake the airfield, one that the marines might not be able to hold back.

"We were just not strong enough to stop them from landing troops at their will," Vandegrift would record. "Even if this will were confined to the night, the night was still ten hours long."

Vandegrift found the casual manner with which Japanese destroyers were able to stand offshore and lob high-explosive shells into his positions and kill his marines infuriating to say the least. Despite the recent losses suffered by the US Navy's light forces, something had to be done to derail the Tokyo Express. On September 2, Vandegrift had the following message transmitted to Admiral Turner:

```
To CTF 62, Info COMSOPAC from CACTUS: Appears
enemy is building up striking force by continuous
small landings during darkness. Due to difficult
terrain areas are beyond range of land opera-
tions except at expense of weakening defense of
airfield. We do not have a balanced force and it
is imperative that following measures be taken:
a) Base planes here capable of searching beyond
steaming range during darkness. b) Provide sur-
face craft, DDs or motor torpedo boats for night
patrolling. c) provide striking force for active
defense by transferring 7th Marines to CACTUS.
If not prevented by surface craft enemy can con-
tinue night landings beyond our range of action
and build up large force.
```

Unbeknownst to the hard-pressed commanding general of the First Marine Division, a squadron of PT boats was already on the way.

## CHAPTER FOUR

# In Harm's Way

ON THE FINAL DAY OF AUGUST 1942, LIEUTENANT COMMANDER ALAN Robert Montgomery found himself "flat on his back and reviling his luck" in the sick bay of the USS *Lackawanna*, somewhere in the South Pacific between Balboa, Panama, and the fleet oiler's final destination, the Allied advanced base of Nouméa, New Caledonia.

Montgomery was the son of a Scottish farmer who in 1882 emigrated to Warrenton, a small town of 1,600 located in the Piedmont region of northern Virginia. His father had prospered in the New World well enough to purchase land and send his sons to the local private school for boys, where it was discovered that young Alan was a gifted student. For secondary school he attended Severn College Preparatory in Maryland and in 1923 won an appointment to the US Naval Academy. An Annapolis plebe can expect to be tagged with at least one nickname, and quite predictably Montgomery was called "Monty" by his fellow midshipmen. Since he was somewhat small in stature, or "far from being a brute in appearance" as the yearbook for the Class of 1927 would describe him, Monty would eventually be issued a second and most unflattering nickname of "Squirt."

After graduation, Ensign Montgomery passed his first year with the fleet aboard the battleship *Mississippi* before being transferred to the destroyer tender *Altair*. He would then embark upon a decade-long stint in destroyers, serving aboard the "four-pipers" *Lawrence, Hale,* and *Wickes* before becoming gunnery officer of the *Case*. Along the way, Monty obtained the requisite qualifications in surface warfare to assume more rank and responsibility, and took a wife with whom he had two children. Like a lot of navy marriages, Montgomery's first would eventually succumb to the stresses of transiency and separation and eventually end in divorce. He would marry for a second time in 1941, the same year that he transferred from destroyers to PT boats.

In January 1942 Montgomery assumed command of MTBRON 4, which was tasked with establishing the new Motor Torpedo Boat Training Center at Melville, Rhode Island. Six months later he received orders to relieve Earl Caldwell as commanding officer of 'RON 2, then operating a complement of fourteen Elco 77-footers in the Panama Canal Zone. Based at the port city of Balboa on the Pacific end of the canal, the squadron trained by day and patrolled the Gulf of Panama by night, searching for the presence of prowling Japanese submarines.

On July 27, 1942, Admiral King issued orders for MTBRON 2 to be split into two separate squadrons. The new squadron was to "stand by with eight motor torpedo boats for action somewhere to the westward," while the remaining six boats were to continue watching over the Panama Canal. A few days later, the CNO's office sent word that the eight-boat element would be designated as MTBRON 3, while the remaining six-boat element would retain the name of MTBRON 2.

Montgomery was chosen to lead this new incarnation of John Bulkeley's old unit, and was relieved as commanding officer of MTBRON 2 by Lieutenant George Brackett. Hoping to get into the action and escape the tedium of duty in Panama, several members of 'RON 2 volunteered to join the new squadron. Montgomery selected Lieutenant Hugh M. Robinson as his XO, and together they compared the list of volunteers with a roster of skilled personnel they considered indispensable. Sixteen line officers, one disbursing officer, and 103 enlisted sailors made the final cut.

Since Bulkeley's squadron was never officially decommissioned, Admiral King's decision to name the new squadron MTBRON 3 inevitably led to confusion within the Navy Department. When Montgomery requested the allotment of start-up funds typically issued to a newly commissioned naval squadron, the Bureau of Supplies and Accounts huffily replied that an allotment for MTBRON 3 had already been issued in 1941. According to an official history of the administration of motor torpedo boat squadrons in the Pacific: "All in all, the selection of some number other than *Three* would have proved more expeditious and less confusing."

Exactly where they were going Montgomery and his men weren't told, but they could certainly make an educated guess. The first Allied offensive to take place in the Pacific, Operation Watchtower, had just commenced with the invasion of Tulagi and Guadalcanal. They had all read the newspaper accounts, listened to the scuttlebutt, and pored over charts of the South Pacific. Spaced at relatively close intervals and separated by multiple channels and reef-lined passages, the Solomon Islands offered a protected littoral environment ideally suited for the deployment of motor torpedo boats. Since PTs operated chiefly at night, it was fairly obvious that they were being sent to counter the main threat to American forces on Guadalcanal: the Tokyo Express.

The PT boats would make the 8,000-mile journey by hitching rides aboard larger ships of the fleet passing through the Panama Canal on their way to the South Pacific Area. Montgomery's leading division of four boats, PTs *38*, *46*, *48*, and *60*, were hoisted aboard the big outbound fleet oilers *Lackawanna* and *Tappahannock*, along with quantities of ammunition, stores, and spare parts. The second division would be led by Hugh Robinson, made up of PTs *37*, *39*, *45*, and *61*, and would follow on the next available transport. On August 1, the motor torpedo boat tender USS *Jamestown* set sail from Melville, with orders to rendezvous with 'RON 3 in the Solomons.

In the final hectic days before their departure, Montgomery found himself growing increasingly short of breath and struggled to keep working through mounting fatigue. The four boat captains of the first division, Henry "Stilly" Taylor, Bob Wark, and the brothers Jack and Bob Searles, all noticed the skipper's eyes shining with fever and tried to convince him to visit the local naval hospital. Monty stubbornly refused, fearing that he would be admitted to a sick ward and forbidden to ship out with his unit.

The first division stood out from Panama aboard the two brand-new fleet oilers on August 29, four days before General Vandegrift's request for "motor torpedo boats for night patrolling" was transmitted to Admiral

Turner. Once the mountains of Central America were no longer visible from the fantail of the *Lackawanna*, Montgomery finally consulted the ship's medical officer, who diagnosed him with pneumonia.

*** 

Montgomery's condition had improved only slightly by the time the two PT-bearing oilers arrived at the port of Nouméa in the Free French colony of New Caledonia on September 19, 1942. Admiral Ghormley's SOPAC area command was still in the process of developing Nouméa Harbor, along with Efate's Havannah Harbor in the nearby Anglo-French territory of the New Hebrides, into advanced naval bases to support Watchtower and subsequent operations to drive the Japanese from the Solomons. Nouméa still lacked the heavy-lift hammerhead cranes found in most modern ports, but the Seabees had mounted a large, stiff-legged crane on a floating barge expressly for the purpose of off-loading the PT boats.

When the barge was brought alongside the giant *Lackawanna*, however, it was discovered that the crane was too short to do the job. The *Lackawanna*'s skipper, Commander Albert Toney, solved the problem by transferring several tons of fuel oil into a bunker on the same side of the ship where the floating crane was located, thereby creating a list and lowering the PT boats just enough to allow the crane to lift them clear.

Once the PTs were back in the water, Montgomery and his four boat captains paid a visit to Admiral Robert Ghormley aboard his flagship *Argonne*, then at anchor in Nouméa Harbor. The SOPAC commander had intended to shift his headquarters from New Zealand to New Caledonia in order to be closer to the Solomon Islands, but found the French colonial government there rather aloof and dismissive. The French were unwilling to provide accommodations for Ghormley and his staff, forcing the admiral to run the South Pacific Area and Operation Watchtower from the cramped and stifling flag quarters of the aged fleet auxiliary.

Though appearing tired and harried, Admiral Ghormley offered a cordial greeting to the PT officers and confirmed that 'RON 3 would, in fact, be sent on to the Guadalcanal-Tulagi area for the purpose of interdicting the Tokyo Express. Ghormley then briefed Montgomery and his men on the many new developments in the Guadalcanal campaign that had occurred during their crossing.

After landing more Japanese troops at Taivu Point just after midnight on September 5, three Tokyo Express destroyers attacked and sank the *Little* and the *Gregory*, two old four-pipers that had been converted into fast transports. Two days later, Merritt Edson's First Raider Battalion performed an amphibious raid against the Japanese encampment at Tasimboko village near Taivu Point, after the presence of the camp was discovered by coastwatcher Martin Clemens and his scouts. The Marine Raiders killed twenty-seven Japanese and drove the rest into the jungle. An INS reporter who had tagged along, a man by the name of Dick Tregaskis, located the Japanese headquarters hut and scooped up an armful of documents for Vandegrift's intelligence staff to analyze. The Raiders then burned the enemy camp along with its stockpile of food and supplies . . . all except for the beer and sake, of course. Returning to the Lunga perimeter, the Raiders settled into a network of positions along the crest of a ridge to the south of Henderson Field, a rather quiet sector where they could hopefully get some well-deserved rest.

On the night of September 12, the Japanese light cruiser *Sendai* and three destroyers appeared in Ironbottom Sound, firing high-explosive shells and illuminating the marine positions with searchlights. Soon afterward the Japanese launched a series of ferocious frontal assaults against the positions occupied by Edson's Raiders and the Marine Parachutists. Over two consecutive nights, 6,000 battle-tested troops of the Kawaguchi Brigade repeatedly hurled themselves against the American perimeter.

Time and again the surging waves of attacking Japanese were bloodily repulsed. Though they managed to overrun several positions, the Japanese were quickly dislodged by determined marine counterattacks, with the savage fighting often hand-to-hand. On the second night, several Japanese managed to break through the lines and made it as far as the aircraft revetments at the edge of Henderson Field. Exemplifying the creed "every marine is a rifleman," combat engineers drove them back with heavy losses. At the end of what came to be known as the Battle of Edson's Ridge, the Lunga perimeter remained intact and Vandegrift's troops were still in possession of the airfield. Over 600 Japanese dead were counted, while the marines had lost 80 of their own.

The following day the aircraft carrier *Wasp*, part of a task force covering the movement of the Seventh Marines to Guadalcanal, was sunk in the waters southeast of San Cristobal Island after being torpedoed by a Japanese submarine. With both *Enterprise* and *Saratoga* under repair, Ghormley now had only one carrier left in the South Pacific, the *Hornet*, to parry the next thrust of the Japanese fleet.

The Tokyo Express, in the meantime, continued to run every night. Hundreds of Japanese troops were known to have been put ashore at Cape Esperance, on the northwestern coast of Guadalcanal. On September 20, four Japanese destroyers bombarded Henderson Field for over an hour, killing two Americans and wounding two more.

Admiral Ghormley was obviously under enormous pressure to stop the Tokyo Express. Frustrations were running deep, and not only among the embattled marines on Guadalcanal, many of whom believed that their navy brethren had run off and abandoned them after Savo Island. An entry made on September 14 in the CINCPAC Running Estimate and Summary expressed the perturbation being felt as far away as Pearl Harbor: "It must be recorded that our surface forces in the South Pacific have done nothing the last 30 days to prevent or interrupt these night landings and shellings of marine positions."

"The bombardments had to be stopped," wrote Jack Searles. "[Ghormley] said he did not care if we sunk any ship or even got any hits. The main thing he wanted us to do was harass the Japanese ships and force them to discontinue the nightly bombardments of Guadalcanal."

"Night after night, with all the gall in the world, the Japs had been pouring down from their Bougainville base," Alan Montgomery would add. "They knew—and they knew the marines knew—that the dark nights belonged almost exclusively to them. Those marine pilots on Guadalcanal could not go out in the dark to hunt them down, nor were there any shore guns on the island big enough to touch them. And the Japs were always mighty careful to be out of there, well out of range, by daylight. If we could put a stop to that, or even scare them into being a little less brazen about it, the situation would be improved."

Ghormley proposed the establishment of a motor torpedo boat base at Espiritu Santo in the New Hebrides, with a temporary operating base in the Guadalcanal-Tulagi area. A rotational system could then be employed; while six boats were engaged in combat operations, the other two could be undergoing periodic maintenance at Espiritu Santo with their crews resting and recuperating. Montgomery was not in favor of the plan, especially after experiencing the difficulties of debarking PT boats from larger ships in Nouméa, which had resulted in damage to the charthouse of one boat and one of his officers, Lieutenant Rosie Ryan, suffering a broken leg. The alternative to transshipment was, of course, the PTs making the trip from Tulagi to Espiritu Santo on their own bottoms, a journey of over 600 miles, which would lead to excessive engine hours and greater wear and tear on the boats. It would be better to have the capability of performing overhauls in the forward area, Montgomery insisted, with the aid of tenders and the full shore establishment of an advanced base. After a great deal of discussion, Ghormley decided to accept the squadron commander's recommendations and issued orders for an advanced PT base to be established at Guadalcanal-Tulagi.

Montgomery then sent Lieutenant (jg) Robert Wark, the squadron gunnery officer and skipper of the *48* boat, ahead to Guadalcanal to find a suitable location for the new base. Accompanying Wark was the thirty-year-old Charles Tufts, a veteran chief boatswain's mate who had served for six years aboard the battleship *Maryland* before transferring to PT boats in 1940. Upon reporting to the First Marine Division command post and paying their respects to General Vandegrift, Wark and Tufts were introduced to Commander James P. Compton, commanding officer of the advanced base support unit known as CUB One, which included the Seabees of the Sixth Naval Construction Battalion.

CUB One had been chiefly concerned with keeping Henderson Field in operation, spending much of their time backfilling the shell holes and bomb craters that liberally pockmarked the dirt runways in the aftermath of Japanese naval bombardments and air raids. Admiral Kelly Turner, however, in his capacity as Commander Amphibious Forces South Pacific, was anxious to have Compton's men set to work on the construction of port facilities as well. On September 11, Turner appointed Compton to the post of Commander Advanced Bases Guadalcanal-Tulagi, the first step in forming the organization that would be responsible for developing both air and naval stations in the eastern Solomons.

Compton, Wark, and Tufts sailed for "Ringbolt"—the navy's code name for the island of Tulagi—where they called upon Brigadier General William Rupertus at his headquarters in the vacated British commissioner's residence. All too happy to hear that the navy was sending a squadron of torpedo boats to deal with the Tokyo Express, the general readily agreed to assist the three navy men in finding a site for 'RON 3 to establish their new base of operations. Following a suggestion from Kelly Turner, they first visited Gavutu-Tanambogo, finding the former Australian-then-Japanese seaplane station a shattered mess. All the buildings and wharves had been razed by the pre-invasion naval and air bombardment, and the sickening stench of decaying Japanese corpses still hung thickly in the humid tropical air.

The fighting had also left the conjoined islets nearly denuded of vegetation, with only a few burned and fragment-scarred coconut palms still standing, which would offer the docked PT boats little concealment from aerial reconnaissance. Gavutu-Tanambogo also stood at the near center of the sprawling bay that encompasses much of the southern coast of Florida Island, and the men agreed that a PT base there would be vulnerable to attack from both air and sea, just as the destroyed seaplane base had been.

Rupertus then suggested they investigate Sesapi Cove, site of a now-abandoned Chinese village and mercantile district on the northeastern shore of Tulagi. Like Gavutu-Tanambogo, the fierce battle to retake Tulagi had left few of the buildings and rudimentary waterfront facilities undamaged. However, they found that although the docks at Sesapi had all been destroyed by fire, their timber pilings remained intact. A small-scale marine railway built into the sloping shoreline had been heavily damaged, but once repaired could be useful in hauling PT boats from the water to conduct hull maintenance. The surviving waterfront shacks, made from mostly bamboo and tin and roofed with tightly thatched palm fronds, could be easily mended and converted into maintenance sheds and administrative offices.

Sesapi was also in a fairly secluded location, on the leeward side of Tulagi facing the much larger and mountainous Florida Island, sheltered from the wind and sea and neatly concealed from the view of ships passing through Ironbottom Sound. Remote and primitive though it was, Sesapi offered the most promising spot in the immediate area for establishing a new motor torpedo boat base. After receiving Turner's approval on October 9, Commander Compton dispatched a civil engineering officer, Lieutenant Benjamin Marcus, and a force of sixty Seabees to assist Bob Wark and Charlie Tufts in making Sesapi ready to receive the first echelon of MTBRON 3.

\*\*\*

Back in Nouméa, the four PT boats were being readied for their departure to the Solomons. Moto-macs made their meticulous, painstaking inspections of the Packard motors, and fuel tanks were filled to capacity with avgas. Each torpedo tube received a slender steel fish, and magazine containers were loaded with hundred-round belts of shiny copper cartridges to feed the .50-caliber machine guns. Fresh water tanks were topped off and galley lockers stocked with cans of flour, dehydrated potatoes, powdered eggs, Spam, and coffee. From stem to stern and from the top of the charthouse to the waterline, each boat was slathered with coats of government-issue olive-drab paint. Overseeing it all was the weary and breathless Alan Montgomery, his normally suntanned complexion replaced by a sickly pallor and his khaki uniform shirt soaked through with sweat, trying his best to push through the alternating fever and chills.

Once the final preparations were completed, the boats were towed to Big Bay on the island of Espiritu Santo by the newly arrived PT tender *Jamestown* and the attack cargo vessel *Bellatrix*. From there they were taken under tow by the more heavily armed destroyer-minesweepers *Hovey* and *Southard* for the remainder of the trip, while the *Bellatrix* and attack transport *Fuller* went on to Tulagi with the squadron's heavy stores. The sea had been kind during the first leg of the journey but not so much on the second, with the PTs bobbing wildly at the end of their tenuous tethers, which "acted like rubber bands." Time and again the tow lines parted in the heavy seas, forcing the boat crews to start their engines and motor ahead to catch up, and for a PT crewman to perform the exceptionally dangerous task of reconnecting the line while waves crashed against the hull.

On the 46 boat commanded by Stilly Taylor, the harrowing job was assigned not once, but several times to a strapping Torpedoman's Mate First Class named Hobert Wisdom. Each time Wisdom would dangle off the bow with one large hand grasping the heaving boat's bullnose and grabbing for the skipping replacement tow line with the other. "Wiz" would then be hoisted onto the foredeck by his attending shipmates, soaked to the bone and emitting a sputtering litany of sailor's curses.

"That's the damndest job I've ever done," he raved. "I won't ever do it again."

"He kept up a running harangue at everyone in sight," Bob Searles remembered. "He bawled the hell out of them all, including Stilly and the exec Stan Thomas . . . it was an education to listen to him."

At three hundred miles out, the PT boats cast off their tow lines and parted company with the two destroyer-minesweepers. Fearing that the slow progress of the towing operation would cause them to arrive in the Solomons well after sunrise and run the risk of being attacked by Japanese aircraft, Montgomery decided that the PTs would complete the trip under their own power.

In the early morning hours of October 12, the four PTs rounded the tiny islet of Rua Sura and entered the black and foreboding waters of Ironbottom Sound. While steering northwest for Tulagi with the strangely quiet, towering form of Guadalcanal looming off to port, the sailors witnessed bright yellow flashes of light on the western horizon, followed by the unmistakable pounding of heavy guns rolling across the sea. In the chartrooms below, radiomen could hear the excited chatter that accompanies close combat on the VHF Talk-Between-Ships (TBS) frequency.

"We slowed our speed and looked the situation over—what we could see of it," recalled Montgomery, who made the crossing aboard the 60 boat skippered by Jack Searles. "Obviously our navy and the Japs were having some sort of altercation near Savo. It might be a quick trading of blows in the dark, or it might be something big. In either case, there was a strong possibility the Japs could come pouring out of the eastern end of the channel and meet us head on. That was bad."

The four boats were not only running low on fuel, they were heavily laden with extra stores and equipment, and carrying several base force personnel in addition to their normal crew complement. Contact with the enemy, therefore, was the last thing Montgomery wanted, and he ordered the boat captains to make a beeline for Tulagi while keeping a sharp eye to the west. The last 20 miles of the journey seemed to last longer than the previous 100 but all four boats managed to arrive safely in Tulagi Harbor at the break of dawn. As the boat crews made fast their mooring lines to the cleats of Government Wharf, the rumble of airplane engines shattered the still morning air. A flight of Marine Corps SBDs had just taken off from Henderson Field on a search-and-strike mission, and were climbing steeply westward over the Sound.

What they had seen and heard hours earlier, the PT sailors would learn, had been a close-range gunnery duel between Japanese and American cruiser forces, which history would remember as the Battle of Cape Esperance. Pressure from Imperial General Headquarters to retake Henderson Field was mounting, and the 8th Fleet at Rabaul had dispatched an unusually large Tokyo Express mission to Guadalcanal for the night of October 11–12. Three heavy cruisers and two destroyers commanded by Rear Admiral Aritomo Goto were assigned to bombard Henderson Field, while a separate convoy of two seaplane tenders and six destroyers were to land 700 Japanese soldiers, field guns, ammunition, and provisions on Guadalcanal. The Japanese bombardment force departed the Shortlands in the late afternoon of October 11, and as it cruised on a southeasterly course down the Slot was spotted by an American B-17.

At the same time, a task force consisting of the cruisers *San Francisco*, *Helena*, *Salt Lake City*, *Boise*, and five destroyers under the command of Rear Admiral Norman Scott was safeguarding the transfer of the 164th Infantry Regiment, one-third of the US Army's "Americal" Division, from New Caledonia to Guadalcanal. A marked increase in enemy radio traffic indicated that the Japanese were up to something, a hunch soon confirmed by the sighting reports of aircraft and coastwatchers.

After completing the escort mission, Scott laid an ambush for Goto's approaching column across the narrow strait between Savo Island and Guadalcanal. Conditions could hardly have have been more favorable; the moonless night was pitch black, with numerous rain squalls passing low over the Slot. None of the Japanese ships were equipped with radar, and their lookouts never saw the American cruisers until it was too late. Scott allowed the Japanese to draw so near before giving the order to open fire that a nervous radar officer aboard the *Helena* blurted out to his shipmates: "What are we going to do? Board them?"

The US Navy was able to give back a little of what it had suffered nine weeks earlier in these very same waters, adding the heavy cruiser *Furutaka* and the destroyer *Fubuki* to the total tonnage of warships resting on the floor of Ironbottom Sound, and pounding the flagship *Aoba* with over forty direct hits. Admiral Goto, who believed that the withering fire had been coming from his own ships, was left mortally wounded after a volley of shells tore through the *Aoba*'s bridge.

"Fools," Goto muttered scornfully with his final breath.

In turn, the Americans lost the destroyer *Duncan*, and the light cruiser *Boise* would be laid up for the next five months after suffering serious damage. In the meantime, the Japanese reinforcement convoy had been able to slip past the raging combatants and managed to land all of its troops and supplies on Guadalcanal before making a clean getaway. Just after the four PT boats arrived at Tulagi, SBDs of the Cactus Air Force sank two Japanese destroyers that had been sent to pick up the *Furutaka*'s survivors.

Despite having just completed an all-night, 300-mile open water run, there was no time for the officers and men of 'RON 3 to rest. While Montgomery trudged wearily up the hill to the Resident Commissioner's house to call upon General Rupertus, the PT boats finished refueling and then motored along the northern shore of Tulagi to Sesapi Cove. Having gotten little to no sleep, the exhausted PT sailors toiled in the hot, velvety air throughout the day, stripped to the waist, slapping at buzzing insects, and enduring the persistent goading of Chief Tufts, who fretted over the boats being caught in the open should Japanese planes appear suddenly overhead.

Ammunition and stores were brought ashore and dispersed into camouflaged dumps; crates of spare parts and tools were carried into the former Chinese warehouse, which would serve as the engineering shop; and boxes of service records, navy forms, and typewriters were delivered to a small A-framed hut floored with teakwood planks, which Bob Wark had set aside for the squadron office. A large wooden disk bearing Disney's mosquito-on-a-torpedo emblem was tacked to a supporting post at the hut's entrance, announcing to all that Motor Torpedo Boat Base Ringbolt was open for business. Covered with netting and palm fronds, the boats were duly stashed into the mouths of shallow creeks along the northern shore of the island, amid the tangled mangroves and beneath the dense rainforest canopy.

"When we first arrived in the area we had no place to live," Chief Tufts explained. "We found it impossible to live on the boats. Every man sort of paired off and built himself a place to live. It was so hot you could not stand it. You could not sleep or rest on the boats. In fact, you couldn't sleep very good anywhere during the day. The place was pretty rough to live in. Every month the high tide came in, covering the entire flat of living spaces with an inch or two of water. Due to the rain the living conditions were pretty tough."

After introducing himself to Rupertus, Montgomery boarded one of the three "yippies"—yard patrol boats—that were constantly plowing the waters between Tulagi and Guadalcanal, and reported to General Vandegrift at his Lunga Point command post. Montgomery was quite taken aback by the warmth of the welcome he received from the haggard and gaunt marines.

"Rumors were rampant on Guadalcanal concerning the prospective arrival of motor torpedo boats," states the navy's official administrative history. "Needless to say, the relatively unopposed shelling of Guadalcanal by Japanese surface ships had a disturbing effect on the morale of the men who were the recipients of these periodic night bombardments. The word that an officer attached to motor torpedo boats had arrived on the island traveled rapidly, and a feeling of over-optimism swept through the rank and file."

"When they found out that our squadron, or half-squadron, of motor torpedo boats had come in to work with them, they may have felt that here at last was recognition, however small, for the job they'd done," Montgomery said. "They hadn't been forgotten after all."

Alexander Vandegrift, however, was a realist. He was under no illusion that a small detachment of four PT boats would be capable of sinking the Tokyo Express, however courageous or skilled their captains and crews might be. Like Ghormley, Vandegrift was more interested in their ability to disrupt and discourage Japanese shore bombardments and the landing of enemy reinforcements. Vandegrift informed Montgomery that despite his authority as commanding general over Guadalcanal and Tulagi, he had no intention of exercising control over the PTs. Compton and Montgomery would be given a free hand to conduct operations as they saw fit, just so long as those operations were aimed at making Admiral Tanaka's life difficult. Montgomery pledged to do his best.

Before boarding a Grumman Duck seaplane for the return trip to Tulagi, Montgomery was approached by a very young but tough-looking marine infantryman with a captured Japanese knife stuck in his belt, emaciated and hollow-eyed after weeks of hard fighting.

"Just teach the bastards to stay home in bed nights where they belong," he said.

\*\*\*

Sickened by malaria and drained of vigor after spending weeks tramping through the jungle with the marines, and with the pages of his black notebook now filled with a day-by-day record of his experiences and assorted musings, Richard Tregaskis packed his few scant belongings and boarded a Flying Fortress bound for Nouméa. There he would begin transforming his notes into a manuscript for a new book, *Guadalcanal Diary*, which would top the New York Times Best Seller List in the final week of February 1943. Later that same year, the film rights for *Guadalcanal Diary* would be purchased by 20th Century Fox.

His would be among the first of an untold number of written accounts, dramatizations, and documentaries about the Guadalcanal campaign to be produced during the war and over the following decades. With their long-held love and admiration for the scrappy underdog, a sentiment dating back to a small band of minutemen making their heroic stand on Lexington's village green, American audiences have remained fascinated by the Guadalcanal story. Countless volumes of history, memoirs, feature articles, cinematic films, and television programs have described how the Americans initiated offensive operations in the South Pacific—on a shoestring—against a cunning and ruthless enemy who had already conquered half the world. Many offer vivid details of the desperate fighting that occurred on land, at sea, and in the air, and how marines, sailors, soldiers, and airmen somehow managed to maintain their tenuous grasp on the Guadalcanal beachhead.

Some of these historical accounts refer to the night of October 13–14, 1942, as "All Hell's Eve," or "The Night of the Battleships." For those who lived through that night, hunkered down in a deep hole within the Lunga perimeter, it is remembered as simply "the bombardment," as if there had been no other. An aging former Leatherneck mentioning "the bombardment" years later while nursing a beer in the dimly lit, smoky bar of his local VFW hall was immediately understood by fellow Guadalcanal veterans in attendance. They didn't have to ask *which* bombardment he was talking about. No further clarification was necessary.

Martin Clemens would call it "our worst night yet," while Alexander Vandegrift would remark with characteristic stoicism that "a man comes close to himself at such times." According to Joe Foss, executive officer of Marine Fighter Squadron VMF-121 based at Henderson Field, the bombardment "was so loud that it overloaded the capacity of the human ear. Those two hours were simply indescribable. Nothing like them could be imagined." Robert Leckie would freely admit that the experience caused him to feel pity for the entrenched Japanese on Peleliu, when he witnessed American battleships bombarding that island later in the war.

Just before 1:30 a.m. on the morning of October 14, the marines began hearing the high-pitched cyclic whirring of a Mitsubishi F1M "Pete" float plane circling high over Henderson Field. Like the Tokyo

Express, these visits were becoming a nightly routine, with float planes buzzing noisily over the field and dropping the occasional light bomb, which usually did little damage other than to add to the sleep deprivation already sapping the strength of the Lunga garrison. The marines had come to call the pesky, anonymous Japanese pilot "Washing Machine Charlie," a reference to the rather annoying, rhythmic whine produced by his nine-cylinder aircraft engine.

On this night, however, it seemed that Charlie was orbiting the airfield at a much higher altitude than normal. Soon a string of parachute flares drifted slowly downward, bathing Henderson Field in a ghostly greenish-blue incandescence. Then came the ominous, faraway thumping of naval artillery and the hair-raising scream of incoming heavy shells, sending infantrymen, engineers, pilots, and mechanics scrambling for foxholes and slit trenches.

The earth itself shuddered mightily with each tremendous impact and detonation, and the air was soon filled with choking, acrid smoke, dust, and swirling debris. Maintenance sheds, tent camps, and parked aircraft were either blown apart by direct hits or shredded to pieces by huge chunks of jagged, whistling shrapnel. Coconut palms toppled. Dugout walls trembled and then caved in, half-burying their inhabitants. A fuel dump containing 5,000 gallons of precious aviation gasoline erupted in flames.

"By God, those aren't 5-inchers they're throwing at us," said Colonel Jerry Thomas, sitting at the bottom of a dugout next to General Vandegrift.

The battleships *Kongo* and *Haruna*, armed with main batteries of massive 14-inch guns, were steadily pummeling Henderson Field and the surrounding defensive positions with nearly a thousand high-explosive fragmentation rounds. The two immense 36,000-ton dreadnoughts, escorted by a light cruiser and nine destroyers, were firing from a distance of 29,500 yards—nearly 17 miles—well beyond the range of American shore batteries.

Vice Admiral Takeo Kurita, commander of Battleship Division Three, had received strict instructions from Admiral Yamamoto: obliterate Henderson Field. Earlier that evening, a convoy of cargo ships and destroyers departed the Shortlands for Guadalcanal, and Yamamoto wanted their delivery of 4,500 Japanese troops to occur unmolested by the planes of the Cactus Air Force. Raizo Tanaka, commanding the destroyers that guarded the battleships, took in the effects of the punishing barrage from the bridge wing of his flagship *Naganami*.

The battleship bombardment "baffled description as the fires and explosions from the [14-inch] shell hits on the airfield set off enemy planes, fuel dumps, and ammunition storage places," according to Tanaka. "The scene was topped off by flare bombs from our observation planes flying over the field, the whole spectacle making the Ryogoku fireworks display seem like mere child's play. The night's pitch dark was transformed by fire into the brightness of day. Spontaneous cries and shouts of excitement ran throughout our ships."

***

Along the northeastern shore of Tulagi, a dozen Packard motors coughed and thundered into life, sending puffs of benzene-scented vapor billowing across the surface of the mangrove-lined creeks. Mooring lines were cast off, transmission levers pushed down into the forward drive position, and throttles steadily advanced. Khaki web belts holding Colt .45 pistols, magazine pouches, and Mark 1 combat knives were slung around waists and buckled. Haze gray steel helmets and kapok life jackets were donned and their straps cinched tight. Propeller locks and safety pins were snatched away from torpedoes and their launching tubes trained outboard. Long belts of .50-caliber bullets were fed into the breach of each waiting machine gun; feed tray covers were slapped shut and charging handles cycled. The four PT boats rounded the southern tip of Tulagi in tactical column, swinging wide past the tiny islet of Songonangona before heading into Ironbottom Sound.

"Prep Monty to all boats—*Baker, Baker, Baker*," Commander Montgomery announced over the TCS radio.

Shifting to a line abreast attack formation at 200-yard intervals, the PTs pointed their bows toward the bright orange muzzle flares on the horizon. With their engine mufflers engaged they cruised southward at half-speed, hoping to avoid leaving the long, sparkling neon-blue wakes caused by the disturbance of thousands of tiny bioluminescent organisms in the water. Minutes earlier the tired PT sailors, sprawled on the dirt floors of bamboo sheds along the Sesapi waterfront, had been jarred from their navy bedrolls by the blasting of 14-inch guns. Montgomery's orders were repeated by the bellowing voices of chief petty officers: *General quarters! Prepare for action! All boats underway immediately!*

Standing beside Jack Searles in the cockpit of the *PT-60*, Montgomery mopped the sweat from his feverish brow with a shirt sleeve and lifted a pair of powerful Bausch and Lomb binoculars to his eyes. Months of training and preparation were coming down to this: a night attack against Japanese capital ships. The current tactical doctrine called for such an attack to be conducted in one of two ways. The first was for an entire squadron of PT boats to assault by divisions, with one division fanned out in the path of the enemy column, while others struck along either flank and from astern. The second option, which took into consideration the presence of darkness or low visibility, was for each division of PTs to approach stealthily in a line abreast, and as the manual advised, "after reaching a favorable attack position, the individual boats should be released to press home their attack."

With only one division of four boats under his command, Montgomery would have to opt for the latter method. It would not be a full-throttle, guns-blazing, pell-mell torpedo attack in the classical sense, the kind loved by navy public relations officers that made for thrilling news copy. Instead, the four boats would creep slowly upon the Japanese formation, probing for gaps in the outer defensive screen. Sneaking under the searchlights and guns of the escorting destroyers, they would launch their torpedoes at the heavies before making smoke and retiring at high speed.

It was an unbelievably dark night, even for the Solomon Islands, with the sky solidly overcast and no visible moon. Unsurprisingly, the four boats quickly lost contact with one another in the darkness and continued ahead to make their own separate attacks. Blinding muzzle flashes from the Japanese guns were reflecting off the surrounding sea and illuminating the low-lying clouds, destroying the fragile night vision of the American sailors.

"You'd blink at the glare and feel the brightness of it eating into your head," Montgomery described. "You could almost feel a kind of physical pain. Then the darkness would come pouring back, deeper and more solid than before."

The Japanese sailor was an unparalleled expert in the art of night combat. For over thirty years, the development of strategy and tactics within the Imperial Japanese Navy had been centered upon the fulfillment of a single objective: drawing the American fleet into a *kantai kessen*, or decisive battle. It was assumed that upon the opening of hostilities, the US Pacific Fleet would sortie in strength from Pearl Harbor and steam westward to attack Japan.

The Combined Fleet's scripted war plans included night surface attacks by torpedo-laden destroyers to steadily diminish the strength of the advancing enemy fleet. Surviving American ships would then be met in a decisive engagement and sunk by the superior gunnery of Japanese cruisers and battleships. Countless tabletop war games and fleet exercises were performed based on this scenario, and generations of Japanese naval officers were trained in adherence to these broad strategic assumptions. It seems that little thought was devoted to the possibility that the Americans might not behave according to plan.

Preparation for these anticipated nighttime attrition operations was greatly emphasized in the years leading up to the Pacific War. The Japanese invested a great deal of time and treasure in refining their nocturnal combat procedures, performing extensive night training, and procuring high-quality low-light optics and other technologies such as powerful searchlights, floating flares, and long-burning starshells. Japanese ships may have lacked radar, but their lookouts were hand-picked for their acute night vision and equipped with huge pedestal-mounted binoculars designed by the Asahi Optical Company, which featured ultra-wide 12-centimeter apertures. Rather than allowing gun batteries to fire at will, Japanese gunnery officers were trained to sound a warning buzzer before firing their guns in coordinated salvos. Lookouts were instructed to cover their eyes upon hearing the buzzer, protecting them from bright muzzle flashes and preserving their night vision.

Considering the fact that such well-drilled and equipped personnel were on the alert for their approach, it is nothing short of remarkable that Jack Searles's *PT-60* managed to shoot the gap between two Japanese destroyers without being seen. At least not at first.

"We ran through the destroyer screen without knowing it," Charlie Tufts recalled. "Neither did the Japs know it."

Searles steered the *PT-60* toward a darkened silhouette in the shape of a Japanese cruiser, the final ship in the enemy column, still methodically loading and firing her deadly salvos toward the distant raging fires that now marked the location of Henderson Field. For several interminable seconds the PT skipper maneuvered to achieve the desired angle on the bow and a satisfactory firing point for two of his steel fish. Standing by the first of the ready tubes and clutching a short-handled mallet was Torpedoman's Mate First Class Willie Uhl, there to deliver a forceful whack to the percussion cap of each torpedo should the remote electrical trigger in the cockpit fail to launch them.

Suddenly a searchlight aboard an unseen Japanese destroyer snapped on, its powerful beam reaching across the sea to find the *PT-60* and bathe her startled crew in its horrifying brilliance. Searles ignored the light and held the boat steady, even as the destroyer opened fire with her main battery and enemy shells passed close overhead with a peculiar ripping sound. The two torpedoes shot out of their tubes and slapped the water. Searles spun the wheel hard to port, advanced the throttles, and called for the engine mufflers to be opened wide.

"We were in their searchlights, and their 5-inch shells were getting closer with each salvo," Searles recalled. "Under high speed we got back through their screen and then laid smoke."

Watching from the fantail as the *60* boat made her escape was Chief Motor Machinist Henry Ramsdell, who reported seeing and hearing two distinct explosions at the target's waterline, which he believed to be the two fish striking home. After running northward for a short distance, Searles eased back on the throttles and called for the smoke generator to be secured.

"I think we can slow down now, Commander," Searles said to Montgomery. The words had hardly left his lips before two Japanese destroyers came charging out of the smoke at flank speed. A 5-inch shell struck the water just astern of the *PT-60* with a tremendous splash, showering her afterdeck with seawater and nearly lifting her stern and spinning propellers from the water. Willie Uhl, who had already made his way aft to secure the smoke generator, was knocked from his feet. Unhurt, the young torpedoman scrambled back to the cylinder and cranked open the valve.

Once again the *60* boat roared away trailing a dense plume of white smoke, zigzagging violently while her machine gunners aimed streams of fiery tracer rounds toward the glaring Japanese searchlights. The destroyers kept on coming, their own machine guns rattling and 5-inch cannon pounding steadily. Towering splashes leapt from the water alongside and ahead of the fleeing PT boat, indicating that the Japanese gunners were quickly finding the range.

Montgomery then ordered a pair of depth charges to be set for 100 feet and rolled overboard. This was yet another untried countermeasure that PT skippers had devised during brainstorming sessions in Norfolk and Melville and practiced on the waters of the Gulf of Panama. The maneuver was designed to trick a Japanese destroyer captain into thinking that his ship had struck a floating mine, while hopefully rupturing some hull plates or perhaps damaging the destroyer's steering gear. The stunning concussion of the two underwater blasts caused the pursuing destroyers to veer off course and discontinue the chase.

"Let's get the hell out of here," Montgomery ordered. He then directed Searles to head for the coast of Florida Island. Free of the weight of two torpedoes, the *PT-60* roared away to the north at 45 knots.

Jack's younger brother Bob was at the helm of the *PT-38*, making his own approach on the Japanese column at a distance quite apart from the other three boats. After the presence of the *PT-60* was finally discovered by Japanese lookouts, searchlights from other screening destroyers began sweeping over the black expanse of surrounding sea. One of the far-reaching beams passed directly over the *38* boat without stopping, eliciting a collective gasp from the men at their topside stations. During their training, new PT officers had been advised by veteran tin can sailors that a small craft cruising at slower speeds was less likely to be detected by a searchlight than one traveling at high speed, and Searles was grateful that the *PT-38* had been idling along at a mere 10 knots.

Seeing the other boats taking enemy fire, Searles began maneuvering into a position to attack the screen of Japanese destroyers. Suddenly the silhouette of a much larger ship appeared off the *PT-38*'s starboard bow. Searles turned toward this new target, which he believed to be a light cruiser, and from a distance of 400 yards launched two fish. The first torpedo shot from the tube and plunged into the water to run "hot, straight, and normal," while the second slid its snubbed nose only a few feet from the end of the tube and stayed there, its internal machinery rattling "like a car running with a burnt-out bearing," as Bob Searles later described.

This was what was known as a "hot run on deck," a problem inherent to the Mark 8 torpedo and one of the more dangerous situations to be faced by a PT crew. When electrically triggered, the black powder stored within the torpedo's launching charge had fizzled, most likely due to the absorption of moisture from the dense tropical air, which caused the weapon to stall in the tube while its turbine engine and propeller continued to spin freely. There was little danger of the 466-pound TNT warhead exploding, since the torpedo needed to travel through the water for some distance before arming itself. The running turbine, however, was designed to be cooled by the seawater through which the torpedo traveled. Without such cooling, there was a good chance that the turbine could overheat and fly apart before its supply of alcohol-based propellent was exhausted, tearing through the torpedo's outer shell and spraying the surrounding area with deadly shrapnel.

There was little that Bob Searles or his crew could do at that point, other than hope for the best. The young skipper decided to press the attack, closing to within 200 yards of the Japanese ship before ordering the boat's quartermaster, Jim Meadows, to fire the two remaining fish. Once again, the first torpedo leapt obediently into the sea and streaked toward the target, while the second remained stuck in its tube on a hot run. Searles put the throttles to the stops and cranked the wheel hard to starboard. Trailing a plume of white smoke, the *PT-38* cut through the churning wake of the enemy vessel, passing just 100 yards from her fantail while Japanese sailors blazed away with 25-millimeter automatic cannons.

"I can't see how she missed," Bob Searles would later remark. The crew of the *38* boat witnessed the flash of two explosions near the target amidships, with every man standing topside claiming to have felt the concussion and heat emanating from the blasts. Now, with two errant torpedoes trembling and knocking disconcertingly in their tubes, Searles turned the *PT-38* about and settled on a northwest heading for the cover of Bungana Island at full speed.

The two remaining PT boats were unable to get past the outer phalanx of Japanese destroyers. The crew of the *PT-46* had been slowly stalking the Japanese column when searchlights lit up the *PT-60* just a few hundred yards ahead. Their view of the *60* boat was suddenly obscured by the spray of near misses falling all around her. The gunfire was coming from Tanaka's flagship *Naganami*, which was bearing down upon the port beam of the *46* with a glittering phosphorescent wave cascading from her bow. The boat captain, Stilly Taylor, spun the wheel to starboard and narrowly avoided a collision with the onrushing Japanese ship.

As she sped away to the west under a smoke screen, the *PT-46* nearly collided in turn with the slowly idling *PT-48*. Forced to put the helm hard to starboard to avoid the fleeing *46* boat, Bob Wark and his crew suddenly found themselves trapped in the beam of the pursuing destroyer's searchlight. Carl Todd, a twenty-year-old Ship's Cook Second Class from Boston manning the port-side twin fifties, sprayed the enemy superstructure with bullets and doused the light. The destroyer continued on at flank speed and disappeared into the dark of the night, passing so close to the *PT-48* that the much smaller craft was rocked violently by her wake, and Japanese voices could be heard shouting from her weather decks. By then the battleships and their cohorts had ceased their fire and were cruising silently to the northwest and into the Slot.

The dazzling bursts of light and violent, deafening noise were swiftly replaced by an eerie silence and the surreal, wildering murk of Ironbottom Sound.

\*\*\*

Stilly Taylor drove the *PT-46* on a high-speed run west-by-northwest, hoping to arrive in the choke point known as Sandfly Passage between the islands of Florida and Savo ahead of the Japanese battlewagons. Had his boat been equipped with the SO-type surface search radar then being installed aboard new PTs in Bayonne and New Orleans, Taylor might have had a chance to intercept them. Instead, the Japanese slipped through the passage and escaped up the Slot under the cover of darkness.

On Montgomery's orders, the *PT-60* was lying-to off the southern coast of Florida Island. The battleship bombardment, the commander reasoned, had more than likely coincided with another reinforcement and supply run of Tokyo Express destroyers. If that were the case, it might afford the *60* boat an opportunity to expend her two remaining fish. Hours passed without any further sign of the Japanese fleet, and dawn soon began to color the horizon to the east. Montgomery decided to call it good and ordered Jack Searles to return to base.

The two moto-macs, DeWayne Parker and George Ebersberger, fired up their engines, which responded with a brief whine and then a rumble, sputtering blue exhaust over the lightening water. Searles advanced the throttles slowly, but to his surprise the boat refused to surge forward. Instead her stern slewed awkwardly to one side, with a spine-shuddering vibration and horrible grinding sound that set every man's teeth on edge. Searles backed off the throttles and tried once more, with the same result. Searles, Parker, and Ebersberger then doffed their kapok jackets and slipped into the warm water to confirm what they already knew. The tide had ebbed slowly and imperceptibly, lowering the drifting boat onto a bed of coral. The *PT-60* was stuck fast. Searles had his radioman, Les Piper, contact Tulagi for assistance, and managed to hail his brother's *38* boat on the VHF voice frequency.

"I asked Bob if I could evacuate to his boat," Jack recalled. "To this day, he has never given me an affirmative answer."

Despite their misfortune the mood of the crew remained upbeat, for they believed that they had torpedoed and possibly sunk a Japanese cruiser. The cook, Nick Carideo, secured his twin machine guns and went below to the galley to prepare breakfast. A few of the men waded across the reef and onto the beach, where they attempted to converse with a handful of curious Melanesian onlookers in pidgin. Later in the morning, the men manned their guns and watched nervously as V-shaped formations of Japanese planes passed overhead on their way to bomb Henderson Field.

Help finally arrived in the form of the *YP-239*, a 113-foot former tuna clipper baitboat of the San Diego fishing fleet that had been purchased by the navy and placed into service as a yard patrol vessel. The crew of the yippie passed over a tow line and the *60* boat was hauled clear of the reef. The squadron flagship then headed for Tulagi with her bilge overflowing and lower deck awash, the bottom of her mahogany hull pierced in a dozen places by razor sharp coral.

***

Even before the outbreak of the war, the sailors of the Mosquito Fleet adopted as their unit motto the famous words of John Paul Jones: "Give me a fast ship, for I intend to go in harm's way." They might have just as easily adopted a bit of military wisdom written in 1871 by the Prussian field marshal Helmuth von Moltke: "No plan survives first contact with the enemy."

In the early days of PT operations, various attack drills had been performed off the Virginia coast and in Caribbean waters with boats maneuvering by divisions and squadrons. The first PT training manuals were filled with hand-drawn diagrams that looked very much like offensive football plays, showing neatly aligned formations of boats spaced at 100-yard intervals, following the tracks of sweeping arrows toward sketched columns of enemy ships. MTBRON 3's fight with Kurita's capital ships had proven that the employment of such intricate tactics during night combat was for the most part impracticable, and that Alan Montgomery's decision to allow the boats to attack individually had been a sound one.

"Our first night against the Japanese showed us that our boats would have to fight on their own," Jack Searles wrote. "There was no way to keep station once the battle was joined. There were distractions of searchlights, 5-inch shell bursts, machine gun tracer bullets, not to mention the concentration of getting off good torpedo shots at the target and then guiding the boat back through the destroyer screen to safety."

In a summary report delivered to Imperial General Headquarters titled *General Progress of Southeast Area Operations (Navy)*, a staff officer of the Combined Fleet wrote, "The bombardment force moved up off Lunga at 2330 hours on schedule, and bombarded the airfield for approximately one hour and ten minutes. The entire area was turned into a sea of flames, resulting in heavy losses. During the bombardment, four enemy PT boats moved in for an attack from the Tulagi area, but were avoided." Tanaka's postwar account would state only that "several motor torpedo boats of the enemy came out to pursue our rear guard ships, but destroyer *Naganami* drove them away."

This was in sharp contrast to the fantastic claims of Radio Tokyo, which reported that Japanese battleships had been attacked off the coast of Guadalcanal by nineteen American motor torpedo boats, and that fourteen of the boats had been sunk. Radio Tokyo went on to admit that a Japanese cruiser had been sunk during the night of October 13–14. Montgomery also received an unconfirmed report that a coastwatcher had witnessed the sinking of a damaged Japanese warship, possibly a cruiser, in the Slot on the morning of October 14. Based on this information, a small Rising Sun flag was painted alongside the mosquito-on-a-torpedo, transforming the sign hanging outside the operations shack at Sesapi into an unofficial scoreboard.

Records of the Imperial Japanese Navy obtained after the war, however, make no mention of a cruiser being lost on that night. None of the Japanese ships involved in the action reported damage from torpedoes. In his diary, Admiral Ugaki declared that the bombardment of Henderson Field "was done with no loss of our own." A chronological record of Japanese combatant and merchant shipping losses in the Pacific War compiled by the Joint Army Navy Assessment Committee (JANAC) lists a Japanese destroyer being sunk by American aircraft on October 12, and another on October 16. No Japanese naval vessels are listed as sunk between those two dates. It is therefore likely that the explosions witnessed by Henry Ramsdell, Bob Wark, and the crew of Bob Searles's

*PT-38* were not the result of torpedoes striking their targets, but were instead the muzzle flares of heavy Japanese guns.

The ability of PT boats to surprise, harass, and confuse an enemy force, however, could not be denied. Samuel B. Griffith of the First Raider Battalion, in his compelling history of the Guadalcanal campaign, would conclude that "the Japanese were sufficiently impressed with the audacity of the attack to recount the episode in their record of the night's work." Samuel Eliot Morison has theorized that the surprise attack of American motor torpedo boats more than likely contributed to Admiral Kurita's decision to cease his bombardment of Henderson Field and retire early. Kurita had no way of knowing how many PT boats were out there lurking in the dark, Morison explained, or whether or not they were the vanguard of a more powerful Allied naval force.

In aggressively pressing home their attack, MTBRON 3 also sent a strong message to Raizo Tanaka: The Tokyo Express now had reason to be afraid of the dark.

# Dangerous Little Ships

THE DAWN OF OCTOBER 14, 1942, REVEALED THE SHATTERED AND smoking mess that was Guadalcanal's Henderson Field. Very slowly the stunned, half-deafened survivors of the battleship bombardment emerged from their dugouts and slit trenches to take in the devastation. Oily black smoke drifted across the heavily cratered runways from still-burning fuel and ammunition dumps. The Lunga plain was littered with shell fragments, distorted sections of perforated steel planking that had once covered the runways and taxiways, fallen palm trees, the tattered remnants of pyramidal tents, and hundreds of dented and crushed cans of Spam, blown high into the air by a direct hit on the ration dump.

A Japanese-built pagoda structure that had served as the airfield's headquarters building—and as an aiming point for the battleships—was smashed flat, and now resembled the proverbial pile of wooden toothpicks. Of the ninety army, navy, and marine planes that made up the Cactus Air Force, forty-eight were completely destroyed and several more seriously damaged. Many would consider it a miracle that only forty-one men had been killed, given the duration and intensity of the bombardment. The majority of the dead were aviation personnel, including a half-dozen pilots.

After surveying the immense damage, Brigadier General Roy S. Geiger, commander of the First Marine Aircraft Wing, was heard to bitterly declare, "I don't think we have a goddamned navy." Geiger's fellow marines were sharing the same hard feelings toward their sister service, despite the best efforts of the Ringbolt PT boats to break up the attack. Unfortunately, their acrimony would only deepen over the next forty-eight hours.

Later that day, as engineers and Seabees worked feverishly to repair the cratered runways and mechanics patched together a handful of SBDs and Wildcats into flyable condition, search aircraft reported that six troop-laden transports, escorted by Tanaka's destroyers, were steaming down the Slot toward Guadalcanal. The tenacious Japanese were continuing to build up their forces on the island, obviously in preparation for another all-out effort to seize Henderson Field, and the US Navy could do nothing to stop them.

Norman Scott's cruisers were in Espiritu Santo, replenishing their fuel bunkers and ammunition magazines after their fight at Cape Esperance. The ships of the *Hornet* task force were also drinking from tankers to the northwest of New Caledonia and were too far away to render assistance. As for the mosquito boats of MTBRON 3, only Stilly Taylor's *PT-46* and Bob Wark's *PT-48* were in battle-ready condition. The *PT-60* was in need of extensive hull repairs after running aground, and *PT-38* had no functional torpedoes left after her first night of combat. Both the *60* and *38* boats would have to wait until the PT tender *Jamestown* arrived in Tulagi Harbor to receive the repairs and replenishment necessary to rejoin the squadron.

The supply of aviation gasoline for the planes of the Cactus Air Force, which had never been overly abundant, was now critically low after the destruction of the fuel dump. Aviation mechanics were forced to drain the gas tanks of demolished airplanes in order to obtain enough fuel to send the four still-flyable SBDs, seventeen Wildcats, and seven army Bell P-39 fighters against the inbound Japanese reinforcement column, an effort that resulted in only minor damage to one destroyer. Working parties were sent to recover barrels of gasoline that had been stashed in nearby swamps, and General Vandegrift transmitted an appeal to Nouméa:

```
Urgently necessary this force receive maximum
support of air and surface units. Absolutely
essential aviation gas be flown here continuously.
```

Rear Admiral Aubrey Fitch, who had assumed the role of COMAIR-SOPAC—Commander Aircraft South Pacific—ordered the Douglas C-47 transport planes based at Espiritu Santo loaded with 55-gallon drums of avgas and flown to Henderson Field. Eight navy SBDs, refugees from the damaged *Enterprise*, were also sent to Guadalcanal along with the twenty marine Wildcat fighters of VMF-212. On Tulagi, General Rupertus ordered all ammunition, supplies, and aviation gasoline that could be spared loaded onto two yippies for transfer to Lunga Point, and asked for the PT boats of MTBRON 3 to provide an armed escort.

At sunset on October 14, the *YP-239* and *YP-284* departed from Tulagi Harbor at the ponderously slow pace of 10 knots, shepherded by PTs *46* and *48*. As they neared Guadalcanal they were engaged by a Japanese artillery battery on Point Cruz, a hatchet-shaped promontory that extended into Ironbottom Sound, the shells plopping into the sea 100 yards ahead of the leading yippie. No sooner had the cargo been transferred to waiting lighters in Lunga Roads than a warning was broadcast over the radio net that the Tokyo Express would soon arrive in Ironbottom Sound. As the PTs and yippies hastened to get underway for Tulagi, the *YP-239* ran hard aground on a sandbar.

Alan Montgomery, who had accompanied Bob Wark and the crew of *PT-48* on the mission, felt obliged to help free the repurposed tuna boat from her predicament, for she was the same craft that had hauled the *PT-60* off the reef near Florida Island earlier in the day. Tow lines were passed over from both PT boats and the *YP-284*, but the evening tide was ebbing steadily and the grounded yippie refused to budge. Suddenly an illumination round burst in the sky over Henderson Field. With an enemy task force bearing down quickly, emotion and sentiment had to be abandoned. The crew of the *YP-239* was put ashore, and the PTs began escorting the *YP-284* to safety.

It was a nerve-wracking two-hour journey back to Tulagi, a trip that would have normally taken an otherwise unencumbered PT boat just over thirty minutes. Unable to leave their slow-moving charge, the PT sailors could only watch with mounting frustration as the heavy cruisers *Kinugasa* and *Chokai* steamed into Ironbottom Sound and gave Henderson Field yet another vicious pasting. The men stood nervously by their guns throughout the entire passage, expecting to be illuminated by the probing searchlights of Japanese screening destroyers at any moment, and forced to fight a desperate rear guard action in defense of the plodding yippie.

After raining another 700 shells onto the tormented airstrip, the cruisers turned onto a northwesterly heading and retired up the Slot. By that time the *YP-284* had gained the shelter of Tulagi Harbor, but the PT boats were too low on fuel for a stern chase. Once the mooring lines of *PT-48* were secured and her motors shut down for the night, Bob Wark went below to his tiny stateroom and returned to the bridge with a pint bottle of Scotch.

"I've been saving this," Wark admitted to his skipper, holding forth the bottle. The ships of the US Navy had been dry ever since 1914, when a teetotaling naval secretary named Josephus Daniels banned the shipboard possession or consumption of alcohol. On this particular occasion, however, Monty decided to look the other way.

*** 

"Dawn of the 15th revealed a spectacle highly humiliating to the marines who saw it, and to the navy that did not," Morison would write. "In full view were enemy transports lying-to off Tassafaronga, unloading troops and supplies with as much ease as if they had been in Tokyo Bay. Hovering around and over them were destroyers and planes."

For the Americans, the third week of October 1942 was another low point in their struggle to wrest Guadalcanal from the Japanese, who had been able to land an additional 15,000 combat troops on the island in preparation for a new offensive. Even though Henderson-based aircraft were able to fly several strike missions against Japanese shipping in the Tassafaronga roadstead on October 15, sinking three of the six now-empty transports, their supplies of munitions and fuel were now running perilously low. Aviators and their mechanics were sick, sleep-deprived, and exhausted, as were the engineers and Seabees who labored under the blazing tropical sun to keep the airfield operational. Vandegrift's malaria-ridden marine infantrymen and American Division soldiers were continuing to hold the 14-square-mile perimeter only by sheer guts and determination.

In the late afternoon of October 16, the seaplane tender *McFarland* arrived in Lunga Roads towing a barge loaded with 650 barrels of gasoline. Even as fuel drums were being transferred onto lighters and marine casualties brought aboard, nine Japanese Val dive bombers pounced on the old converted four-piper, striking her stern with a bomb that killed a dozen men, destroyed her steering gear, and blew the barge with its priceless cargo sky high.

Whatever satisfaction the Japanese pilots derived from their successful air strike was short-lived. One of the Vals was splashed by the *McFarland*'s antiaircraft guns, and as the remaining eight climbed away over Ironbottom Sound, they ran headlong into the Wildcat fighters of VMF-212 just arriving from Espiritu Santo. The 212 squadron commander, Lieutenant Colonel Harold "Indian Joe" Bauer, personally sent four of the dive bombers down in flames. After sundown, the stricken *McFarland* was taken under tow by the *YP-239*, back at work after a recent flood tide had lifted her clear of the reef. With the *PT-48* standing watch alongside, the *McFarland* was taken to the upper channel of Tulagi Harbor, where she underwent temporary repairs before setting sail for Pearl Harbor. For this action the *McFarland* would be awarded the Presidential Unit Citation.

The gasoline crisis not only hampered the operations of the Cactus Air Force, but those of the PT boats stationed in Tulagi Harbor as well. Fuel economy had not been a chief concern for the designers of the 1,500-horsepower V-12 Packard marine engine, and procuring a sufficient and reliable supply of 100-octane gasoline posed a significant challenge for Montgomery and his men. With a bit of luck, the PT boats might get the chance to refuel from a passing fleet oiler or convince the captain of a heavy cruiser equipped with seaplanes to part with a few hundred gallons from his onboard avgas tanks. Otherwise, the squadron's meager allotment of gasoline was transferred to Tulagi from rear area bases in 55-gallon drums. It took sixty such containers to refuel a single PT boat, with the transfer having to be performed with the use of hand-operated pumps while straining the gas through a chamois to avoid contamination. This painstaking process took several hours, and led to extended downtime between missions and the risk of the boats being unavailable when needed, as was the case on October 16.

That night, the heavy cruisers *Myoko* and *Maya* and their accompanying destroyers fired over a thousand 8-inch and 5-inch shells into the Lunga perimeter. In a message transmitted to Admiral Ghormley the following morning, the deeply frustrated Vandegrift urged the SOPAC commander to "take and maintain control of the sea area adjacent to Cactus to prevent further enemy landings and enemy bombardment such as this force has taken for the last three nights."

"It now appears that we are unable to control the sea in the Guadalcanal area," read an October 16 entry in the CINCPAC war diary. "Thus our supply of the positions will only be done at great expense to us. The situation is not hopeless, but it is certainly critical."

At a press conference held the following morning in Washington, DC, a newspaper reporter asked Secretary of the Navy Frank Knox, "Do you think we can hold Guadalcanal?"

"I certainly hope so, and expect so," was the best Knox could offer. "I will not make any predictions, but every man will give a good account of himself. There is a good stiff fight going on, everybody hopes we can hold on."

In the early morning hours of October 16, COMSOPAC received a report relayed from a radio station in Canberra, Australia, claiming that a Japanese aircraft carrier had been spotted steaming to the west of Ndeni Island, just 350 miles east of Guadalcanal. The report, which later proved false, prompted Ghormley to transmit an urgent dispatch to Pearl Harbor at 4:40 a.m.:

```
This appears to be all out enemy effort against
Cactus possibly other positions also. My forces
totally inadequate to meet situation. Urgently
request all aviation reinforcement possible.
```

Chester Nimitz was already deeply concerned over Robert Ghormley's ability to command. During a recent inspection tour of the South

Pacific, the Commander-in-Chief Pacific Fleet had been disturbed by the sight of his old friend, who appeared to have aged considerably over the past months. Nimitz was astonished to learn that Ghormley had not been ashore in weeks, but remained sequestered aboard the *Argonne* in Nouméa Harbor, working long hours with very little rest. Ghormley had yet to conduct any inspection tours of his own, and had never set foot on Guadalcanal. During their discussions of the Guadalcanal operation, Nimitz found Ghormley to be pessimistic, apprehensive, and woefully out of touch with the dynamics of his own combat theater. The tone of this latest dispatch only confirmed what Nimitz and his staff already suspected: Ghormley was very clearly overwhelmed, and simply not up to the task.

"Although he did not say so directly, it was obvious that he felt that Ghormley had handed over command of the sea to the Japanese," recalled Commander Ed Layton. "We proposed that personalities should be set aside and that the Commander South Pacific should be replaced by someone who could do a more effective job."

A top-secret dispatch was soon transmitted from Pearl Harbor to Washington:

```
OCT 16 0937 CINCPAC to COMINCH: For Admiral King
Only. Ultra from CINCPAC. Halsey, his chief of
staff and intelligence officer will be with Ghorm-
ley sixteenth our date. In view Ghormley's 160440
and other indications including some noted during
my visit I have under consideration his relief
by Halsey at earliest practicable time. Request
your comment.
```

Nimitz soon received a characteristically blunt reply from Ernest J. King:

```
Your 160937 approved.
```

\*\*\*

The huge four-engined Consolidated PB2Y Coronado flying boat banked low over the city of Nouméa, offering its passengers a splendid view of the tidy palm-lined avenues, red-roofed bungalows, ornate French provincial buildings housing the shops and offices of the downtown, and the majestic Romanesque towers of the Cathédrale Saint-Joseph, all overlooking the deep cobalt waters of Mosselle Bay.

It was a scene from one of the colorful posters one might find prominently displayed in the front window of a travel agency back in the States, advertising the many exotic destinations available to passengers of the Pan American Clipper before the war. Excepting, of course, the dozens of prefabricated, utilitarian Quonset huts that had sprung up along the waterfront, the ugly snouts of antiaircraft guns pointed skyward from their sandbag emplacements, the thirty-odd dull gray Liberty cargo ships crowded into the anchorage, and the many thousands of unpainted wooden crates piled in a seemingly haphazard fashion in the dockyards. Cargo vessels were still sailing from the United States without being properly combat-loaded, causing immense log jams in the ports of Nouméa and Espiritu Santo and forcing the SOPAC command to waste many precious man-hours on the unloading, sorting, and reloading of supplies for the troops on Guadalcanal.

The Coronado drifted slowly downward to settle upon the waters of the harbor, skimming along the surface for a quarter mile before coming to rest, the tail pitching sharply upward from the forward surge of wake and the big reversible-pitch propellers radiating a flat roar. Gazing through a porthole from his seat in the seaplane's cavernous cargo bay, Vice Admiral William F. Halsey Jr. watched as a motor whaleboat approached and an officer Halsey recognized as Robert Ghormley's flag lieutenant passed a sealed manila envelope through the open hatch.

Halsey had journeyed to New Caledonia to acquaint himself with its advanced base facilities and the key personnel stationed there, in anticipation of his carrier task force being deployed to the South Pacific Area as soon as repairs to the bomb-damaged *Enterprise* were completed at Pearl Harbor. Whatever was in the envelope must be pretty important, Halsey thought, since he would be piped aboard the *Argonne* in only a matter of minutes.

Halsey tore open the envelope and stared at the enclosed message form for several seconds, his bushy white eyebrows angled downward into a deep frown. Then he handed the message to his intelligence officer, Colonel Julian Brown.

"Jesus Christ and General Jackson!" Halsey exclaimed. "This is the hottest potato they've ever handed me!"

Brown read the typewritten words:

```
You will take command of the South Pacific Area
and South Pacific Forces immediately—NIMITZ.
```

\*\*\*

"I held nothing personal against Ghormley, whom I liked," Vandegrift wrote. "I simply felt that our situation called for the most positive form of aggressive leadership at the top. From what I knew of Bill Halsey he would supply this like few other naval officers."

Halsey was certainly a fighter, of that there is no doubt. Time would reveal that his natural aggressiveness could sometimes lead to impetuous or even reckless decisions, often with costly results. In the South Pacific in October 1942, however, Halsey was the right man for the job. The situation required bold, decisive leadership and a willingness to take risks, qualities that Robert Ghormley unfortunately lacked but Bill Halsey possessed in spades. Halsey's appointment not only had an immediate and far-reaching impact on the esprit de corps of the sailors, soldiers, and marines fighting in the South Pacific, it was a windfall for war correspondents and their editors back home.

"Shift to Offensive Is Seen in Washington Selection of Fighting Admiral Halsey as Commander in the South Pacific," read a front-page headline in the *New York Times*. "Halsey is known among navy men as a rough, tough fighting man who is as quick with his praise as he is with his blame when it is warranted. He is the sort of leader men will follow right to hell and back," wrote the columnist Foster Hailey. Shortly after Halsey took command, a reporter asked about his plans for prosecuting the war in the South Pacific.

"Kill Japs, kill Japs, and keep on killing Japs," Halsey replied.

Lieutenant Commander Roger Kent, an air operations information officer at Henderson Field, would recall hearing the news that Halsey had assumed command of SOPAC: "One minute we were too limp with malaria to crawl out of our foxholes; the next, we were running around whooping like kids. . . . If morale had been enough, we'd have won the war right there."

According to Motor Machinist's Mate First Class Albert Sackett of the *Jamestown*, "It was just electrifying, the change in morale, the enthusiasm. Halsey was just magnetic along those lines. He was a sailor's admiral."

On October 23, Alexander Vandegrift boarded a plane for Nouméa to meet with the new SOPAC commander. While listening to the general tell of the daily air raids, nightly naval bombardments, rampant shortages, and the exhausted state of his troops, Halsey sat chain-smoking cigarettes and drumming his fingers on the *Argonne's* wardroom table.

"Can you hold?" Halsey asked abruptly.

"Yes, I can hold," Vandegrift answered without hesitation. "But I have to have more active support than I've been getting."

"You go on back there, Vandegrift," Halsey told him. "I promise to get you everything I have."

\*\*\*

On October 22, the motor torpedo boat tender *Jamestown* finally stood into Tulagi Harbor after spending several weeks in emergency service as a supply vessel, shuttling gasoline and aerial bombs to Guadalcanal from Espiritu Santo. The 1,780-ton converted luxury yacht was equipped with boat cranes capable of hoisting a PT from the water, and had onboard repair and machine shops staffed by journeyman mechanics, machinists, carpenters, and electricians. She also carried torpedoes, spare parts, supplies, and provisions along with 40,000 gallons of clean aviation gas. The presence of the *Jamestown* helped improve the austere living conditions of the Ringbolt base as well, by providing mess and shower facilities for the PT crews and berthing space for the officers.

After taking soundings from a motor whaleboat, Commander Charles Beasley eased the *Jamestown* beneath the overhanging trees that lined the banks of the Maliala River on Florida Island, just across the upper loch of Tulagi Harbor from Sesapi. The leaking *PT-60*, with her badly chewed-up hull and two engines inoperable after being cannabalized for spare parts, was then craned aboard the *Jamestown* and the work of restoring her to a seaworthy condition begun.

Three days later, on October 25, the second echelon of MTBRON 3, consisting of PT boats *37, 39, 45,* and *61,* cruised into Tulagi Harbor and tied up at the Sesapi docks. The following morning, Lieutenant Hugh Robinson relieved Alan Montgomery of command. Not only had Montgomery's pneumonia worsened since his arrival in the Solomons, he had also contracted malaria and shed 25 pounds from his already diminutive frame. In need of more extensive treatment than the local evacuation hospitals could provide, Monty was being sent home.

For leading his division of four PT boats into action against the Japanese in Ironbottom Sound on the night of October 13–14, 1942, Montgomery was awarded the Silver Star. He would spend the next six months in the naval hospital in Oakland, California. After regaining his health Monty took over the "shakedown center" in Miami, where newly delivered Higgins PT boats were inspected and tested before being admitted to the fleet. He would return to sea duty in 1944, this time in command of a squadron of amphibious landing ships during MacArthur's return to the Philippines. Alan Montgomery retired from the navy in 1949 at the rank of rear admiral.

Like many of his fellow PT skippers, Hugh Robinson was a New Englander. Originally from Longmeadow, Massachusetts, he had lived and studied in Paris and Zurich and was fluent in French. Robinson's father had been an officer in the Naval Reserve and encouraged his sons to apply to the US Naval Academy. After graduating with the Annapolis Class of 1938, Robinson seemed destined for a career in destroyers, first serving aboard the ancient four-piper USS *Bainbridge.* While on leave in March 1941, he visited his detailing officer in Washington to request a transfer, hoping to be assigned to one of the new *Fletcher*-class destroyers then being readied for service. Two days later, Robinson was detached from the *Bainbridge* with orders to report to the New York Navy Yard.

"I hope you're not going to one of those PT boats I've heard about," his intuitive new bride Peggy had remarked. "I know those would be dangerous little ships to be on."

Sure enough, Robinson soon found himself in Key West assigned to Motor Torpedo Boat Squadron 2. He quickly proved a capable PT skipper and became fast friends with John Bulkeley, who in September 1941 put in a request for Robinson to join his new MTBRON 3 for their deployment to the Philippines. Earl Caldwell had the authority to deny the request, which he did, explaining that Robinson's talents were sorely needed in his own squadron—a decision that may have saved Robinson's life. Now, a little over a year later, command of the Tulagi PTs "was more or less dumped on" the twenty-six-year-old lieutenant, according to Chief Tufts. Fortunately, Robinson was able to rise to the challenge of leading the squadron in Montgomery's absence, exhibiting not only a genuine concern for the welfare of his men, but a willingness to share in the dangers they faced.

"The men had supreme confidence in him," Tufts recalled. "They would have followed him anywhere against any enemy vessels."

"I put my faith in the squadron commander, Mr. Robinson, and in fact all of the officers did a wonderful job," stated Chief Machinist's Mate Arthur Stuffert. "They were all good and showed plenty of courage and guts while in action and at other times."

For his executive officer Robinson chose the redoubtable Jack Searles, who had been busying himself with overseeing the project of dredging the shallow channel between Tulagi and Florida Island while his *60* boat awaited repairs. The eastern approach had been the only way in or out of Sesapi Cove, and the newly opened channel offered the PT boats an alternate escape route should Japanese destroyers venture into Tulagi Harbor.

The arrival of the *Jamestown* and the second division of PT boats at Tulagi coincided with two major actions of the Guadalcanal campaign. It had taken several weeks for the Tokyo Express to land enough Imperial Army troops, heavy weapons, ammunition, and supplies on Guadalcanal to launch another offensive to retake Henderson Field. On the evening of October 23, after several days of struggling through dense jungle terrain to reach their assigned objectives, the Japanese assaulted the marine positions along the Matanikau River to the west of Lunga Point. The marines held the line, inflicting heavy casualties among the two attacking infantry battalions and destroying nine enemy light tanks.

Over the following two nights, 7,000 Japanese troops of the 2nd Sendai Division attacked Henderson Field from the south, falling upon a sector defended by the 1st Battalion/7th Marines commanded by the legendary Lieutenant Colonel Lewis B. "Chesty" Puller. Dug in alongside the 1/7 was the stalwart 3rd Battalion of the US Army's 164th Infantry.

"The Second Division had little combat experience, as it had engaged only in the Java campaign," Admiral Ugaki would record in his diary. "Though high-spirited, they were not expert fighters."

Once again the Japanese attempted to overwhelm the American defenders by making frenzied bayonet charges against prepared positions, only to have their ranks decimated by intense rifle, machine gun, and artillery fire. The Battle of Henderson Field cost the Japanese nearly 3,000 men while gaining absolutely nothing; the Americans would lose fewer than a hundred. In the confusion of battle, an erroneous signal that Henderson Field had been recaptured was transmitted by a Japanese officer. Believing that they no longer had anything to fear from the Cactus Air Force, 8th Fleet Headquarters in Rabaul ordered two columns of warships loaded with infantry to steam for Guadalcanal's Koli Point in the broad daylight of October 26, to cut off an anticipated retreat of American forces to the east.

The first column, made up of the destroyers *Akatsuki*, *Shiratsuyu*, and *Ikazuchi*, darted into Ironbottom Sound at 34 knots at around 10:30 a.m. Two old destroyer-minesweepers, *Trevor* and *Zane*, the fleet tug *Seminole*, and the hard-working *YP-284* were traversing the Sound at the time, shuttling 120 men of the Tenth Marines along with their howitzers and ammunition from Tulagi to Guadalcanal. Instead of landing their own embarked troops, the Japanese destroyers attacked the American vessels, sinking the *Seminole* and *YP-284* and damaging the *Zane* with gunfire before being driven off by aggressively strafing Wildcats that weren't supposed to be there. Miraculously, all but three men aboard the two sinking boats were rescued. Later that morning, as the second column of Japanese ships cruised through the Indispensable Strait to the east of Florida Island, they were attacked by marine SBDs and army P-39s from Henderson Field and B-17s from Espiritu Santo. The light cruiser *Yura* was left on fire and sinking.

Even as this was going on, four Japanese aircraft carriers supported by four battleships, ten cruisers, and twenty-five destroyers were closing in on the Solomon Islands from the north. Admiral Isoroku Yamamoto, the avid gambler, had ordered this powerful force to sortie from the huge fleet base at Truk Atoll, hoping that the Japanese ground offensive on Guadalcanal would cause the American carrier task forces to come to the aid of their embattled marines. With any luck, the enemy carriers could be lured into a decisive battle and destroyed, an outcome that had eluded Yamamoto at the battles of Coral Sea, Midway, and the Eastern Solomons.

This time the gamble nearly paid off. On the night of October 25 the Japanese task force, commanded by Vice Admiral Chuichi Nagumo, was steaming a southerly course 450 miles to the north of the Santa Cruz Islands, approximately 550 miles northeast of Guadalcanal. The combined *Enterprise* and *Hornet* task forces, under the overall tactical command of Rear Admiral Thomas C. Kinkaid, were also on a sweep to the north of the Santa Cruz island group. Just after midnight the Japanese fleet was spotted by a patrolling PBY Catalina, and Kinkaid received a three-word message from Admiral Halsey:

ATTACK REPEAT ATTACK.

An intense, two-day-long slugging match between the two opposing carrier fleets then ensued. American dive bomber pilots managed to inflict heavy damage on the *Shokaku* and *Zuiho*, knocking those two Japanese carriers out of action, and scored several direct hits on the cruiser *Chikuma*. The Japanese "sea eagles" would in turn ravage the *Hornet* so badly that she had to be abandoned. The *Enterprise* and battleship *South Dakota* would also suffer significant bomb damage, and the destroyer

*Porter* was sunk by a Japanese submarine. Eighty-one American aircraft were destroyed in the battle, while the Japanese would lose ninety-nine planes along with sixty-nine more of their highly trained naval aviators.

The Battle of the Santa Cruz Islands would be considered a draw, since afterward both fleets repaired to their respective bases to lick their wounds. The Imperial Japanese Navy would loudly proclaim that they had achieved another signal victory in the Pacific War, greatly inflating the number of American ships sunk and airplanes destroyed in their broadcast communiqués, just as they had after Midway. Likewise, the generalship of the "invincible" Japanese Army would refuse to admit, especially to their bitter rivals in the navy, that their latest attempt to conquer Guadalcanal had been an utter debacle.

***

The radio station for Commander James Compton's Advanced Naval Base Guadalcanal was located inside a 250-foot-long tunnel that the Seabees bored through a hillside on the banks of the Lunga River, some 800 yards to the west of Henderson Field. In its center, the tunnel branched off in either direction for 50 feet, with one branch serving as a coding room and the other housing a powerful array of radio transmitters and receivers. Lumber left behind by the airfield's former custodians, much of it still marked with Japanese writing, was used to shore up the walls and roof.

Additional wooden planks were laid down to create a deck, but these were usually covered by a thick layer of sludge. When it rained, which was quite often, the tunnel floor was quickly transformed into a swift-running brook. Radio operators and coding officers were therefore required to don rubber boots whenever they entered the dank space. Japanese generators, wiring, and switch boxes were used to provide electrical power and lighting, and 250-watt lightbulbs were placed beneath the delicate radio equipment to keep it dry and functioning. The measure worked, but also raised the air temperature inside the already stifling tunnel.

Blowers were installed near the eastern entrance to inject some of the fresh sea breeze drifting across the airfield, and while this offered a blessed relief for the radio watchstanders, it also tended to blow paper dispatch forms from the makeshift tables and desks. Dispatches therefore had to be entered into logbooks as soon as they were decoded, just in case the originals were blown away or floated downstream. Both the tunnel and its signal towers were well camouflaged, and while Japanese bombers made several attempts to locate the site by homing in on the radio beams it generated, it was never successfully bombed.

Base Radio Guadalcanal, known by the call sign "Cactus Control," employed around 20 officers and 160 enlisted personnel, maintaining twenty-four-hour watches over a dozen major radio circuits and processing thousands of messages each day. It was conveniently located next to the headquarters of COMAIRCACTUS and another underground radio station known by the call letters KEN, operated by Lieutenant Commander Hugh Mackenzie of the Royal Australian Navy and established at Henderson Field to receive teleradio reports directly from Ferdinand coastwatchers.

The arrangement allowed intelligence officers to make a timely analysis of sighting reports from coastwatching stations and search aircraft, and compare them against the latest signals intelligence from Melbourne and Pearl Harbor to develop a reasonably accurate picture of Japanese air and naval activity in the upper Solomons. Notifications of the enemy's movements were then sent by messenger or broadcast to the various combatant commands in the South Pacific Area, including Motor Torpedo Boat Base Ringbolt.

This vital intelligence permitted Hugh Robinson and his PT skippers to plan their nocturnal forays into Ironbottom Sound to intercept the Tokyo Express. With the arrival of four additional PTs and the support of the tender *Jamestown*, 'RON 3 now had the ability to perform regular combat patrols in division strength. Among the PTs' favorite haunts were the channels to the north and south of Savo Island, the 12-square-mile lump of jungle-covered volcanic rock and coral that marked the southeastern end of the Slot and the entrance to Ironbottom Sound. Savo lies 9 miles to the northeast of Guadalcanal's Cape Esperance, and 16 miles to the southwest of Florida Island. Upon receiving a report that the Tokyo Express was on the move, PT boats would sortie from Tulagi after nightfall, hoping to catch Tanaka's destroyers as they navigated these relatively narrow passages.

"While patrolling, we would leave Tulagi about seven o'clock at night and take certain patrols which would keep us up all night, and come in in the morning at about six thirty," remembered Chief Stuffert. "We would bring the boats up into the bushes and hide them out in the little waterholes along the shore and try to sleep, and do all the repairs during the day because that night we would have to go out again. It wasn't long before we got into action, around the first of November during the dark period. About every other night we ran into the Japanese ships. Some nights we couldn't find them, other nights we did."

"We did get involved in sixteen different engagements with Japanese destroyers and larger ships," Hugh Robinson recalled. "Those were some hairy times."

One of the "hairiest" occurred on the night of October 29–30. Late in the afternoon, Cactus Control reported that two Japanese destroyers, *Shigure* and *Ariake*, had departed the Shortlands and were bound for Guadalcanal. Desperate to regain the initiative and preserve the honor of the Japanese military, Imperial General Headquarters sent yet another infantry division and an independent mixed brigade to Rabaul, and ordered the navy to ferry them to Guadalcanal via the Tokyo Express.

At the time, only six of the eight PTs at Tulagi were seaworthy. Both the *PT-60* and *PT-39* were sitting aboard the *Jamestown*, the *39* having two propellers replaced after striking a coral head while on patrol the night before. The *PT-39*'s skipper was Ensign James Brent Greene, a husky, towheaded Kentuckian who had studied economics at North Carolina's Davidson College and joined the Naval Reserve just before Pearl Harbor. On this night Greene went to sea in command of the *PT-48*, replacing the ailing Bob Wark, who had been stricken by tropical disease and would soon become a patient of the hospital ship *Solace* in Espiritu Santo.

The six boats stood out from Sesapi just after sunset, with Robinson at the wheel of *PT-61* and Jack Searles accompanying his brother Bob aboard *PT-38*. Robinson decided to deploy three of the boats around Savo Island to act as scouts, while the remaining three laid in ambush. He sent Greene and the *PT-48* west to reconnoiter the Slot, directed Stilly Taylor's *46* boat to patrol the northern Sandfly Passage, and posted the *PT-38* in the strait between Savo Island and Cape Esperance. Satisfied that all western approaches were covered, Robinson cruised the dark reaches of Ironbottom Sound along with Leonard Nikoloric's *PT-37* and Thomas Kendall's *PT-45*. Nikoloric was a twenty-three-year-old New Yorker who had studied at Princeton with the Searles brothers. Kendall, the former XO to Wark aboard *PT-48*, had been a college student living with his parents in Racine, Wisconsin, when the war broke out and was barely old enough to be allowed into an officer's club.

Around midnight Greene's lookouts spotted the gleaming bow waves of the two destroyers through the misty rain.

"Two enemy ships sighted, ten miles west of Esperance, headed for Savo at high speed," Greene's radioman announced over the tactical frequency. Greene attempted to follow the Japanese ships, but lost track of them after they faded into a rain squall.

Aboard the *PT-38* idling in the midst of the Savo-Esperance channel, the crew stood tensely at their battle stations and peered westward into the deepening gloom. On the bridge Bob Searles made minor adjustments to the helm while his brother Jack and XO Bill Kreiner scanned the sea ahead with binoculars. In the blacked-out chartroom just below and forward of the cockpit, Radioman First Class Paul Stephenson fiddled with the squelch dial on his Collins TCS radio to mute the static in his headphones, hoping to catch some fragments of Greene's next contact report. Every man knew the Tokyo Express was barreling eastbound in their direction, and they were standing on the tracks.

"It was very dark," Bob Searles recalled. "It was always very dark out there when the Japs attacked Guadalcanal."

Above the muffled gurgle of the *38*'s motors came the startling roar of a fast-approaching airplane. Quickly recognizing the deep, throaty sound of Pratt & Whitney radial aircraft engines, the sailors began to breathe again. Apparently the PT boats weren't the only ones out hunting for the Tokyo Express. It was a Black Cat—a PBY Catalina of the navy's Patrol Squadron VP-12, covered entirely in matte black paint for night combat missions.

"Cats reporting two enemy DDs* off Tassafaronga," Cactus Control announced. A few seconds later a parachute flare burst beneath the scattered clouds to illuminate the seascape below, revealing the shadowy form of a Japanese destroyer steaming at high speed along the shores of Guadalcanal. Almost immediately the destroyer's searchlights reached out for the prowling seaplane, and fire spat from the muzzles of her antiaircraft guns. Blazing tracer rounds streamed upward into the night sky.

"God, that PBY pilot has a lot of guts," Bob remarked to his brother while swinging the bow of *PT-38* toward the destroyer. In the cockpit beside him, Quartermaster Jim Meadows stood ready to fire the two forward fish on command, while Torpedoman's Mate First Class Scottie Lueckert positioned himself between his torpedo tubes and the smoke generator at the stern, ready to deliver a whack from his mallet or scurry aft to make smoke, whatever the skipper called for.

"All of a sudden, we were the target," Jack Searles later wrote. "The Japanese just lowered his searchlight and guns on us."

"Make smoke!" Bob shouted, spinning the wheel hard aport and pushing the throttles forward. To his great horror, the three Packard engines failed to respond with the expected burst of horsepower, the kind that caused a great surge of kinetic energy and left you feeling as if the boat were about to shoot forward and leave you paddling in its wake. Instead the bow raised sluggishly and only slightly, as if the *PT-38* were indifferent to the fact that the Japanese destroyer had turned in her direction and 5-inch shells were now tearing through the water close aboard. Chugging along at a mere 22 knots, she contributed great clouds of rich exhaust to the trailing smoke screen. Several hours of idling through the Savo-Esperance channel at slow speeds had caused the Holley carburetors to load up and the spark plugs to become badly fouled.

Jack Searles opened the door to the charthouse as Japanese tracer rounds streaked overhead. "Tell Robbie what's happening!" Jack told Stephenson. "Tell him we're coming!"

---

* US Navy hull designation for a destroyer.

Stephenson keyed the radio mic. "One enemy can coming from east through Cape Esperance and Savo! Am being chased! Am being fired on! Course northeast! Hurry! *Hurry!*"

Bob Searles steered the *PT-38* deeper into Ironbottom Sound, hoping to close the distance with the boats of the striking force, all three of which were racing west in response to Stephenson's desperate radio call. Aboard the *PT-37*, Chief Quartermaster John Legg urged Leonard Nikoloric to push their three Packard motors to the limit: "Skipper, you can't go home and face Mrs. Searles if both those guys get it tonight."

The *PT-38*'s wild zigzag course allowed the smoke screen to spread across her wake and conceal her from Japanese gunners, but the 34-knot destroyer was quickly gaining, and it would only be a matter of minutes before she ran down the faltering PT boat. Suddenly the *PT-48* roared out of the night with her .50-caliber machine guns blazing and launched three torpedoes at the *38*'s pursuer from just 400 yards. The destroyer veered sharply to comb the wakes of the inbound fish and turned her own guns upon the *48* boat, blasting several holes in the hull and charthouse but causing no casualties.

Now drawing the enemy's full attention, the *PT-48* wheeled about in a tight heeling turn and made for Tulagi at high speed behind a smoke screen, while the *PT-38* puttered off into the darkness and likewise escaped. Brent Greene and the *48*'s quartermaster, Lee Bagley, both reported seeing an explosion and the destroyer settling by the stern, leading them to believe that one of their fish had found its mark. However, the operational histories of *Shigure* and *Ariake* make no mention of torpedo damage being sustained by either ship on the night of October 29–30, and both destroyers returned safely to their base in the Shortlands.

The shortcomings of the fickle Mark 8 torpedo, rather than poor marksmanship on the part of the PT skippers, may have been to blame for the failure to inflict any serious damage on Japanese ships during the night action off Savo Island or on the night of October 13–14 against Kurita's battleships. Like the air-dropped Mark 13 and the submarine-launched Mark 14 torpedoes used by American naval forces early in the war, the Mark 8 suffered from a multitude of technical problems, apart from its tendency to "run hot" in the tube. The torpedo's contact exploder often failed to detonate the warhead unless it struck its target at a near 90-degree angle, and at just 466 pounds the warhead itself was too small to do any appreciable damage to an armored ship. By comparison the Japanese Type 93 torpedo, often referred to as the "Long Lance," packed a deadly 1,080-pound punch.

The Mark 8's internal gyro tended to become unstable when the torpedo struck the water, often leading to wild, erratic runs. Once destabilized the Mark 8 might "porpoise" along the surface or even turn in circles. During an engagement between PT boats and Axis forces in the Mediterranean Sea in the fall of 1943, a fiery exchange occurred over the radio between two PT skippers: "How many fish have you fired?" one of them asked. "None!" replied the other. "I've been too damned busy dodging yours!"

Later in the war, PT boats would carry the more reliable modified Mark 13 torpedo deployed from newly designed depth charge–style racks rather than the temperamental launching tubes. For the time being, however, the PT boats assigned to "Operation Shoestring" would have to make do with what they had. While they had yet to sink a Japanese ship, the hell-for-leather PT crews had once again forced the Tokyo Express to run away without completing its mission, and they had somehow managed to come through another close-quarters gunfight without anyone being seriously wounded or killed.

"The next morning Bob found a couple of pieces of shrapnel on the cabin top forward of the wheel and only two feet from where we stood," Jack Searles wrote. "Our luck was unbelievable."

Two of the US Navy's experimental PT boats conducting test runs off the Virginia coast in 1939. The 70-foot Scott Paine–designed *PT-9* is in the foreground, accompanied by the 58-foot Fisher Boat Works *PT-3*. (Naval History and Heritage Command)

The 78-foot PT boat built by Higgins Industries of New Orleans. (National Archives)

An 80-foot Elco PT boat launches a salvo of torpedoes. (Naval History and Heritage Command)

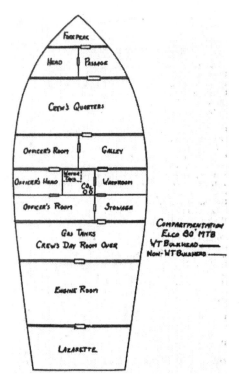

The belowdecks layout of an 80-foot Elco PT boat. (Naval History and Heritage Command)

Two 77-foot Elco PT boats of MTBRON 1, *PT-28* and *PT-29*, escort the aircraft carrier *Hornet* into Pearl Harbor upon her return from the Doolittle bombing raid on Tokyo, April 1942. (National Archives)

US Marines landing on Guadalcanal, August 7, 1942. (Naval History and Heritage Command)

The *PT-47* being off-loaded from a transport ship in Nouméa, New Caledonia, November 1942. (Naval History and Heritage Command)

A PT sailor mans a turret containing two Browning .50-caliber machine guns. (Naval History and Heritage Command)

Sharing a meal aboard a PT boat in the South Pacific. (Naval History and Heritage Command)

The MTB base at Sesapi Cove on Tulagi, British Solomon Islands, 1942. (PT Boats, Inc.)

Ensign John F. Kearney of the *PT-39* stands outside the MTBRON 3 operations shack on Tulagi. Shown is the mosquito-on-a-torpedo emblem designed by Disney cartoonist Hank Porter, transformed into a scoreboard of Japanese ships claimed sunk. (PT Boats, Inc.)

The 77-foot Elco *PT-37* skippered by Leonard Nikoloric cruises into Tulagi Harbor. (PT Boats, Inc.)

The "Tokyo Express"—three *Fubuki*-class destroyers of the Imperial Japanese Navy. (National Archives)

Six PT skippers who saw a great deal of action in the Guadalcanal campaign. Back row, left to right: John Searles, Thomas Kendall, Charles Tilden. Front row, left to right: Robert Searles, Henry Taylor, Leonard Nikoloric. The men in the front row have just been decorated with the Silver Star by Admiral Halsey. (PT Boats, Inc.)

Admiral William F. Halsey Jr., Commander South Pacific Area. (Naval History and Heritage Command)

Willis A. "Ching" Lee, victor of the Naval Battle of Guadalcanal, shown here wearing the rank of vice admiral. (National Archives)

Richard Tregaskis (left) and Major General Alexander A. Vandegrift. (US Marine Corps)

Rear Admiral Raizo Tanaka, commander of Japanese destroyers during the Guadalcanal campaign. (Naval History and Heritage Command)

Alan R. Montgomery, skipper of MTBRON 3 during its initial deployment to Guadalcanal-Tulagi, shown here as a full commander. (Naval History and Heritage Command)

The crowded PT docks at Tulagi's Sesapi Cove, British Solomon Islands, 1942. (PT Boats, Inc.)

Lieutenant Rollin Westholm, commanding officer of MTBRON 2 at Tulagi. (PT Boats, Inc.)

Lieutenant Hugh Robinson, upon whom command of MTBRON 3 "was more or less dumped on" after Alan Montgomery's evacuation.
(PT Boats, Inc.)

PT sailors enter "Calvertville," the enlisted housing area on Tulagi named after Commander Allen Calvert of MTB Flotilla One. (Naval History and Heritage Command)

The *PT-109* entering Tulagi Harbor after the Battle of Tassafaronga, her decks crowded with survivors from the sunken cruiser *Northhampton*. In the background is the *New Orleans*, still afloat after having her bow blown off by a Japanese torpedo. (Naval History and Heritage Command)

The wreck of the *PT-43* on the beach at Aruligo, Guadalcanal. To prevent her from falling into enemy hands, the *43* boat was destroyed by gunfire from a Royal New Zealand Navy corvette. (National Archives)

Lieutenant (jg) John F. Kennedy, skipper of the *PT-109*. (National Archives)

The crew of the *PT-109*. (National Archives)

Robert Searles, Leonard Nikoloric, and Henry "Stilly" Taylor on the cover of the May 10, 1943, edition of *Life* magazine. (Time-Life Inc.)

CHAPTER SIX

# Bitch Patrol

"MY ANXIETY ABOUT THE SOUTH PACIFIC IS TO MAKE SURE THAT EVERY possible weapon gets into that area to hold Guadalcanal," President Roosevelt wrote in an October 24 memorandum to the Joint Chiefs of Staff, "and that having held it in this crisis that munitions and planes and crews are on the way to take advantage of our success."

Much to the chagrin of stubborn "Germany first" proponents like Army Air Forces chief Henry H. "Hap" Arnold, and to the great annoyance of General Douglas MacArthur, who believed his Southwest Pacific Area was always being short-changed when it came to resources, "Operation Shoestring" was being reinforced by order of the president of the United States.

Even though the Allied invasion of North Africa, Operation Torch, was set to begin in early November, additional aircraft from the Army Air Forces were being sent to bolster the ranks of the Cactus Air Force, including a squadron of the new twin-engined Lockheed P-38 Lightning fighters. Admiral King soon informed the president that one battleship, six cruisers, two destroyers, twenty-four submarines, thirty transports, and twenty Liberty cargo ships were en route to the South Pacific Area, along with additional squadrons of motor torpedo boats, fighter aircraft, dive bombers and torpedo planes. True to his promise, Bill Halsey had already sent Vandegrift the Second Raider Battalion and the Eighth Marine Regiment, and would soon transfer a second regiment of the Americal Division, the 182nd Infantry, to Guadalcanal from New Caledonia.

With these badly needed reinforcements arriving, and with the Imperial Japanese Army still reeling from the wallop it received at the Battle of Henderson Field, General Vandegrift decided to launch an offensive of his own. The Fifth Marines, now under Merritt Edson's command and backed by the 3rd Battalion/7th Marines, attacked across the Matanikau on the first day of November. To provide on-call naval gunfire support for the assault, Admiral Halsey sent the cruisers *San Francisco* and *Helena* and the destroyer *Sterett*.

Despite the challenges posed by jungle topography and the stubborn resistance of the Japanese, by the afternoon of the second day the marines had pushed their way westward for over a mile. Some 300 Japanese were cut off and trapped on Point Cruz, where they were annihilated by air strikes, marine artillery, and naval bombardment. Forced to plug the holes in his line with the sick and wounded, Lieutenant General Harukichi Hyakutake, commander of Japanese forces on Guadalcanal, put in a desperate call for more troops. That night 1,500 men of the 228th Infantry Regiment boarded seventeen destroyers and set sail from the Shortlands.

In doing so the Japanese assumed the enormous risk of having their ships within range of the Cactus Air Force after sunrise, but the nighttime departure allowed them to avoid detection by search planes and coastwatchers, and to slip past the patrolling PT boats who had no advance word of their arrival. The Japanese soldiers were landed on the beach at Tassafaronga without incident and immediately marched into the front lines.

In the meantime, some 2,000 members of the battered Sendai Division who survived the Battle of Henderson Field had regrouped and were marching around the eastern flank of the Lunga perimeter. Their commander, Colonel Toshinaro Shoji, had received radioed instructions to make for Koli Point, where they would be resupplied and reinforced by Tanaka's destroyers. That message was intercepted and decoded by US Navy signals intelligence and forwarded to Admiral Halsey, who alerted Vandegrift and the new Commander Advanced Naval Base Cactus-Ringbolt, Captain William Greenman.

Lieutenant Colonel Herman Hanneken's 2nd Battalion/7th Marines were dispatched to deal with the new threat, and Hugh Robinson was ordered to deploy his PT boats in the waters off Koli Point. Robinson was further instructed to conduct patrols between Cape Esperance and Kokumbona, a coastal village just to the west of the new marine lines, to keep Hyakutake's men from receiving any further reinforcements by sea.

But as Chief Stuffert described, "Some nights we couldn't find them." Robinson's boat crews stayed out all night on November 1 through November 4 but returned to Tulagi each morning empty-handed, having failed to make contact with the Tokyo Express. Not only was the weather horribly foul, with frequent rain squalls, high winds, and heaving seas, but the waning lunar cycle caused Ironbottom Sound to be even darker than usual. November 3–4 was especially gloomy, a moonless night with heavy rain. Consequently, one Japanese cruiser, three destroyers, and a transport vessel were able to evade searching PT boats and around midnight put reinforcements, food, and supplies ashore at Gavaga Creek, about a mile east of Koli Point.

The three boats patrolling that sector, PTs *38*, *39*, and *46*, had run across the wakes of the larger ships, but without radar had little hope of locating them through the driving rain and pitch blackness of the Sound. Visibility was so poor, in fact, that as they made for Tulagi in the pre-dawn hours, two of the boats collided. Bob Searles's *38* boat got the worst of it, after being struck in the starboard side amidships by the bow of Stilly Taylor's *PT-46*. An 8-foot-long gash was torn in the *38*'s mahogany hull below the waterline, flooding the wardroom and officer's quarters. Fortunately the crew had set Condition Z for battle cruising, with all watertight doors between compartments slammed shut and dogged tight, and the flooding was easily contained. Back at Tulagi a temporary patch was applied to the hull and the compartments drained of seawater. The *PT-38* would spend the final two months of 1942 under repair.

Four PT boats formed the night patrol for November 5–6. Robinson was once again at the helm of the squadron flagship, *PT-61*. Lenny Nikoloric commanded *PT-37*, while Tom Kendall now skippered the *PT-48*. With the bow of his *46* boat being repaired, Stilly Taylor took out the *PT-39*. Even as the individual PTs were standing out from Tulagi Harbor and steering for their assigned patrol sectors, two columns of Japanese ships were steaming at high speed down the Slot. The first column was made up of ten destroyers, while the second consisted of five destroyers led by the light cruiser *Tenryu*. Both columns had the remaining troops of the Japanese 228th Infantry Regiment embarked and were bound for Tassafaronga and Cape Esperance, respectively.

By now the PT sailors had figured out that the Tokyo Express, which usually departed from the Shortlands in the late afternoon, could be expected to arrive off the shores of Guadalcanal between the hours of 10:00 p.m. and 2:00 a.m. Setting sail too early or lingering in Ironbottom Sound for too long would, of course, leave the Japanese ships vulnerable to daylight observation and attacks by Allied aircraft. The PT crews had therefore learned to be especially vigilant during this four-hour window, when they were most likely to make contact with the enemy. And on this night, they did.

Stilly Taylor had the *PT-39* at a slow idle just off the northwestern beaches of Guadalcanal between Cape Esperance and Kokumbona, a dangerous and therefore unpopular sector the PT sailors had come to call the "bitch patrol." Around 12:30 a.m. the boat was rocked by the wakes of two passing ships. Taylor and his crew were unable to visually acquire any targets, but guessed correctly that the ships were headed for Tassafaronga and began heading west in pursuit. An American searchlight, most likely from a shore battery or antiaircraft gun emplacement situated around Henderson Field, suddenly switched on and began sweeping out to sea, the beam coming to rest on a *Shiratsuyu*-class destroyer cruising through the Sound. Just as suddenly the light was prudently extinguished before drawing fire. Now having knowledge of the enemy's whereabouts, Taylor steered a course to intercept.

After forty minutes of searching, Taylor finally spotted the *Murasame* and moved in to attack. At almost the same time, lookouts aboard the destroyer picked up the approaching *PT-39*. Illuminating the PT boat with her searchlights, the *Murasame* unleashed a withering fusillade from her main and secondary guns. Lee Bagley triggered two torpedoes on Taylor's command, one of which missed the target while the other failed to launch. Taylor gave the order to make smoke and spun the wheel to port, sending the *PT-39* into a wide turn through a deluge of enemy bullets.

A 5-inch shell burst just off starboard quarter of the *PT-39*, throwing torpedomen Ben Goddard and Emil Stayonovich from their feet. The concussion also lifted Gunner's Mate Second Class Teddy Kuharski completely out of his starboard machine gun turret and sent him sprawling onto the foredeck. Despite the pitching and rolling of the zigzagging PT, the now-furious twenty-four-year-old sailor managed to pick himself up, climb back into the turret, and begin hammering away with the twin fifties. Kuharski fired seventy-five rounds before both guns jammed, but that was enough. The *Murasame*'s searchlight exploded with a shattering crash and the enemy guns fell silent. Almost immediately another Japanese destroyer, most likely the *Murasame*'s sister ship *Harusame*, turned her searchlight upon the *PT-39* and opened fire. Shell splashes leapt from the *39*'s wake, but she outran her pursuers with the aid of a smoke screen.

"Speculation has it," wrote the squadron intelligence officer, Lieutenant Samuel Savage, "that the Japs aboard at least one destroyer have a healthy respect for the PT's .50-caliber fire."

On the following night of November 6–7, Robinson decided to deploy three boats in the Lengo Channel to ambush an expected Tokyo Express run to Koli Point. Colonel Shoji's hard-pressed troops had been conducting a fighting withdrawal toward the sea, fending off attacks from not only the Seventh Marines but the US Army's 164th Infantry, and were in danger of being surrounded. Several radio transmissions between Shoji and General Hyakutake had been intercepted, which included Shoji's pleas for more troops, ammunition and provisions.

Robinson led the patrol in *PT-61*, followed by Nikoloric's *PT-37* and the *PT-48*, skippered by the recently arrived Lieutenant Lester Hollis Gamble. A blond-haired, blue-eyed, ruddy-faced twenty-five-year-old who had studied at Fresno State, in June 1941 Gamble was tending bar at the opulent Mark Hopkins Hotel on San Francisco's Nob Hill when he decided to enlist in the Naval Reserve. Despite his landlubbing past, Gamble quickly adapted to the life of a seaman and became a skilled boat handler. Friendly, charismatic, and seemingly fearless, he would soon make a name for himself among the officers and men of the Mosquito Fleet.

The wind was up that night, the seas were choppy, and as the two o'clock hour approached the Tokyo Express had yet to put in an appearance. Aboard the pitching and yawing *37* boat, Lenny Nikoloric found himself silently hoping that they wouldn't. He looked forward to the appointed time when they would knock off for the night, and with coffee and sandwiches doled out, they could begin the long, steady, hour-long cruise back to Tulagi.

The mental and physical strain caused by the recent increase in operational tempo was beginning to take its toll on everybody. Eight boat crews were doing the job of twelve, and the nights were long. Sleeping during the daylight hours was difficult under the bright light and oppressive heat of the equatorial sun, made worse by the aches, fever, and cramps of tropical ailments. Little time could be devoted to sleep anyway, since the boats demanded constant care and maintenance in order to be ready for the next patrol. As combat missions are so often described, the patrols consisted of many hours of dull monotony punctuated by a few moments of stark terror. So far the members of 'RON 3 had been lucky: None of their PT boats had been seriously damaged or sunk by enemy fire, and no one had been grievously wounded or killed. Sooner or later, Nikoloric knew, their luck was bound to run out.

Standing in the cockpit beside him was Chief Quartermaster John Legg, an old salt of a dozen years' service, carefully scanning the surrounding sea through a pair of binoculars.

"How many boats are out here, sir?" Chief Legg asked Nikoloric.

"Two besides us," the skipper replied.

"I see three," the chief said.

Legg lowered the binoculars, removed the leather strap from around his neck, and handed the glasses to Nikoloric. Five thousand yards to the north, a Japanese destroyer was running at 20 knots in the direction of Koli Point.

"Enemy ship on my starboard beam," Nikoloric called over the radio.

"Deploy right," Robinson ordered.

"We were the only boat that was able to see this destroyer," Chief Legg said later, "and we notified the other boats naturally, but we found that we were going to be the only one having to attack it, so we maneuvered into position and let her have four fish."

The torpedoes plunged into the water and sped off into the darkness, each leaving a faintly glowing trail of phosphorescence. Seconds ticked by, then a minute, then three, and then five. Unbothered, the destroyer continued on for Koli Point. All four of the *37*'s fish had missed, passing well ahead of the Japanese vessel. Legg would admit that everyone aboard the *PT-37* was "pretty jittery," and that the torpedoes had been fired from too great a distance.

"I would say two and one-half miles," Legg said. "That's much too far for a good torpedo run."

Farther to the southeast aboard the *PT-48*, Les Gamble spotted the Japanese ship rounding Koli Point and turning toward shore. Closing to within just 400 yards, Gamble fired a spread of four torpedoes before dashing away with engine mufflers wide open and smoke generator hissing. Seconds later came a blinding flash and the stunning report of an explosion. The destroyer replied with a single shot from one of her 5-inch guns, which rocketed over the zigzagging *PT-48*.

"We got a hit!" Gamble's radioman Elden Alvis announced. "All torpedoes gone. We're heading for the barn. There's another ship to the north."

"Where the hell is he?" Robinson asked. His *PT-61* had been too far away to engage the first destroyer. The squadron commander would spend the next ninety minutes trying to locate the second, to no avail.

While the records of the Imperial Japanese Navy cannot confirm Gamble's claim of a torpedo hit on the destroyer, an oil slick and floating debris were spotted in Lengo Channel the following morning. It can be said with certainty that the destroyer did not sink, as JANAC lists no Japanese ships lost on the night of November 6–7, 1942. The explosion may have been the result of one or more of Gamble's fish detonating prematurely, another maddening tendency of their unreliable torpedoes that plagued the Americans early in the war. But along with the presence of oil and flotsam in the water, it is compelling that the destroyer fired her guns only once and never tried to pursue the *PT-48*.

\*\*\*

General Vandegrift watched apprehensively as the olive-drab Flying Fortress carrying Vice Admiral Halsey made its final approach to Henderson Field. Forgoing the customary orbit of the airfield so as to not attract the attention of Japanese machine gunners in the surrounding hills, the army pilot pushed the big four-engined bomber into a steep angle of descent from a height of 1,000 feet, flared abruptly at the last moment, and then settled onto the packed earth of the airstrip in a near-perfect three-point landing.

When telltale puffs of dirt billowed from the airplane's tires, Vandegrift emitted a sigh of relief. Recent heavy rains had turned Henderson Field into a swampy quagmire, forcing flight operations to be suspended until the afternoon on most days. By that time the sun had dried the mud sufficiently for takeoffs and landings to resume with an acceptable level of risk, leaving an upper layer of red dust to be whipped across the airfield by the trade winds. The Canal, as many a marine has said, was the only place on earth where you could be standing knee-deep in mud and have dust blowing in your face.

Halsey returned Vandegrift's warm greeting before embarking upon a tour of Henderson Field, the previous battle sites of Edson's Ridge and Alligator Creek, and finally the front lines west of the Matanikau. The admiral had chosen a well-worn, standard-issue working khaki uniform for the trip, making him indistinguishable from any other officer. When his new flag lieutenant, William Kitchell, suggested that he stand in the jeep and wave in order to be recognized by the troops, Halsey flatly refused, stating that such a gesture would "smell of exhibitionism."

"During a tour of the area, [Halsey] showed extreme interest and enthusiasm in all phases of the operation, concurring with my existent positions and future plans," Vandegrift wrote. "More important, he talked to a large number of marines, saw their gaunt, malaria-ridden bodies, their faces lined from what seemed a nightmare of years. I believe then and there he decided to get us out as fast as possible."

To drive the admiral's jeep, Vandegrift selected Lieutenant Frederic Gehring, a Roman Catholic chaplain who spent much of his time in the field with the marines and knew the terrain of Guadalcanal well. At one point during the tour, Gehring turned to Halsey and bravely announced, "You know, Admiral, some of the men are afraid that this will be another Bataan."

"This won't be another Bataan, damn it!" Halsey shot back. "We're going to win, and you and I will both see Yamamoto in hell!"

That night the admiral and his accompanying staff bedded down in Vandegrift's quarters. "Soon after we turned in, an enemy destroyer somewhere near Savo Island began lobbing shells, and our artillery started an argument with the Japs," Halsey recorded in his memoirs. "It wasn't the noise that kept me awake, it was fright. I called myself yellow—and worse—and told myself, *go to sleep, you coward*. But it didn't do any good; I couldn't obey orders."

***

Even as Admiral Halsey was restlessly tossing and turning in his borrowed cot, PT boats were out on the waters of Ironbottom Sound stalking the Japanese destroyers. Earlier in the day Hugh Robinson received word from Cactus Control that reconnaissance aircraft had spotted five of the enemy ships pounding down the Slot at 30 knots, on a course of 120 degrees southeast. At that speed, they would arrive off Savo Island at around 11:00 p.m. Captain Greenman ordered every available PT boat to sortie after dark to "intercept and destroy" the Japanese force, which was actually larger than the sighting reports had advised, consisting of a light cruiser and nine destroyers.

Like the sailors who manned them, the boats themselves were being gradually worn out by the relentless pace of night operations. Despite the fact that President Roosevelt and the Joint Chiefs had recently doubled down on the Guadalcanal campaign, shortages of spare parts, lubricants, and other essential items continued to be a problem. A lack of adequate shore facilities on Tulagi made it difficult to conduct the extensive maintenance the boats required, and the tender *Jamestown* could only accomplish so much. Greenman may have wanted an all-out effort from MTBRON 3 for the night of November 8–9, but Robinson could muster just three boats: PTs *37*, *39*, and his own *61*. Lenny Nikoloric's *37* boat would go to sea with only three torpedoes, which represented the last of the *Jamestown*'s stock of replacement fish.

At 10:45 p.m. the three PTs were idling off the southern end of Savo Island at slow speed, and were turning onto a southeasterly course toward Guadalcanal when Brent Green suddenly broke radio silence.

"Jap can on my starboard bow."

Robinson signaled for the boats to assume a line abreast attack for-mation, and as they moved to comply the shapes of two more destroyers were seen skulking in the darkness behind the first. From a distance of 800 yards Greene in the *39* boat sent two fish barreling toward the destroyer in the van, both of which passed harmlessly through the churn-ing wake of the ship. Nikoloric had in the meantime singled out another destroyer, the *Mochizuki*, and let fly with all three torpedoes.

"We got up pretty close to this baby," Chief Legg would recount. "We had a good broadside shot at him. We fired our three torpedoes and then they started shooting. There was quite a lot of it. There was so much fire going on around there that it lit up the whole side of Guadalcanal. We immediately laid smoke and turned about to get out."

One of Nikoloric's torpedoes struck the *Mochizuki* but exploded with a low order of detonation and did little damage. Hugh Robinson, whose line-of-sight had been blocked by the silhouette of the *PT-37* as Nikoloric maneuvered for the shot, was forced to turn away with-out launching any torpedoes of his own. By now all three tin cans had turned to give chase, and were attempting to fix their searchlights on the scattering PT boats while their main and secondary guns poured out a murderous volume of fire.

As the boats fled the scene, machine gunners aboard the *PT-61* raked the superstructure of the lead destroyer with 250 rounds of .50-caliber ammunition. The *61* boat was also equipped with a deadly 20-millimeter Oerlikon on her fantail, which contributed another 60 high-explosive rounds to the effort to fend off her pursuers. Robinson zigzagged his boat wildly and gave the order to drop depth charges at a shallow setting. The "ash cans" were rolled overboard at random intervals and exploded, caus-ing the destroyers to veer off course momentarily and cease their fire. At least one of the destroyers quickly resumed the chase and closed to within

500 yards of Robinson's stern, indicating that the Japanese destroyer skippers were getting wise to the trick.

One of the *61* boat's three moto-macs, "seeing that he didn't have anything to do," appeared on deck brandishing a 1903 Springfield rifle and crouched behind one of the boat's torpedo tubes.

"What are you going to do with that?" Chief Art Stuffert asked.

"I'm going to start shooting when he does," the sailor replied. As if to answer the challenge, the main battery of the destroyer erupted with a deafening roar. A 5-inch shell whistled over the stern of the *PT-61*, passed between the cockpit and the forward torpedo tube, and struck the bow with a shuddering crash.

"We thought it was all over for Robbie and his gang," said Nikoloric, watching from just 300 yards away. "If that shell hadn't finished them, the next hit certainly would. The Japs were sending everything they had at her."

"The Japs kept firing at us and landed quite a few salvos near our stern and kind of knocked me off my feet," Stuffert recalled, "and while I was down there mostly watching the .50-calibers firing, it seemed to take everything off my mind."

Very slowly, the stunned chief machinist's mate pulled himself to his feet and went below to the engine room. Sensing a marked decrease in the boat's speed, and unaware that the *PT-61* had taken a direct hit that removed most of her bow, Stuffert assumed that the three Packard motors must be struggling.

"Still the engines wouldn't get up the speed and I started wobbling gas up to the engines thinking it would help out a bit," Stuffert remembered. "One of the engineers kept saying to me, he said, 'Don't let the engines stall, there is a Jap destroyer right astern of us.' This destroyer had chased us for about 20 minutes and we finally lost them."

Fortunately, the boat's speed was sufficient to keep the shattered bow out of the water. Back in Tulagi Harbor, Robinson and his crew took stock of the damage. The Japanese shell had penetrated the foredeck of the *PT-61* and passed through the bulkhead that separated the crew's quarters from the head. There the shell had struck the washroom sink and detonated, blowing the hull apart on both sides, leaving a gaping hole in the main deck above, and punching several large shrapnel holes through the bottom.

The sorely needed *61* boat would be out of action for the next thirteen days. While her demolished bow section was being pieced back together, moto-macs took the opportunity to replace her tired engines with three spares stored aboard the *Jamestown*. All throughout the intense gun battle on the night of November 8–9, the incredible luck of the PT sailors had held out, for none had yet earned a Purple Heart, or their mothers at home a gold star.

*** 

On November 9 Admiral Halsey returned to Nouméa, where his new headquarters ashore had been established. Fed up with the intransigence of French colonial officials, in late October Halsey ordered a detachment of sailors and marines to seize the offices of the High Commissioner and, ironically, the former Japanese consulate. Shortly thereafter the SOPAC staff moved into these spacious new quarters and raised Halsey's three-star flag.

Upon his arrival, Halsey was handed an "ultra top secret" message from Commander-in-Chief Pacific Fleet:

```
Indications that major operation assisted by
carrier striking force slated to support move-
ment army transports to Guadalcanal.
```

The message went on to list the Japanese air, surface, and subsurface units expected to take part in the next great effort to seize Guadalcanal—and the list was lengthy—which had been compiled by the cryptanalysts at Station HYPO.

Yamamoto was sending two battleships, *Hiei* and *Kirishima*, a heavy cruiser, and fourteen destroyers under Vice Admiral Hiroaki Abe to pulverize Henderson Field and destroy the Cactus Air Force on the ground. Then a dozen of Tanaka's destroyers would escort eleven transports to the beaches of Tassafaronga, where they would land 14,500 troops of the Imperial Army's 38th Infantry Division and the Special Naval Landing

Force to sweep the Americans from the island once and for all. An additional six cruisers and six destroyers were being assigned to support the landing. A formidable task force of two carriers, two battleships, four cruisers, and nineteen destroyers were to keep station 75 miles north of the Solomons to provide air cover and a tactical reserve of surface ships. These forces were already steaming south from Truk or gathering in Rabaul's Simpson Harbor. Codebreakers were still trying to determine the planned date and time of the assault.

After delivering this dreadful news, Nimitz closed with a word of encouragement to his subordinate commander, which, knowing Halsey, must have inspired a chuckle followed by a long string of profanity:

```
While this looks like a big punch I am confi-
dent that you with your forces will take their
measure.
```

***

For the Japanese already on Guadalcanal, the situation was growing increasingly desperate. To the east of the Lunga perimeter, Colonel Shoji's men had been pushed into a narrow pocket around Gavaga Creek, and many had already taken their own lives to avoid capture. General Hyakutake's troops manning the defensive line west of Point Cruz weren't faring much better. During the day they were subjected to relentless bombing and strafing attacks by the planes of the Cactus Air Force, and were receiving punishing indirect fire from army and marine artillery around the clock. Ammunition, food, and medicine remained in short supply. Daily rations had been cut by two-thirds, and fully half of the men were sick from malaria, dengue fever, or dysentery. Reports transmitted from Rabaul to Combined Fleet Headquarters in Truk touted the number of "successful" reinforcement and supply runs made by Tanaka's destroyers, and stopped short of conveying the ugly truth: "Rat Transportation" wasn't getting the job done.

On the night of November 10–11, five Japanese destroyers unloaded supplies onto the beaches of Cape Esperance along with 600 fresh troops, among them Lieutenant Commander Masatoshi Funabashi, a naval gun-fire liaison officer who was to act as a spotter for the coming battleship bombardment of Henderson Field. Most of these men would be replacements rather than reinforcements, for after they were put ashore, 585 sick cases were embarked and the destroyers were soon underway for the Shortlands. As they passed to the south of Savo Island, they were spotted by a three-boat element being led by Hugh Robinson aboard the *PT-45*, accompanied by Kendall's *PT-48* and Nikoloric's *PT-37*.

The PT boats were in turn detected by Japanese lookouts, and just as they closed to within torpedo-firing range they were lit up by destroyer searchlights. In order to defend themselves against the American "devil boats," as the Japanese sailors had begun to call them, the destroyers assumed a cruising disposition that allowed for interlocking arcs of fire, creating a kill zone for any unsuspecting PT captain that might blunder into it.

"By this time the Japs were getting smart," said Chief John Legg. "They had their ships arranged so in case a boat did get in for a shot, they would get several of us."

Tangled streams of 12.7-millimeter tracer bullets and 25-millimeter shells that looked like "flaming baseballs" crisscrossed the night sky; towering 5-inch shell splashes rose from the sea. In the face of this withering fire, Robinson selected a destroyer as his target and triggered a pair of torpedoes before cranking the *PT-45* into a hard turn and making smoke. Nikoloric's *PT-37* launched a single fish before doing the same. All three torpedoes missed. At the same time, gunners aboard Tom Kendall's *48* boat were doing their best to lay down suppressive fire, but the sheer volume of the incoming fusillade was just too much. Kendall was forced to turn away without launching any torpedoes of his own.

A large-caliber Japanese shell exploded close aboard the fleeing *PT-37*, nearly standing the boat onto her beam ends. Everyone standing topside was thrown to the deck except for Chief Legg, who had already been bracing himself against the cockpit handrail. Nikoloric received a blow to the head that left him momentarily stunned, and the chief had to step over his skipper's sprawled-out figure to grab the wheel.

"I saw that we were going to get sunk," Legg later reported, "so I pushed the throttles down and gave her a hard right. We had our smoke on already. I zigzagged for about three minutes, laying smoke. . . . We got through it all right that night."

For his quick and skillful action, which surely saved the *PT-37* and the lives of her crew, Chief Quartermaster John Legg would be awarded the Silver Star. Lieutenant Nikoloric managed to regain his senses, get back to his feet, and relieve Chief Legg at the helm. The *PT-37* had traveled about half the distance to Tulagi when, quite unexpectedly, a sailor crawled from the open end of the boat's empty torpedo tube.

"I don't know how he did it, because it was trained out," Legg explained. "He considered himself pretty lucky. It was quite a joke around the squadron."

Radioman First Class Owen Peale, whose battle station was located inside the thinly walled plywood charthouse, had scrambled into the open steel tube seeking cover from the intense enemy fire.

"He happened to have the torpedoman's jacket on," Legg said. "It was pretty greasy, so they had quite a squabble over that."

\*\*\*

"On six days, November 2, 5, 7, 8, 9, and 10, a total of two cruisers and sixty-five destroyers succeeded in landing operations," read the 8th Fleet summary report to Imperial General Headquarters. "However, interference from PT boats and planes necessitated a change from the existing unloading procedure to shorter interval unloadings."

Less time spent by Tanaka's destroyers off the beaches of Guadalcanal meant fewer soldiers being put ashore to reinforce or replace the sick and starving men of the garrison. It meant fewer sacks of rice, fewer bottles of medicine, and fewer boxes of bullets. The aggressive American PT crews, in spite of their small numbers and temperamental torpedoes, were having their impact. Patrols by the Ringbolt PTs were again conducted on the following night of November 11–12, 1942. No enemy contact was reported, and all boats returned safely to base. The Tokyo Express, it seemed, had decided to take the night off.

It would prove to be the calm before the storm.

CHAPTER SEVEN

# Friday the Thirteenth

"*TALLY HO!* BANDITS! TWO O'CLOCK LOW!"

High over the glistening blue waters of Ironbottom Sound, Captain Joe Foss was leading a formation of sixteen Grumman F4F-4 Wildcats from VMF-121, trailed by a flight of eight shark-nosed Bell P-39 Airacobras of the US Army's 67th Fighter Squadron. Far below, two dozen Japanese "Betty" bombers, laden with torpedoes and escorted by nine Zero fighters, were racing at wave-top height for the American ships riding at anchor off Lunga Point.

"Let's go, gang!" Foss called over the radio as he rolled the stubby Wildcat into a screaming power dive.

The nearest Betty grew ever larger in the front windscreen of Foss's canopy, completely filling the reflector gunsight mounted atop the instrument panel. Closing to within just 100 yards, Foss squeezed the trigger on the joystick and opened fire with all six .50-caliber machine guns mounted in the Wildcat's wings. Lacking armor and self-sealing fuel tanks, the Betty had a reputation for easily catching fire after absorbing just a few rounds of incendiary ammunition, leading American fighter pilots to nickname the twin-engined naval bomber "The Flying Zippo." This Betty proved no exception. Immediately bursting into flames and streaming black smoke, the bomber skidded sideways, buried the tip of its starboard wing into the waves and cartwheeled wildly across the surface of the channel, scattering burning chunks of its airframe in every direction.

"As I passed the ships, a Zero came diving from somewhere and made a run on me," Foss said later. "He chose an annoying time, for I had a bomber up front and was just ready to shoot. I had to haul up and give a short burst, which happened to be dead on the Zero. He blew up practically on the water."

Foss would go on to splash another Betty for his twenty-second air-to-air kill before running out of ammunition and returning to Henderson Field. Sixteen of the Japanese bombers were shot down by pilots of the Cactus Air Force and another four were destroyed by shipboard antiaircraft fire. The survivors managed to stagger back to their base on Bougainville but were so badly shot-up that they would never fly again. Seven Zeroes were also sent down in flames during the brisk dogfight, while the Americans lost three Wildcats and one Airacobra. The pilot of one flaming Betty, either in a final gesture of devotion to his Emperor or because he was already dead, crashed his plane into the aft superstructure of the heavy cruiser *San Francisco* and killed thirty of her crew.

The target of the failed Japanese air strike had been Rear Admiral Kelly Turner's four transport ships, which were busily debarking the soldiers of the 182nd Regimental Combat Team onto landing craft in the Lunga roadstead. Escorted by the heavy cruiser *Portland* and four destroyers, the transport flotilla had rendezvoused with Task Group 67.4 in the Solomon Sea the previous afternoon before proceeding to Guadalcanal. Made up of the *San Francisco*, the light cruisers *Helena* and *Juneau*, and six destroyers, Task Group 67.4 was commanded by Rear Admiral Daniel J. Callaghan, former naval aide to President Roosevelt and chief-of-staff to Vice Admiral Robert Ghormley during the latter's tenure as COMSOPAC.

Already waiting for them in Lunga Roads was Rear Admiral Norman Scott, flying his flag from the light cruiser *Atlanta* and accompanied by four destroyers. In the meantime, Rear Admiral Thomas Kinkaid's Task Force 16 had set sail from Nouméa, with the carrier *Enterprise* and battleship *South Dakota* still smarting from wounds received in the Battle of Santa Cruz.

"The *South Dakota*'s number one turret was completely out of commission, but the *Enterprise* was crippled far worse," Admiral Halsey wrote. "When we sent her back to sea, 85 repairmen were still aboard, one of her tanks was still leaking oil, and her forward elevator was still jammed, as far as we knew, at flight deck level. I say 'as far as we knew,' because we didn't dare test it. If we had lowered it and been unable to raise it again, she would have been useless. As it was, she could conduct flight operations at slow speed, and this was a time when half-ships counted."

Halsey was sending everything that could still float into the lower Solomons in order to thwart Isoroku Yamamoto's latest effort to reconquer Guadalcanal. Reports from coastwatchers, reconnaissance aircraft, and submarines confirmed the previous warning issued by Nimitz's codebreakers. Vice Admiral Hiroaki Abe's bombardment group, centered on the battleships *Hiei* and *Kirishima*, had been sighted some 300 miles northwest of Guadalcanal. Not far behind were Rear Admiral Raizo Tanaka's twelve destroyers shepherding eleven transport vessels loaded with Japanese troops.

Before departing for Espiritu Santo with his empty transports on the evening of November 12, Kelly Turner ordered the *Portland* and Norman Scott's five ships to join Callaghan's task group. As the more senior of the two flag officers, "Uncle Dan" Callaghan was given overall tactical command of the combined force. Turner's adherence to this long-standing practice would prove unfortunate, for Scott of Cape Esperance had already met and defeated the Japanese at their own game of night combat, while Callaghan had never before commanded a task group in battle and lacked a thorough understanding of modern radar and its capabilities.

Now consisting of two heavy cruisers, three light cruisers, and eight destroyers, Task Group 67.4 shadowed Turner's transports on their journey eastward until 10:10 p.m., when Callaghan ordered a change of course to 270 degrees due west. Entering Lengo Channel at midnight, they continued westward across Ironbottom Sound in the direction of Savo Island. Callaghan had his ships arrayed in a single column formation, with four destroyers in the van and four bringing up the rear, an arrangement that greatly limited their ability to launch torpedo attacks against the Japanese. A former captain of the *San Francisco*, Callaghan insisted on having her as his flagship, even though she did not possess the latest SG surface search radar. The *Helena* was so equipped, but Callaghan placed her behind *San Francisco* in the formation.

At 1:24 a.m., *Helena* reported two surface contacts on a true bearing of 310 degrees northwest at a distance of 18 miles. Eleven minutes later, *Helena* announced, "We have four in a line," followed by, "We have about ten targets," at 1:42 a.m. Precious minutes ticked by with no orders coming from the flag bridge of the *San Francisco*. Finally, at 1:50 a.m., Callaghan issued the perplexing command: "Odd ships fire to starboard, even ships fire to port." By then it was too late; Callaghan had squandered the technological advantage, and sharp-eyed Japanese lookouts had spotted the American column.

What followed was a wild, confused, murderous mêlée at close quarters, which one American officer would liken to "a bar room brawl after the lights had been shot out." The first Japanese destroyer to illuminate the American ships with searchlights, *Akatsuki*, was pummeled by gunfire and quickly sank, taking all but eighteen members of her 197-man crew down with her. The *Atlanta* was struck by a torpedo, which gutted her forward engine room; shortly thereafter an errant salvo of 8-inch shells from the *San Francisco* destroyed her bridge and killed Admiral Scott.

The *Portland* was struck by a torpedo in her starboard quarter that wrenched off two screws, flooded her steering engine rooms, and jammed her rudder at 5 degrees right. Steaming in a series of aimless circles, the *Portland* nevertheless remained in the fight and continued trading blows with the Japanese. The *Juneau* would also fall victim to the Long Lance, receiving a torpedo hit in her forward fireroom. As she limped eastward toward Espiritu Santo later that morning, *Juneau* would be torpedoed again by the submarine *I-26* and sunk with heavy loss of life, including five brothers belonging to the Sullivan family of Waterloo, Iowa.

Before meeting her own demise, the destroyer *Laffey* peppered the bridge of the *Hiei* with gunfire, wounding Admiral Abe and killing his chief-of-staff. A salvo fired by the *Kirishima* then crashed into the forward superstructure of the *San Francisco*, ending the life of Admiral Dan Callaghan. The same explosion killed the ship's captain, Cassin Young, who had received the Medal of Honor for gallantry displayed during the attack on Pearl Harbor. Before she retired, the outgunned *San Francisco* was able to score several direct hits on the *Hiei*, ravaging the battleship's topside and destroying her steering engines and fire control systems. At around 2:20 a.m., both Admiral Abe and Captain Gilbert Hoover of the *Helena*, the senior surviving American officer, ordered their respective forces to break off the engagement.

\*\*\*

A stratified layer of pungent black smoke hung low over Ironbottom Sound in the dawnlight of Friday the Thirteenth, emanating from a half-dozen drifting, burning hulks that just hours before had been proud ships of the line. Shining slicks of fuel oil spread with the ocean currents across the slate-blue surface of the channel, interspersed with great patches of floating debris and a good number of lifeless bodies, both Japanese and American. Here and there an oil-smudged life raft could be found gently rising and falling on the morning swells, packed with the burned and bleeding survivors of the night's ordeal.

The US Navy had been able to save Henderson Field from another "Night of the Battleships," but at a tremendous cost. Two new light cruisers, *Atlanta* and *Juneau*, had been lost along with destroyers *Laffey*, *Barton*, *Cushing*, and *Monssen*. Of the thirteen ships in Task Group 67.4, only the destroyer *Fletcher* had escaped damage. Some 1,400 Americans were dead, including two admirals. Along with the *Akatsuki* being sunk in the first chaotic moments of the battle, the Japanese also lost the destroyer *Yudachi*. With her number one boiler room wrecked by 5-inch shells from the *Sterett*, the powerless *Yudachi* was abandoned by her crew and finished off by gunfire from the *Portland* later that morning.

At first light, dive bombers and torpedo planes of the Cactus Air Force and B-17s from Espiritu Santo caught up with the foundering *Hiei* northwest of Savo Island. With fires raging out of control from multiple bomb and torpedo hits, *Hiei* would be abandoned and scuttled later that evening, the first Japanese battleship destroyed by Allied forces in the Pacific War.

The vicious "bar room brawl" that would go down in history as the Naval Battle of Guadalcanal was far from over, however. Abe had failed in his mission to bombard Henderson Field, forcing Tanaka's destroyers and transports to reverse course and return to the Shortlands. Bill Halsey knew that the respite would be brief, for the Japanese would surely regroup and try again. A message was sent to Thomas Kinkaid aboard the *Enterprise*, ordering the fast battleships *Washington* and *South Dakota* and four destroyers to peel away from Task Force 16 and steam for Guadalcanal. Designated as Task Force 64, the battleship-destroyer detachment was placed under the command of Rear Admiral Willis Lee, flying his flag from the *Washington*.

"The dispatches I had received that morning made it obvious that the remnants of Callaghan's force were in no condition to fight another battle," Halsey wrote. "Yet if I did not take positive action, if I let the enemy enter the combat zone unmolested, to bombard our troops and their positions and their airfield and to land reinforcements, not only would he increase his strength at the expense of ours but our morale would be riddled. Lee's ships were my only recourse, so I sent them in."

*Washington* and *South Dakota* would have their rendezvous with destiny, but not this night. The two battlewagons had been shadowing *Enterprise* ever since Task Force 16 put to sea on November 11. Much like the original six frigates that made up the early US Navy, the modern aircraft carrier was reliant upon the fortunes of the wind to perform the functions for which it was designed. In order to conduct flight operations in support of the Cactus Air Force, *Enterprise* had been forced to steer southerly courses into the wind, greatly slowing Task Force 16's progress toward Guadalcanal. By the time Kinkaid received Halsey's directive, his ships were some 150 miles farther south than Halsey realized.

"What does he think we have? Wings?" Lee asked Kinkaid over TBS. Even by steaming throughout the night at high speed, there was no way Lee's battleships would arrive in time to counter the next Japanese move into Ironbottom Sound. That job would fall to the men of MTBRON 3.

There had been five PT boats on patrol during the fateful night of November 12–13, but all had steered well clear of the furious sea battle going on in the Savo-Esperance channel. Lacking surface search radar or Identification Friend or Foe (IFF) transponders, it would have been nearly impossible for PT skippers to distinguish Japanese from American ships, and the darting PT boats would have likely become the targets of friendly as well as enemy fire. For these reasons, PT sailors had little desire to get mixed up in a slugging match between capital ships. At the same time, the regular navy's "Gun Club" of battleship and cruiser officers preferred for motor torpedo boats to stay out of the battlespace and not add to the chaos of a night engagement with the Japanese.

"During those big battles we did nothing but lay on the sidelines because we had no information on who was who," Charlie Tufts would later remark.

"None of our task force commanders wanted the PTs out when our big ships—our major combatants—were engaging the Japanese major combatants," Hugh Robinson explained. "So on any of the nights when the Japanese and our major combatants were there, we were not involved."

After sinking the derelict *Yudachi*, the damaged *Portland* made for Lunga Roads on the morning of November 13. At 2:47 p.m. *Portland* received instructions from Cactus Control to make for safe harbor at Tulagi. With the seagoing tug *Bobolink* nudging her in the proper direction, the "Sweet Pea" got underway at the creeping pace of 3 knots. Sunset came at 6:20 p.m., and shortly afterward five PT boats put to sea with Jack Searles commanding the patrol from the *PT-39*. Bob Searles's *PT-37* and Les Gamble's *PT-45* proceeded west to scout the passages around Savo Island, while Tom Kendall's *PT-48* maintained a security patrol outside the entrance to Tulagi Harbor.

At around 7:00 p.m. Cactus Control announced that a large Japanese vessel, possibly a battleship, was steaming down the Slot toward Sandfly Passage in the company of several destroyers. This prompted a request for PT boats to escort the wounded *Portland* to safety. Searles's *PT-39* and Stilly Taylor's *PT-46* patrolled in two oblong tracks along the path of the slow-moving cruiser, north to south and east to west, keeping a watchful eye for any prowling enemy surface ships or the glowing phosphorescent wake of a periscope. Just after midnight, with the black mountains of Florida Island looming ahead, a motor launch bearing the Tulagi harbor pilot emerged from the darkness, and the two PT boats sped away to join the others still on patrol.

"There's always some poor bastard who doesn't get the word," as the old navy expression goes, and on this particular night that poor bastard was Tom Kendall.

"An MTB had been stationed off the entrance to Tulagi Harbor and the boat captain had been instructed that any vessel that approached was to be considered an enemy ship," the navy's official account states. "As this order was never countermanded, when the *Portland* approached the harbor entrance the motor torpedo boat, without further ado, made an attack. Fortunately the boat captain overestimated the speed of the crippled *Portland* and all four torpedoes passed ahead. This unfortunate incident, however, served to emphasize the need for better communications."

Whether it was deserved or not, this near calamity would have a detrimental impact on the reputation of the Mosquito Fleet. Many officers in the surface navy already regarded the young PT skippers and their crews with a mixture of curiosity and suspicion. After all, any man who would *volunteer* to live in some far-flung malarial cove amid the rats and snakes and go up against Japanese destroyers in a wooden boat must not be in full possession of his faculties. In the wake of the *Portland* incident, more than a few line officers began viewing their counterparts in the PT boats as not only unconventional, but high-strung and reckless.

"The battlewagon navy didn't think very much of us," recalled Clark Faulkner, "a bunch of crazy young kids running around in speed boats."

Fortunately, the PT sailors would be given the opportunity to at least partially redeem themselves just an hour and a half later, when parachute flares began bursting in the night sky above Henderson Field, followed by the cracking thunder of 8-inch guns. Rear Admiral Shoji Nishimura's force of two heavy cruisers, *Maya* and *Suzuya*, the light cruiser *Tenryu*, and six destroyers had slipped into Ironbottom Sound, hoping to finish the job that Admiral Abe had not. Just after 1:30 a.m., General Vandegrift transmitted the message AM BEING HEAVILY SHELLED to COMSOPAC headquarters in Nouméa.

Pounding across the waves at full throttle, four PT boats raced in for the attack. "Our boat got into a good position and fired four torpedoes at one destroyer but saw no apparent hits before retiring in their searchlights and under 5-inch salvos," said Jack Searles. Headed back to Tulagi with empty torpedo tubes, Searles hailed the passing *PT-45*. Leaving *PT-39* in the hands of her exec, Ensign John Kearney, Searles boarded Gamble's *45* boat and returned to the fight.

Bob Searles's *PT-37* also launched a full spread of torpedoes toward a Japanese destroyer in Sandfly Passage before banking into a tight turn and heading for Tulagi behind a smoke screen. All four fish missed the target. Stilly Taylor, in the meantime, was stalking a Japanese cruiser that was busy shelling Henderson Field.

"After closing in to about a thousand yards, I decided that if we went in any further, we would get tangled up in the destroyer screen, which I knew would be surrounding him at about 500 to 700 yards," Taylor remembered. Guided by bursts of orange flame billowing from the cruiser's main guns, Taylor lined the front sight of his torpedo director against the darkened silhouette of the big ship and triggered all four fish. One stubbornly refused to launch, while the remaining three plunged into the water and began running hot and straight.

"I am positive that at least one of them found its mark," Taylor said later, having witnessed a blinding flash followed a half-second later by an explosion. The *PT-46* then turned for Tulagi and retired at high speed while making smoke. Shortly thereafter, the *45* boat closed with one of the screening destroyers and launched two torpedoes. Les Gamble would enter the phrase "observed two explosions, results undetermined" in the boat's deck log. Jack Searles, however, believed Gamble had scored "one definite hit."

Once again, Japanese sources do not support the claims of torpedo damage, but the PT sailors had nevertheless accomplished their vital mission. The whirlwind attack of the "devil boats" thoroughly rattled Nishimura, who ordered his ships to cease fire and beat a hasty retreat up the Slot. Later that morning, Vandegrift would report that the cruiser bombardment had for some reason stopped abruptly at 2:40 a.m.

"None of us at Nouméa could imagine why," Halsey wrote. "Later we learned that a squadron of PT boats, Lieutenant Hugh M. Robinson commanding, had dashed out from Tulagi and harried the enemy ships until they broke off and fled."

Nishimura's flight in the face of the PT counterattack and his failure to neutralize Henderson Field would cost the Japanese dearly. At 7:50 a.m., the bombardment group rendezvoused with Vice Admiral Gunichi Mikawa's task force in the Solomon Sea to the south of the New Georgia island group. Throughout the morning of November 14, the combined force was repeatedly bombed and strafed by the vengeful pilots of the Cactus Air Force as well as search-and-strike missions from the *Enterprise* air group. The heavy cruiser *Kinugasa* was sent to the bottom, along with 511 of her crew. Mikawa's flagship, the heavy cruiser *Chokai*, received extensive damage from armor-piercing bombs, as did the heavy cruiser *Maya* and light cruiser *Isuzu*.

At the same time, Raizo Tanaka's destroyers and transports were steaming for Guadalcanal in broad daylight, under the assumption that Nishimura's destruction of Henderson Field would afford them clear skies under which to land their embarked troops.

"I had a premonition that an ill fate was in store for us," Tanaka remembered. At 9:08 a.m., the Japanese reinforcement column was subjected to the first in a series of aggressive American air strikes that would continue until sundown. The "Buzzard Patrol," as the pilots who flew the many sorties that day would call themselves, was made up of navy and marine Dauntless and Avenger bombers from Henderson Field and the *Enterprise*, along with army B-17s from the New Hebrides.

"In detail the picture is now vague," Tanaka wrote, "but the general effect is indelible in my mind of bombs wobbling down from high-flying B-17s, of carrier bombers roaring toward targets as though to plunge full into the water, releasing bombs and pulling out barely in time; each miss sending up towering columns of mist and spray; every hit raising clouds of smoke and fire as transports burst into flame and take the sickening list that spells their doom. Attackers depart, smoke screens lift and reveal the tragic scene of men jumping overboard from burning, sinking ships."

Six of the transports were set afire and would eventually sink, while a seventh was heavily damaged and forced to return to the Shortlands in the company of two destroyers. Before departing the scene these three ships plucked over 1,500 survivors from the sea, including the commanding general of the 38th Infantry Division. Nearly 450 Japanese soldiers and sailors perished or were counted as missing. Just before sunset, as his destroyers were busy collecting another 3,200 men from the water, Tanaka learned that a newly formed task force under Vice Admiral Nobutake Kondo, consisting of the battleship *Kirishima*, two heavy cruisers, two light cruisers and nine destroyers, was steaming down Indispensable Strait on its way to bombard Henderson Field.

"Thus it was with a feeling of relief that I gave the order to proceed with the operation," Tanaka wrote. After nightfall his four remaining transports and their escorting destroyers, now packed to the gunwales with waterlogged survivors, assumed their normal cruising disposition and pressed on for Guadalcanal.

*** 

At 9:00 p.m. on November 14, Task Force 64 was steaming north-by-northeast at 20 knots, skirting the outer islands of the Russell group about 24 miles to the west of Guadalcanal. It was fairly clear for a November night in the Solomons; so clear, in fact, that young bluejackets found themselves marveling at the sight of thousands of stars reflecting upon the surface of a flat, calm sea. In the van were the destroyers *Walke*, *Benham*, *Preston*, and *Gwin*, followed by the battleships *Washington* and *South Dakota*. The task force continued north until 10:09 p.m., when it changed course to 090 degrees due east to place Savo Island off the starboard beam.

For the past several hours the ships had been at General Quarters, with all hands at their battle stations, maintaining the highest levels of material readiness. Lookouts reported the dull glow of Tanaka's burning transports over the horizon to the northwest, and the light of a camp-fire about halfway up a hillside on Savo, likely belonging to a group of shipwrecked Japanese from the previous night's battle. Several miles ahead and slightly to starboard, a red signal rocket rose into the night sky, flickered briefly, then disappeared. A light surface wind caused the fragrant scent of gardenia flowers on nearby Florida Island to waft across the weather decks, intermingled with the rich smell of bunker oil still floating on the water. For some, the smell of gardenias would linger in their subconscious for the rest of their lives, instantly transporting them back in time to this night and this place.

Stationed on the navigation bridge of the *Washington* was the task force commander, Rear Admiral Willis Augustus Lee Jr. The flagship's captain, Glenn Davis, and two junior officers were surveying the dark expanse of Ironbottom Sound through binoculars. An enlisted sailor stood ready at arm's length, wearing a set of headphones and a microphone in a cumbersome harness plugged into the battleship's command circuit. Lee much preferred to be outside in the open air of the bridge wing when leading his forces into battle, rather than remaining below in the cramped confines of the flag plot.

Born in Kentucky in 1888, Lee was a distant relative of the Confederate general Robert E. Lee and the son of a county judge. From an early age he had shown a flair for science and mathematics and a penchant for mischief. At the age of eleven, the precocious and inquisitive child was nearly blinded by the explosion of a homemade bomb fashioned from a tin can and the gunpowder of several shotgun shells. A local physician managed to save the boy's eyesight, but Lee was required to wear thick glasses for the rest of his life and tended to squint narrowly in all but the dimmest of light. With the help of his father's political connections, Lee gained an appointment to the US Naval Academy, where despite his poor eyesight he proved a crack shot and became a top performer on the academy's rifle team.

Inspired by his Chinese-sounding surname and deep perpetual squint, Lee's classmates assigned him the nickname of "Ching." Today such a breach of decorum would see the offending midshipmen standing tall before the commandant, but this was in 1904. Lee accepted the new moniker with good humor and for many years afterward even signed unofficial correspondence with the Chinese character for the name "Li." In 1907, while still at the Naval Academy, Lee became the first competitive marksman in history to win national championships in both pistol and rifle shooting, and after graduation would return to Annapolis to serve as captain of the rifle team.

In 1914, Lee commanded a party of armed sailors from the battleship *New Hampshire* during the landings at Vera Cruz. He went ashore toting a Springfield rifle in addition to his officer's sidearm, and used it to kill three snipers who were firing on American troops. As a member of the Olympic rifle team, Lee represented the United States during the 1920 Summer Games in Antwerp and won seven medals—five gold, one silver, and one bronze—a record that would stand for the next sixty years.

Lee was no spit-and-polish naval officer. In fact, he was rather apathetic about his appearance and somewhat unkempt. Subordinates would note that his uniform was often disheveled, as if he had slept in it, and that he rarely bothered to clean his Coke-bottle eyeglasses. He was savant-like when it came to the practice of higher mathematics, and astounded others by being able to calculate complex equations of calculus and physics in his head. The science of naval gunnery was Lee's professional forte. Between tours of sea duty, Lee served with the Bureau of Ordnance and in the Fleet Training Division, participating in the research, development, instruction, and quality control of naval artillery, munitions, and fire control systems.

Unlike some of his contemporaries in the Gun Club, Lee refused to remain stuck in the dreadnought era and enthusiastically embraced new technologies that promised to enhance the fleet's warfighting capability. It was said that "Ching" Lee knew more about surface search and fire control radar systems than the men who operated them. On the night of November 14–15, 1942, Lee would demonstrate that knowledge to deadly effect.

Having been alerted by sighting reports from reconnaissance aircraft and the submarine *Flying Fish*, Lee was aware that both Kondo's bombardment force and Tanaka's reinforcement column were rapidly closing on Guadalcanal. At 10:23 p.m., Lee had a coded message transmitted to Vandegrift's headquarters, asking for any new intelligence on the disposition of the Japanese fleet to be relayed over the local VHF voice tactical circuit. As his task force entered Ironbottom Sound, there was a burst of chatter over that very same voice frequency as patrolling PT boats began sighting Lee's battleships.

"There go two big ones," someone said, "but I don't know whose they are."

Earlier in the day, the PT skippers had been briefed about the possible arrival of Lee's force. "We may have a battleship task force, Admiral Lee's outfit, coming up here to meet the Japs, but we're not sure," they were told. "Even if they do come, we don't think they'll get here in time. We want you fellows to sift through the destroyers and cruisers and get the transports."

COMSOPAC had neglected to issue a radio call sign to Lee after designating him Commander Task Force 64, so the admiral was compelled to improvise in his communications. The conversation that followed is now legendary, and like all good sea stories the accounts vary slightly depending on who is doing the telling. According to Hugh Robinson, who was patrolling Ironbottom Sound with four PT boats and listening to local radio traffic at the time, the exchange went something like this:

"Cactus Control, Cactus Control, this is Ching Lee, over."

"Ship or station hailing Cactus, we have no information as to your identity," replied the coldly suspicious voice of Base Radio Guadalcanal.

"Cactus Control, tell your big boss that Chinese Ching Lee is here and wants the latest information. There are PT boats after us. Call off your boys, over."

After an elongated pause, Cactus Control answered, "Roger, standby." The same officer returned to the airwaves a few minutes later, after consulting General Vandegrift's headquarters as to the identity of the curious stranger broadcasting in plain language over the radio net. "Ching Lee, this is Cactus Control. The big boss has no new information, over."

"Roger, Cactus. Ching Lee out." Hoping to avoid another *Portland* incident, Lee then hailed the commander of MTBRON 3 with the signal words for "PT" in the current version of the US military's phonetic alphabet.

"Peter Tare, Peter Tare, this is Ching Lee, over."

Robinson then answered, "Ching Lee, this is Peter Tare. I recognize you. We are not after you, over."

"Peter Tare, this is Chinese Ching Lee. Stand clear, we are coming through, over."

"Roger, wilco," Robinson responded.

At around 11:00 p.m., Robinson's PTs spotted three strange ships steaming through the Sandfly Passage to the northwest of Savo Island, and a sighting report was transmitted to the *Washington*. In obeyance with Admiral Lee's order to "stand clear," two of the PT boats lingered along the coast of Florida Island to watch, their crews sipping hot coffee and munching tuna fish sandwiches while waiting for the action to begin. The other boat crews returned to Tulagi. Back at the Sesapi docks, they secured their craft, grabbed binoculars, and climbed to the top of a hill overlooking Ironbottom Sound, where they would have a grandstand seat to the first of only two battleship-versus-battleship duels of the Pacific War.

"It was just like sitting at Ebbets Field," one man said. "Only different."

\*\*\*

Vice Admiral Nobutake Kondo was quite aware of Ching Lee's presence. One of his cruiser float planes spotted Task Force 64 in the rapidly fading twilight of November 14 and flashed an urgent warning to Kondo's flagship *Atago*. The Japanese pilot, however, had mistaken both *Washington* and *South Dakota* for cruisers, leading Kondo to believe that he would be facing an American task force with considerably less firepower than it actually had.

As his bombardment unit approached Savo from the east, Kondo detached the light cruiser *Sendai* and three destroyers to make a clockwise sweep around the island, while his remaining ships headed for the southern passage between Savo and Guadalcanal. A single destroyer, *Ayanami*, sheared away from the sweeping group and headed south, down Savo's western shore. At 10:31 p.m., the *Sendai* group spotted Lee's force, steaming on a southeasterly course on its own clockwise circumnavigation of Savo Island.

At 10:52 p.m., Lee ordered a change of course to 270 degrees due west, putting Task Force 64 and Kondo's main body on a collision course.

Within seconds of receiving Robinson's sighting report, the ships of the *Sendai* group appeared on the SG radar scope of the *Washington*. Almost simultaneously, they were picked up by the fire control radar of the battleship's main battery. At 11:16 p.m. Lee gave the order "fire when ready," and all nine of *Washington's* 16-inch guns unleashed a thunderous salvo.

Less than a minute later the big guns of *South Dakota* opened fire from 18,500 yards, her armor-piercing shells glowing bright red as they arched lazily through the night sky. The huge shells slammed into the sea within yards of the *Sendai* and her two accompanying destroyers, sending them scampering away to the north under a smoke screen. In the meantime, the *Ayanami* had maneuvered into a position to the south of Savo and began trading 5-inch shell fire with the leading American destroyer *Walke*.

By that time the destroyers of Task Force 64 had entered the Savo-Esperance channel from the east, two miles ahead of the battleships. All four were about to encounter serious trouble, for the main body of Kondo's bombardment force, led by the light cruiser *Nagara*, was rounding the southwest corner of Savo Island. The destroyer *Preston* spotted them first and opened fire with her 5-inch guns, provoking an immediate and overwhelming response.

Pounded by enemy shellfire, *Preston* rolled over and sank at 11:37 p.m., leaving just 42 survivors from a crew of 158 officers and men. The *Walke* was smashed by several direct hits before taking a torpedo just forward of the bridge, touching off an explosion in her forward magazine that killed 80 men and sent the *Sims*-class destroyer to the bottom. Wracked by shellfire, *Gwin* turned west-by-southwest and retired along the coast of Guadalcanal, as did *Benham* after receiving a torpedo hit in the starboard bow.

That left *Washington* and *South Dakota* to face Kondo's main force of ten warships on their own. After *Washington* trained her guns upon the pesky *Ayanami* and promptly ended that destroyer's service life, Lee ordered both battleships to change course to 282 degrees west, bringing their powerful broadsides to bear upon the Japanese column. The *South Dakota*, however, chose this most critical juncture to suffer a massive electrical failure that killed power to her radio, radar, and fire control systems.

Now "deaf, dumb, and blind," *South Dakota* was quickly located by Japanese searchlights, and the concentrated fire of Kondo's main body was soon directed upon her. Over the next four minutes, she would receive several hits to her topside but managed to evade a flurry of torpedoes launched by the Japanese destroyer screen, and continued to return fire with her gun batteries under local control.

The furious action would effectively mask the *Washington*, cruising several hundred yards off the embattled *South Dakota's* port bow, from the view of Japanese lookouts. Just after midnight, with her fire control radar locked onto the battleship *Kirishima*, the unseen *Washington* let fly with the first of several devastatingly accurate salvos from her 16-inch and 5-inch guns.

"The performance of the individual battleships and the conduct of the battleship personnel were uniformly excellent," Lee would write in his after-action report. "In the *Washington* particularly, control and battery functioned as smoothly as though she were engaged in a well-rehearsed gunnery practice."

Watching awestruck from the crest of a hill on Guadalcanal with a group of his fellow marines was Robert Leckie, who would later record his impressions of the great sea battle in his wartime memoirs.

"I think of Judgement Day, I think of Götterdämmerung," Leckie wrote, "I think of the stars exploding, of the planets going off like fireworks; I think of a volcano; I think of a roaring and an energy unbelievable; I think, of holocaust; and again I think of night reeling from a thousand scarlet slashes and I see the red eye of hell winking in her wounds—I think of all these, and I cannot tell you what I have seen, the terrible spectacle I witnessed from that hillside."

Radioman First Class Eldon Alvis of the *PT-37* was perhaps not as eloquent as Bob Leckie in his running commentary of the naval battle, but no less expressive or passionate.

"Jesus Christ, what a sight!" Alvis kept saying. "I never saw anything like it!"

The horror quickly dissipated the picnic-like mood among the PT sailors. "In less than five minutes after the first shot was fired," Chief

Tufts would recall, "I personally saw nine ships afire, burning right in my vicinity."

"What a terrible loss of men and equipment we have witnessed in an hour," another man told his shipmates.

"No one could think of anything really intelligent to say until later, when it was all over," Leonard Nikoloric recalled. "The immensity of the thing had stunned us, the awful noise and confusion, the flames and smoke and the sight of big ships being smashed as though by some power beyond human control."

Slammed by at least twenty of the *Washington*'s 2,700-pound armor-piercing projectiles and a like number of 5-inch shells, the *Kirishima* was soon blazing fiercely from stem to stern and shuddering from internal secondary explosions. Rapidly taking on water and listing to starboard with her steering gear destroyed, the Japanese battleship unwittingly sheared away from the column and began to founder. *South Dakota* was then able to partially restore her electrical power and signal the flagship that she was beginning a withdrawal west-by-southwest, following the path of the staggering destroyers *Gwin* and *Benham*. To draw the enemy away from the damaged *South Dakota* and his shattered destroyer screen—and still hoping to find Tanaka's inbound transports—Admiral Lee ordered the *Washington* to check fire and turn onto a northerly course to make an end run around the Japanese column.

With great caution, Kondo's flagship *Atago* and heavy cruiser *Takao* shadowed the formidable *Washington* as she made her northward turn and fired several torpedoes from long range, all of which missed. In the meantime, *Nagara* closed with the burning *Kirishima* to pass over a tow line, but by then the battleship's list had increased to a steep 18 degrees and the effort was given up as hopeless. With the most powerful ship of his command now a total loss, Kondo decided to cancel the bombardment of Henderson Field and ordered a general withdrawal. At 3:25 a.m. the *Kirishima* would capsize and sink, taking 212 members of her crew with her to the bottom of New Georgia Sound.

***

Despite the fact that Henderson Field had been left untouched by his bombardment force, Kondo nevertheless directed Tanaka to proceed to Guadalcanal with his remaining destroyers and transports. For both Japanese admirals, at least a partial completion of the reinforcement mission was of critical importance, if for no other reason than to allow themselves and the Imperial Navy to save face. Knowing full well that his ships would become the targets of relentless air attacks as they boated and landed troops and supplies off Tassafaronga in broad daylight, Tanaka proposed a rather unorthodox and desperate plan of action to his superiors. Mikawa immediately nixed the idea but was quickly overruled by the more senior Kondo, who flashed the go-ahead to Tanaka's flagship:

```
Run aground and unload troops.
```

"As we approached Tassafaronga by the early light of dawn I gave the fateful order which sent the four transports hard aground almost simultaneously," Tanaka would later write. "Assembling my destroyers, I ordered immediate withdrawal northward, and we passed through the waters to the east of Savo Island."

Lodged firmly on the Tassafaronga reef, the four *marus* were left squatting in the shallow water like sitting ducks. Forward observers quickly detected their presence and called down fire from the US Army's 155-millimeter howitzers and Marine Corps 5-inch coastal defense guns. Soon Dauntless and Avenger strike aircraft from Henderson Field and the *Enterprise* were stacked overhead and selecting their targets. The destroyer *Meade* appeared offshore and for the better part of an hour pounded the transports with 5-inch gunfire, then strafed the hapless soldiers on the beach with her 40-millimeters. The four ships sat burning for the next several days, along with most of the supplies, ammunition, and provisions that had been piled at the water's edge. Only 2,000 Japanese troops made it ashore alive, and most of them had lost their weapons and equipment.

At the end of the three-day Naval Battle of Guadalcanal, 1,732 Americans and 1,895 Japanese were dead. The Japanese lost two battleships, one heavy cruiser, three destroyers, ten transports, and forty-one aircraft. American losses were two light cruisers, seven destroyers, and twenty-six aircraft. These grisly box scores tell only part of the greater story.

The immense industrial base of the United States, which in late 1942 was only beginning to hit its wartime stride, was capable of replacing such losses, while the Japanese war machine was not. In 1943, for example, Japanese shipyards would lay down the keels of 12 new destroyers, while the Americans would build and launch 128. That same year America's aircraft manufacturers produced five warplanes for every one built in Japan.

Both sides would declare victory in the battle, though it is difficult to see how the Japanese could claim success with the American airfield on Guadalcanal still bustling and only a tiny fraction of their 38th Division making it ashore. The Imperial Japanese Navy would adhere to their usual practice of exaggerating American losses while refusing to acknowledge the stark reality of their own failures, for the benefit of their public image as well as their own pride. Matome Ugaki, for one, would indulge in this very sort of self-deception in the pages of his diary, after watching the remnants of Kondo's bombardment force stand into Truk Lagoon on November 18: "It was lonely indeed when we couldn't see *Hiei* and *Kirishima* among them. Morale was lifted as it became almost certain, as a result of an investigation conducted by the advance force, that two or three enemy battleships had been sunk."

A few Japanese officers, like Raizo Tanaka, were more willing to accept the hard truth: "It was certainly regrettable that the Supreme Command did not profit or learn from repeated attempts to reinforce the island. In vain they expended valuable and scarce transports and the strength of at least one full division. I believe that Japan's operational and planning errors at Guadalcanal will stand forever as classic examples of how not to conduct a campaign."

The Naval Battle of Guadalcanal "was decisive, not only in the struggle for that island, but in the Pacific War," Samuel Eliot Morison would write. "The Imperial Army did not give up Guadalcanal for another ten weeks, but the navy performed its ferryboat duties with increasing reluctance and made no further bid to rule the adjacent waves."

For the US Marines on Guadalcanal, the looming fear of their tenuous beachhead becoming "another Bataan" was finally beginning to fade.

"All Guadalcanal was alive with hope and vibrant with the scent of victory," Bob Leckie described. "We were as doomed men from whose ankles the iron bands had been struck. A great weight was lifted from our shoulders."

"We believe the enemy has suffered a crushing defeat," Alexander Vandegrift wrote in a message to Bill Halsey. "We thank Lee for his sturdy effort of last night. We thank Kinkaid for his intervention yesterday. Our own aircraft have been grand in their relentless pounding of the foe. Those efforts we appreciate but our greatest homage goes to Scott, Callaghan and their men who with magnificent courage drove back the first hostile stroke and made success possible. To them the men of Cactus lift their battered helmets in deepest admiration."

CHAPTER EIGHT

# Starvation Island

BEGINNING WITH THE HEROIC DASH TO MINDANAO THAT SAVED THE life of General MacArthur and secured a Medal of Honor for John Bulkeley, PT boats and the gallant young men who sailed them began receiving a great deal of attention within the fleet and on the home front. In mid-October 1942, William Lindsay White's *They Were Expendable* climbed to the top of the *New York Times* Best Seller List and was excerpted in both *Life* magazine and *Reader's Digest*. Dramatic feature articles describing the daring exploits of PT crews at Guadalcanal, many of them highly sensationalized, were already appearing in popular magazines and newspapers. By November, navy detailers and fleet personnel offices were receiving scores of applications for transfer to "Specht Tech," the Motor Torpedo Boat Training Center in Melville, now under the command of William Specht.

When his Atlantic Fleet destroyer *Ellyson* paid a call on Boston, Lieutenant (jg) Ed Hoagland asked for and received two days of shore leave, which allowed him to visit the local BuPers office and request a transfer to PTs.

"Are you out of your mind?" the detail officer asked. "Leave the destroyer navy, get your ass shot off in the boats, and live like a pirate?"

"I want the boats," Hoagland replied.

\*\*\*

After bombarding the four Japanese transports stranded off Tassafaronga on the morning of November 15, 1942, the destroyer *Meade* withdrew to the waters south of Savo Island. There she began collecting the scattered survivors from the sunken *Walke* and *Preston*, many of whom were clinging to floating wreckage or drifting solitarily among the waves with the aid of their kapok life jackets. There to assist *Meade* was Lenny Nikoloric and the crew of *PT-37*, pulling aboard every forlorn, oil-drenched sailor they could reach. In all, 266 men were rescued and taken by the *Meade* to Government Wharf, then transferred to a navy field hospital on Tulagi for medical treatment.

The latter half of November was relatively quiet in the bitterly contested waters surrounding Guadalcanal, as the naval forces of both Japan and the United States sought to recover and regroup after the epic three-day battle that claimed over two dozen ships and thousands of lives. Ringbolt-based PT boats patrolled Ironbottom Sound on the nights of November 15–19, but there had been no sign of the Tokyo Express. On November 22, the PTs escorted *Portland* from Tulagi Harbor into the open Solomon Sea, on the first leg of her journey to Sydney, Australia, for permanent repairs.

The lull in the fighting was certainly welcome, brief as it was. A solid month of continuous night combat operations had left the men of MTBRON 3 on the brink of total exhaustion and their boats in a sorry state of repair. The original complement of 120 officers and men was proving inadequate for performing nightly patrols and the required upkeep of the boats. A general malaise settled over the squadron as a lack of sufficient rest and the scourge of tropical disease continued to take its toll. Every day more and more men were being added to the binnacle list, with the number being especially high among the motor machinists, who were suffering from various degrees of carbon monoxide and lead poisoning in addition to the usual fatigue and jungle maladies.

Joseph Nemec, an unobtrusive twenty-four-year-old moto-mac from Buffalo, New York, who went by the nickname of "Silent Joe," was sent to the field hospital on Tulagi after being stricken by a severe case of peritonitis. He died a month later.

"It's exciting here, and naturally I'm scared," Joe had written in an earlier letter to his mother. "But I guess the Japs are scared too."

One man lost his mind. He had been aboard the *California* when the battleship was bombed and torpedoed at Pearl Harbor, and after the fleet tug *Seminole* was shot out from under him in October, he volunteered to serve as a gunner aboard a PT boat. When his new shipmates decided that a little hazing was in order and tossed his bunk over one of Tulagi's cliffs, the man snapped. Gathering several weapons from his boat's small arms cache, including a Tommy gun, he withdrew to his tent and threatened to shoot anyone who came near him. Chief Tufts was somehow able to calm the distressed young sailor, who was evacuated to a rear area hospital for psychiatric treatment.

To replace the sick men and adequately staff the boat crews, a number of sailors were recruited from the refugee tent camp at Lunga Point, where survivors from the *Atlanta* and the carrier *Wasp* were being temporarily housed. Most had never seen a PT boat at close range, but there was little time for their indoctrination and training. If a man was capable of firing a weapon, operating a radio, repairing an electrical short, or adjusting a carburetor, the paperwork was done to transfer him into the squadron and he was immediately put to work. He was trusted to familiarize himself with the boats, and with the subtleties of PT duty.

It was soon discovered that the cause of the mysterious illness affecting the moto-macs was the noxious fumes leaking from worn-out exhaust mufflers. A stopgap fix had to be applied, as there were no spare parts available to make the proper repairs. Crates of engineering and electrical parts were arriving in the ports of Espiritu Santo and Nouméa from the United States, but they were not given priority for shipment to Tulagi, an issue that would not be addressed until an adequate logistics organization for the PT squadrons was finally put into place. A complement of twenty-six officers and men had, in fact, been sent to Nouméa to establish a rear echelon administration, logistics, and repair base for motor torpedo boats, but were assigned to other duties by the port director.

On any given evening, only three or four of the eight PT boats based at Tulagi were fit for service. Work on the *PT-61*'s shattered bow was completed on November 21, two days after *PT-39* ran aground while on patrol, sustaining damage that would take at least three weeks to repair.

Bent propeller shafts and torn hulls were commonplace, often resulting from collisions with jagged coral heads in the shallow waters surrounding Guadalcanal and Tulagi. Larger combat vessels were given priority for service in the navy's floating dry docks, so salvage divers were often utilized to perform rudimentary underwater repairs to the PTs.

According to the Packard Company's specifications, motors were supposed to be replaced and overhauled after 600 hours of running time, a standard that was seldom if ever achieved in the combat theater. Neither the makeshift engineering shop at Sesapi nor the repair facilities aboard the *Jamestown* was capable of performing complete engine overhauls, even if the proper spare parts could somehow be obtained. In October, a supply of forty-two spare Packard motors had been placed aboard the *George H. Himes* for shipment to Tulagi, but the Liberty ship was torpedoed by a Japanese plane off the coast of Guadalcanal. Salt water had flooded her cargo hold, completely immersing the precious spare engines.

Setbacks and shortages such as these prevented crews from keeping up with daily wear and tear, inevitably resulting in a progressive degradation of their boats' performance. One squadron wag summed up the exasperation of the PT crews, as bored and frustrated sailors are wont to do, by composing a sardonic ditty on the subject:

*Oh, some PTs do seventy-five,*
*And some do sixty-nine;*
*When we get ours to run at all*
*We think we're doing fine.*

The arrival of MTBRON 2 at Tulagi during the third week of November, therefore, helped alleviate some problems while serving to compound others. In early September the squadron received orders to move from Panama to a new base in the Galapagos Islands, but the move was canceled before the appointed date of departure. By that time the first elements of MTBRON 5, equipped with a dozen new 80-foot Elco PT boats, began arriving in Balboa. Six of the 80-footers were transferred to MTBRON 2 in order to bring the squadron up to full strength, and shortly thereafter orders were received for their deployment to the South

Pacific. The first two divisions of four PTs from 'RON 2, made up of the 77-foot boats *36*, *40*, *43*, *44*, *47*, and *59*, along with the 80-footers *109* and *110*, stood into Tulagi Harbor between November 20 and 25.

The new skipper of MTBRON 2 was Lieutenant Rollin E. Westholm, a husky thirty-one-year-old from Moose Lake, Minnesota, and a graduate of the Annapolis Class of 1934. Westholm served aboard the battleship *Texas* and the destroyers *Barry* and *McCall* before being recruited for PT duty by John Bulkeley in 1940. He then spent six months in England as an Assistant Naval Attaché and Special Naval Observer, learning everything he could about doctrine and tactics from the veteran MTB operators of the Royal Navy. Upon taking command of 'RON 2, Westholm selected as his flagship what would become the most famous PT boat of them all, the *PT-109*. Once they arrived in-theater, the squadron wasted little time in getting to work. In fact, the *36*, *40*, and *47* boats patrolled the Savo-Esperance channel on the night of November 20–21, just hours after their arrival in the combat zone.

\*\*\*

"Almost daily came radio messages reporting the critical situation on the island and requesting immediate supplies," Raizo Tanaka wrote, describing the desperate plight of Japanese soldiers on Guadalcanal. "It was indicated that by the end of November the entire food supply would be gone, and by the latter part of the month we learned that all staple supplies had been consumed. The men were now down to eating wild plants and animals. Everyone was on the verge of starvation, sick lists increased, and even the healthy were exhausted. Realizing these circumstances, every effort was directed to relieve the situation."

By mid-November, Lieutenant General Harukichi Hyakutake could list just 4,200 combat-effective troops from among the 30,000 soldiers of his 17th Army on Guadalcanal. One infantry regiment in particular could muster just 60 men still capable of fighting. On November 22, Lieutenant General Hitoshi Imamura arrived in Rabaul to take command of the newly formed 8th Area Army, which was to oversee the operations of the 17th Army on Guadalcanal and the 18th Army in New Guinea. Imamura contacted Hyakutake by radio, asking for an honest appraisal of the supply problem. That was exactly what he got, for Hyakutake held nothing back.

"An average of 100 men starve to death daily," Hyakutake told his new commander. "This average will only increase. By the time we get reinforcements, doubtful how many troops here will be alive."

The Imperial Japanese Navy, the service responsible for keeping the Guadalcanal garrison supplied, was losing control of the adjacent sea. Japanese naval forces in the South Pacific were suffering unsustainable losses and becoming more hesitant to engage, while the Americans were growing stronger and more willing to assert themselves. Concerns were being raised by many senior Japanese naval officers over the number of destroyers being lost in combat. A dozen had been sunk since the beginning of the Guadalcanal campaign, a rate of attrition that would eventually lead to an insufficient number of destroyers being available to screen carriers and battleships, and prevent the Combined Fleet from meeting the Americans in a much sought-after decisive battle.

Night-flying patrol bombers and motor torpedo boats continued to harrass every run of the Tokyo Express, and while they had yet to sink any Japanese destroyers, they were bound to get lucky sooner or later. New methods had to be devised to keep food, medicine, and ammunition flowing to the Japanese troops on Guadalcanal, while at the same time limiting the exposure of destroyers to attack while off-loading supplies close to shore.

On November 22, the submarines *I-17* and *I-19* departed the Shortlands for Kamimbo Bay, a shallow inlet just west of Cape Esperance where a primitive forward base for Japanese two-man midget submarines had been established. Each submarine was carrying 20 tons of food and other badly needed supplies. The I-boats arrived off Guadalcanal on the afternoon of November 24, where they remained submerged until darkness. After sunset they came to the surface and inched slowly into the bay to begin unloading their cargo. The operation was halted suddenly when an American PT boat—most likely the *PT-36* commanded by Lieutenant (jg) Mark Wertz—was spotted cruising down the coastline on patrol. Both subs quickly submerged and left the area without being detected. The *I-17* had been able to off-load only about half of her supplies, while the *I-19* still carried all 20 tons.

Returning the following night, the submarines were able to finish unloading their cargo and embark several sick and wounded army personnel before returning to the Shortlands. The operation was deemed a success, and for the remainder of the Pacific War the Japanese would continue employing submarines to supply their bypassed outposts as the Allied "island hopping" campaign advanced toward Tokyo. These "mouse runs," as the resentful Japanese sub commanders would call them, would end up diverting the I-boat force from its primary mission of hunting enemy surface ships, thus decreasing the overall lethality of the Combined Fleet in battle, while delivering only a fraction of what was needed to sustain the isolated garrisons.

An alternate method of delivering food and supplies was developed using steel oil drums dropped by destroyers. After being scoured, the drums were partially filled with food and medical supplies, then sealed with enough empty air space remaining to ensure buoyancy. Between 200 and 240 drums were then loaded onto the weather decks of a destroyer and lashed together with rope. Approaching the northwestern coast of Guadalcanal at night, the destroyer crews would shove their load of drums overboard and rapidly depart. Japanese sailors in a power boat would retrieve the running end of the rope, which was attached to a buoy, and deliver it to soldiers on the beach who would then haul the drums ashore. The fact that the Japanese Navy would resort to such desperate measures speaks to the intense pressure being applied by Imperial General Headquarters to save Hyakutake's troops from starvation, and to the ability of American PT boats to effectively harass enemy supply lines.

The Tokyo Express would make their first attempt to deliver supplies using this new method on November 30, which would result in yet another brutal night clash with the US Navy. A force of eight destroyers led by Rear Admiral Tanaka aboard the *Naganami* departed the Shortlands for Tassafaronga after sundown on November 29. Tanaka meandered on an westerly course for several hours in an effort to mislead Allied coastwatchers and search planes, but a radio message informing

Hyakutake of the supply mission was snatched from the airwaves and deciphered by US naval intelligence.

Admiral Halsey then directed Task Force 67, commanded by Rear Admiral Carleton Wright and made up of the cruisers *Minneapolis*, *Northhampton*, *New Orleans*, *Pensacola*, *Honolulu*, and six destroyers, to lay a trap for the Tokyo Express. At 11:20 p.m. on November 30, Wright's task force surprised the Japanese destroyermen just as they began unloading their supply drums off Tassafaronga Point. The closest ship to the American column, *Takanami*, was decimated by a torrent of heavy shells and sunk, but the landmass of Guadalcanal served as a cluttered backdrop for the remaining Japanese vessels and confused American fire control radar. Tanaka's destroyers would turn about and flee under a smoke screen, but not before sending a deadly school of forty-four Long Lance torpedoes streaming toward the American cruisers.

Struck by two torpedoes in her port side, the flagship *Minneapolis* suffered severe structural damage to her bow and lost all propulsion and steering. Another Long Lance slammed into the *New Orleans* and exploded her forward magazine, blowing off the entire bow section forward of the number two turret. The *Pensacola* also took a hit amidships, and while the *Honolulu* escaped serious damage, the last ship in the column, *Northhampton*, was torpedoed twice and would sink three hours later.

Tassafaronga would be Raizo Tanaka's finest hour as a fighting admiral. For the loss of the *Takanami* and 196 men, he had dealt a severe beating to an American naval force several times more powerful than his own. One American heavy cruiser had been sunk and three severely damaged, along with 417 officers and men killed or missing. The victory did little to help the starving Japanese soldiers on Guadalcanal, however, for only a handful of supply drums were jettisoned before the battle was joined.

Even before the mangled and listing cruisers of Task Force 67 were able to stagger into Tulagi Harbor, five PT boats stood out to comb the waters of Ironbottom Sound for survivors from the *Northhampton*. Several hours later they came cruising back slowly with their hulls low in the water, their main decks completely covered with drenched and exhausted sailors lying shoulder-to-shoulder. The *PT-109* managed to rescue ninety-four men from the water while *PT-37* collected another eighty-six, one of whom died of his wounds before reaching Tulagi.

"After half an hour," Lenny Nikoloric recalled, "there wasn't room on board to move. They were lying in rows on the deck and standing and sitting in a solid jam below. You had to watch your step, or down you'd go in a heap on top of some poor devil who would not thank you for it. And there were still hundreds of men in the water, patiently waiting for Robbie, Brent or Tom to pick them up."

During the search, Nikoloric and his crew came upon one frantic *Northhampton* survivor struggling to tread water while at the same time trying to fight off a large gray shark that kept nudging him in the chest. One of the PT crewmen drove the shark away with a few bursts from a Thompson submachine gun, and the man was pulled to safety. He had been in the water for over five hours.

"Boy, am I glad to see you guys and get rid of that bastard!" the sailor exclaimed.

\*\*\*

Tanaka would try again on December 3. His Tokyo Express run of eight destroyers was spotted by a coastwatcher in the early afternoon and attacked by Henderson-based planes 160 miles northwest of Guadalcanal, resulting in only minor damage to the *Makinami*. The destroyers continued on to Tassafaronga Point, evaded the patrolling PT boats, and dropped 1,500 tethered supply drums before making a clean getaway.

Only 310 of the drums would make it onto the beaches of "Starvation Island," as Japanese soldiers had begun to call Guadalcanal. An insufficient number of men had been assigned to the hauling teams, and most of them were already weak from hunger and sickness. Many clusters of floating barrels simply drifted away with the current before they could be recovered, or the ropes that connected them parted under tension. All were sunk by strafing Wildcats after they were discovered bobbing in the swells of Ironbottom Sound the following morning.

"The loss of four-fifths of this precious material was intolerable when it had been transported at such great risk and cost, and when it was so badly needed by the starving troops on the island," wrote the highly frustrated Tanaka.

Three days later, on December 6, Admiral Halsey ordered Ching Lee's Task Force 64, now consisting of the battleships *Indiana* and *Washington*, to rendezvous with the *Enterprise* task force and the battleship *North Carolina* in the Coral Sea to the south of Rennell Island. Halsey, who on Thanksgiving Day received the fourth star of a full admiral, wanted the aircraft carrier and fast battleships to be in a position to block the next attempt by the Japanese fleet to reinforce Guadalcanal. At dusk on December 7, one year to the day after the attack on Pearl Harbor, an Allied search plane spotted a group of eleven Japanese destroyers speeding down the Slot on a course for Tassafaronga.

This latest effort to keep the 17th Army alive was being led by Captain Torajiro Sato aboard the *Oyashio*. Eight of Sato's destroyers were heavily laden with supply drums, which under Tanaka's orders were lashed together in clusters of no more than one hundred, a measure intended to ease the burden on the undernourished and depleted men who would have to haul them through the surf. The remaining three ships were stripped for action and carrying their full load of torpedoes, in the event another force of American cruisers should suddenly appear out of the darkness. Halsey might have relished the thought of obtaining retribution for the trouncing received on November 30, but his heavy forces were still steaming westward from Nouméa and Espiritu Santo and were too distant to intervene. Once again, it would be up to the pilots of the Cactus Air Force and the mosquito boats of Ringbolt to stop the Tokyo Express.

A squadron of Marine Corps SBDs located Sato's destroyers in the Slot just before dusk, landing a half-ton bomb close aboard the *Nowaki*, which killed seventeen sailors, dished several hull plates, and flooded her fire rooms. Another near miss damaged the *Arashi*, the very same destroyer that had unwittingly led American dive bombers to Nagumo's carriers at Midway. Sato ordered *Naganami* to take the powerless and drifting *Nowaki* under tow and return to the Shortlands, followed by *Arashi* with a fourth destroyer acting as escort. His task force now cut down to just seven ships, Sato pressed on for Guadalcanal.

As darkness fell, eight PT boats sortied from their base on Tulagi under the tactical command of Rollin Westholm aboard *PT-109*. Message traffic between the Japanese destroyer base in the Shortlands and Hyakutake's headquarters on Guadalcanal, along with the presence of so many supply drums adrift in the sound after the failed supply mission of December 3, had served to tip the enemy's hand. Westholm had a clear idea of Sato's destination and intentions, and was able to deploy his boats accordingly.

The squadron commander assigned himself the "bitch patrol" between Cape Esperance and Kokumbona, along with the *PT-43* skippered by Lieutenant Charles Tilden. Bob Searles in *PT-48* and Stilly Taylor in *PT-40* were ordered to take up scouting positions in the Slot to the northwest of Guadalcanal. A designated striking force of four boats roamed the waters of Ironbottom Sound east of Savo Island, led by Jack Searles and made up of PTs *36*, *37*, *44*, and *59*.

Before departing the Solomons for rear area bases following the naval battles of Guadalcanal and Tassafaronga, several heavily damaged cruisers like *San Francisco*, *Portland*, and *New Orleans* had left their Curtiss SOC Seagull reconnaissance seaplanes and their aircrews behind in Tulagi with orders to assist the PT boats. On the night of December 7–8, the Seagulls were tasked with maintaining a constant vigil over Ironbottom Sound between the hours of 11:00 p.m. and 2:45 a.m., on the lookout for Japanese destroyers and standing ready to drop parachute flares as directed. This would be the first of many nights the Seagulls were partnered with PT boats to hunt for the Tokyo Express. It was dangerous work for the men flying these underpowered and lightly armed biplanes, who were forced to brave pitch darkness and often-foul weather in addition to prowling Japanese aircraft.

At 11:20 p.m. both Bob Searles and Stilly Taylor spotted the Japanese formation. The *Oyashio* was in the van, steaming directly for the two scouting PT boats at 34 knots with a glowing "bone in her teeth." George Bockemuehl, the *48* boat's radio operator, began transmitting a contact report by TCS radio, alerting the striking force to the presence of at least five enemy ships roughly 3 miles north-northwest of Savo Island, on a course of 130 degrees southeast for Guadalcanal. Just as the two boats were motoring into a position to flank the Japanese destroyers and launch torpedoes, the tired portside motor aboard *PT-48* sputtered, coughed, and then finally died. Despite the frantic efforts of Chief Otis Cline and moto-mac Bill Nelson, the obstinate Packard steadfastly refused to start. Searles cranked the wheel and gunned the two remaining motors in a desperate bid to get clear of the onrushing destroyers.

"Get that smoke going!" Searles roared. Bockemuehl was still in the midst of transmitting his contact report, and his skipper's urgent order could be heard in the background. This caught the attention of Stilly Taylor, who quickly shot a glance across the water. Five-inch shells were tearing into the sea all around the plodding *PT-48*, showering the men topside with salt water.

Taylor ordered his own smoke generator opened and then put the wheel of the *PT-40* hard over, reversing course to trace a tight circle directly in the path of Sato's destroyers. Japanese searchlights swept forward, attempting to locate the new threat through the billowing smoke and glistening spray. Seeming to forget all about the crippled *PT-48*, the first two Japanese ships swerved away from the main column in pursuit of the *PT-40* as she sprinted away to the southeast at full throttle. The five remaining destroyers, their decks jammed with supply drums and their captains evidently hell-bent on completing their mission, steamed past the wallowing *48* boat at over 30 knots. Deciding to seek cover in the black shadow of Savo Island, Searles nosed the crippled *PT-48* close to shore before dropping anchor just 2 yards from the beach. Then the young skipper and his crew, still somewhat rattled after what had been an exceedingly close brush with death, settled in to watch and wait for what came next.

"Visibility was excellent, and I could see the Japanese heading in three columns from Savo to Cape Esperance," Jack Searles remembered. Alerted by the *PT-48*'s sighting report, the four boats of the striking force were roaring in from the northeast in attack formation. Selecting the leading destroyer *Oyashio* as his target, Searles began maneuvering the *PT-59* for a torpedo shot.

"I soon realized that we were on head-on collision courses, and rather than run away from him behind smoke, I thought we would give it to him with our guns," Searles wrote. "All hands were alerted to get ready to shoot everything they had at the bridge, all gun positions, and all search-lights, and to sweep their deck. We continued on at 28 knots, estimating his speed at 30. I fired our two torpedoes across his bow, hoping he would see us and swerve to his starboard right into our fish, but he never altered his course. I had forgotten our depth charges, but that's all I forgot. Once the torpedoes were on the way, we opened fire, passing him port-to-port at about 30 to 50 yards. I was proud of my crew. They really let that 'can' have it."

A violent hailstorm of .50-caliber slugs and 20-millimeter cannon shells swept through the bridge of the *Oyashio*, killing or wounding ten men and sending Captain Sato scrambling for cover. Standing in the open hatchway of the *PT-59*'s engine room, even Motor Machinist's Mate George Ebersberger was plugging away with a Springfield rifle. The two vessels passed so close to each other that the *Oyashio* was unable to depress her 5-inch guns low enough to get a clean shot at the *PT-59*, but one of her machine gunners was still able to rake the devil boat's topside. A pair of Japanese bullets punctured the *59*'s portside gun turret, narrowly missing Gunner's Mate Third Class Cletus Osborne and strik-ing an ammunition belt, which "started a lively blaze," in the words of one official account. Quickly grabbing a delinking tool, Osborne snapped the belt in two and tossed the flaming portion from the turret before resuming fire on the destroyer. The sizzling band of bullets landed on the deck at the feet of Quartermaster Harold Johnson, who stopped firing his Tommy gun long enough to kick it over the side.

Within three minutes of Searles making his brazen strafing run on the flagship, the Japanese destroyer skippers suddenly found themselves in "torpedo water." Lookouts spotted the tracks of eight fish streaking toward the Japanese column, fired by Lieutenant (jg) Marvin Pettit's *PT-36* and Lieutenant Frank Freeland's *PT-44*. More than a few supply drums toppled or skittered wildly across the weather decks as the destroy-ers heeled over into high-speed turns to avoid the inbound torpedoes.

Apart from ten small-caliber holes and a number of fish blown onto her deck by near misses, the *PT-59* and her crew came through their close encounter with the *Oyashio* unscathed. Spending those few seconds on the business end of a PT boat had apparently taken the fight out of Captain Sato. A radio message was sent to Tanaka's new flagship, the big 2,500-ton antiaircraft destroyer *Teruzuki*. Sato informed the admiral that he was ordering his ships to return to base without pausing to drop their supply drums.

"On the way I learned that the rest of the force which had continued toward Guadalcanal had fought off six torpedo boats west of Savo Island," Tanaka later wrote. "It was prevented from conducting unloading operations, however, by the presence of enemy planes and more torpedo boats. Accordingly it was on its way back to base without having made delivery. Under the circumstances I was forced to agree with the decision. Another attempt had failed."

While the four boats of the striking force retired toward Tulagi behind a cloud of white chemical smoke, the *109* and *43* were racing toward Cape Esperance from Kokumbona, hoping to catch the retreating Japanese in the narrow confines of the Savo-Esperance channel. Westholm broke off the chase at 12:25 a.m. on December 8, after receiving a radio report from the Seagull scout plane orbiting overhead. Sato's destroyers had already put 15 miles behind them, and were high-tailing it northwest for the Shortlands.

***

One day later, and 125 days after the first Higgins landing boat ran ashore onto the sands of Beach Red, Major General Alexander A. Vandegrift relinquished command of the Cactus-Ringbolt area to Major General Alexander M. Patch of the US Army. The men of the First Marine Division had been relieved, and were finally departing The Canal for a long-deserved period of rest and recuperation in Melbourne, Australia.

Gaunt, filthy, and with their faded green dungarees looking more like rags than uniforms, the marines formed long queues according to regiment and waited on the beach at Kukum for the landing craft that would whisk them out to a flotilla of transport ships anchored in Lunga Roads. Many were so weak that they struggled to make the long climb up the cargo nets that dangled from the transports and had to be hoisted aboard by healthy young sailors who regarded each of the shambling, vacantly staring combat veterans with a deep sense of reverence and awe.

Of the original force of 16,000 marines and their organic naval support personnel that stormed the beaches of Tulagi, Gavutu-Tanambogo, and Guadalcanal back in August, 680 had been killed in action and 1,300 wounded. Over half, some 8,500 men, were stricken with malaria and other tropical diseases. After its four-month ordeal on Guadalcanal, it would take an entire year to rehabilitate the First Marine Division, which would not see action again until the December 26, 1943, landings at Cape Gloucester.

"I could not muster the strength to swing over the gunwale," Bob Leckie wrote, "and I hung there, breathing heavily, the ship's hot side swaying beneath me—until two sailors grabbed me under the armpits and pulled me over. I fell with a clatter among the others who had been so brought aboard, and I lay there with my cheek pressed against the warm, grimy deck, my heart beating rapidly, not from this exertion, but from happiness."

***

At noon on that same day across the channel, Jack Searles was summoned to the bamboo shack on the Sesapi waterfront that Rollin Westholm had recently taken over and converted into an office. Westholm had pinned on the rank of full lieutenant two years before Hugh Robinson, and as the senior PT officer on Tulagi was now directing the operations of both motor torpedo boat squadrons.

Searles could see that "Westy" was on edge. The skipper was sitting at his makeshift desk holding two radio dispatch forms, both of which were stamped "Top Secret" in red ink. One of the decoded messages had been transmitted from Commander-in-Chief Pacific Fleet in Pearl Harbor to South Pacific Area Headquarters in Nouméa, and the other had been sent directly from Admiral Halsey to Westholm. CINCPAC's message stated that a large Japanese I-boat would be arriving off Cape Esperance at 11:00 p.m. local time on December 9 to deliver supplies and evacuate casualties from Guadalcanal.

Just how Admiral Nimitz had obtained this intelligence was obviously a closely guarded secret. COMSOPAC's dispatch to Westholm contained the same basic information, but went on to state that the Ringbolt PT boats would be the "only navy in area," and that it was "imperative you meet and sink sub." True to character, Halsey signed off with a special instruction for the PT boat commander:

```
Get the big SOB.
```

The PT boat had been designed as an anti-ship platform and was not a particularly efficient submarine hunter, despite its being armed with depth charges and often assigned to perform in that role. Unlike the navy's destroyers, PTs were not equipped with sonar and their crews did not receive the extensive antisubmarine warfare training of tin can sailors. An early attempt to turn a squadron of PT boats into subchasers had been given up as impracticable, after it was discovered that the noise and vibration of their big V12 engines rendered the installed sonar and hydrophone equipment useless. Apparently Admiral Halsey was concerned that the presence of sonar-pinging destroyers would spook the submarine, and was relying upon the PT boats to make the intercept. They would have the advantage of surprise, with the foreknowledge of when and where the submarine would surface.

"You want the job?" Westholm asked.

"Hell, yes," Searles responded. After going up against the blazing searchlights and roaring 5-inch guns of Japanese destroyers night after night, attacking a submarine on the surface would seem like a walk in the park. Westholm then asked if Jack's *PT-59* would be ready in time. Searles assured the skipper that she would be; it was standard practice for the crew of *PT-59* to restore their boat to a ready condition immediately following each night patrol. Upon their return to Tulagi, the boat was always fully refueled and restocked with ammunition and torpedoes. Cleaning, inspections, and maintenance were then performed on the engines and guns. That usually took until noon on most days, after which the crew would knock off for a bite of lunch and a few hours of sleep before their next outing.

Westholm wanted a second boat to accompany *PT-59*. Searles suggested the *PT-44*, skippered by the newly arrived Frank Freeland. Westholm agreed reluctantly but without protest. The captain and crew of the *44* boat were still green, but they were rested and ready, and needed the combat experience. Searles called for his new executive officer, Lieutenant (jg) Alfred Snowball, along with Freeland and his XO, Ensign John Chester, to begin planning the mission. In order to deceive any Japanese that might be watching, Searles told them, they would leave Tulagi Harbor at dusk and cruise westward along the coast of Florida Island toward the Slot. After dark, they would turn south and head for Cape Esperance, where they would lie in ambush.

The "big SOB" in question was the *I-3*, a 2,800-ton cruiser submarine skippered by Commander Ichiro Togami, running her sixth supply mission to Guadalcanal. The *I-3* had been equipped with a 46-foot Daihatsu motorized barge for landing cargo, which was clamped to her main deck just abaft the conning tower. At 11:00 p.m. Togami brought the *I-3* to periscope depth 3 miles to the northeast of Kamimbo Bay, and after making a cautious survey of the surrounding waters ordered his crew to surface the boat and launch the Daihatsu. Idling on the surface nearby were PTs *44* and *59*, which Togami had somehow missed during his periscope observation.

"Do you see what I see?" Freeland asked Searles over the VHF voice frequency. "On the surface to starboard?"

With amazing swiftness the well-drilled submariners launched the supply barge and the *I-3* submerged once again, apparently without seeing the PT boats. Undeterred, Searles turned the *PT-59* toward shore, trying to anticipate where the submarine might resurface.

"I've got a barge out here," Freeland called. "What should I do with it?"

"Strafe it," Searles ordered. With that the *PT-44*'s machine gunners opened fire, riddling the barge with .50-caliber bullets. Freeland then maneuvered his boat alongside the Daihatsu, only to find it abandoned— apparently the frightened coxswain and crew had jumped overboard. Suddenly the *I-3* returned to the surface, a mere stone's throw from the *PT-44* and just 400 yards directly off the bow of *PT-59*—point-blank range for a torpedo shot. Without hesitation Searles triggered two fish, both of which leapt from their tubes to run hot and straight.

"*Now* what do I do?" the nonplussed Freeland asked, his boat now stern-to-stern with a Japanese submarine.

"Stuff some cotton in your ears," Searles coolly replied. "Two fish are on the way."

As Freeland and his crew watched, the first torpedo zipped toward them at 29 knots and passed beneath the keel of the *PT-44*, completely missing the intended target. Every man knew that the minimum running depth of the Mark 8 was greater than the draft of a PT boat at full displacement, but it was a discomfiting experience nonetheless. This had only begun to register in their minds when the second torpedo blew the stern off the submarine, the tremendous explosion raining a mixture of seawater and diesel oil onto the decks of their boat.

"You got him!" Freeland shouted over the radio. "Beautiful!"

At that very moment on Guadalcanal, several army, navy, and marine officers were gathered around a radio speaker at the Lunga Point headquarters, listening with great anticipation to the voice tactical frequency. Among them was Bob Searles, serving as liaison officer for the Mosquito Fleet. Upon hearing Freeland's exultation the crowd erupted into loud, raucous cheers, "just as if they were back home listening to a baseball game."

The bow of the *I-3* lifted skyward and the submarine slipped beneath the boiling surface for the final time, taking Commander Togami and all but four of the ninety-man crew down with her. One junior officer and three able seamen somehow managed to survive and made the long swim to Guadalcanal to join their beleaguered comrades. Their mission accomplished, the two PT boats returned to base with the captured Daihatsu in tow. As it turned out, Freeland's eager machine gunners had done their job a little too well, for their shot-up prize sank before reaching Tulagi. With Westholm's permission, Jack Searles dictated the radio message that was sent to COMSOPAC headquarters:

```
Met and sank sub with torpedo. One less big SOB.
```

***

"They are performing heroic services," Admiral Halsey wrote in praise of the Ringbolt-based PT crews in a message to Admiral Nimitz on December 10, 1942, "and it is confidently expected that they will achieve a high record of valor and achievement in service of their country."

For his "exceptional bravery, aggressive leadership, and outstanding devotion to duty" on the night of December 9, Jack Searles would be awarded the Navy Cross, while the remaining officers and men of *PT-59* received the Silver Star. There was no time for resting on laurels, however. Though the sinking of the *I-3* would discourage further attempts to resupply the Japanese troops on Guadalcanal by submarine, "Tenacious Tanaka" and his Tokyo Express were still in business. Another major effort to deliver supplies and provisions to Guadalcanal by destroyer was being organized for the night of December 11–12.

As preparations for the mission were being made, the corresponding increase in radio chatter between Combined Fleet Headquarters in Truk, 8th Fleet Headquarters in Rabaul, and the IJN advanced base in the Shortlands caught the attention of Station HYPO in Pearl Harbor. One of the signals was a personal note from Admiral Yamamoto himself to his subordinate commanders, emphasizing the critical importance of the coming mission. The Imperial Army and Navy, whose leaders still arrogantly refused to believe that Americans were capable of grasping the intricacies of the Japanese language, let alone break their complicated radio codes, were continuing to conduct highly sensitive military communications with a compromised cipher. The fact that Allied forces were so often in the right place at the right time to disrupt Japanese operations was written off as mere coincidence, or the hand of fate.

After reviewing the decoded intercepts, cryptanalysts at Station HYPO forwarded their conclusions to the CINCPAC staff. South Pacific Forces were then advised that a Tokyo Express run of eleven Japanese destroyers was expected to arrive in Ironbottom Sound at around midnight on December 11–12, an intelligence estimate that would prove highly accurate. The Japanese squadron, led by Tanaka aboard the *Teruzuki*, stood out from the Shortlands on the afternoon of the eleventh.

Six of the destroyers were loaded with a total of 1,200 supply drums, while the remaining five ships were detailed to the escort. Dive bombers from Henderson Field once again confronted the Tokyo Express in the Slot, just after Tanaka's fighter cover retired for the night, but were unable to inflict any serious damage.

While Tanaka's destroyers were busy dodging bombs, six PT boats were getting underway from Tulagi. Entrusting the care of *PT-59* to Ensign Bill Kreiner, Jack Searles climbed aboard *PT-109* and headed west into the Slot to act as forward scout. The *59* boat, along with Stilly Taylor's *PT-40* and Les Gamble's *PT-45*, formed the striking force in Ironbottom Sound. Frank Freeland's *PT-44* and Charlie Tilden's *PT-61* were assigned to patrol the waters off Kamimbo Bay and watch for supply-bearing submarines.

Just before midnight, the crew of an SOC Seagull scout plane reported "at least nine" Japanese destroyers in the Slot headed southeast. Shortly thereafter, the Japanese ships were spotted by the crew of *PT-109*. Jack Searles announced that the Tokyo Express was "passing through Rye," the designated halfway point between Guadalcanal's Cape Esperance and Savo Island. Immediately the boats of the striking force, with Gamble's *PT-45* in the lead, roared westward into the Savo-Esperance channel on a course to intercept. The two boats of the antisubmarine patrol also began heading in that direction from their station off Kamimbo Bay.

Maneuvering as close to shore as they dared, Tanaka's destroyer crews pushed their supply drums overboard and continued east toward Ironbottom Sound. Soon their lookouts detected the wakes of incoming PTs and raised the alarm. From the bridge of the *Teruzuki*, Admiral Tanaka watched as his ships accelerated to flank speed, swept the sea ahead with their searchlights, and opened fire on the devil boats as they came within range.

"We took course to maneuver around them and attacked, but took an unexpected torpedo hit on the port side aft, causing a heavy explosion," Tanaka wrote. "The ship caught fire and became unnavigable almost at once. Leaking fuel was set ablaze, turning the sea into a mass of flames. . . . Directing operations of my force on the bridge when the torpedo struck, I was thrown to the deck unconscious by the initial explosion. I regained consciousness to find that *Naganami* had come alongside to take off survivors."

All three boats of the striking force had launched full spreads of four torpedoes toward the Japanese column. It is thought that a fish triggered by Les Gamble was the one to have found its mark, tearing through the hull of the *Teruzuki* and leaving her dead in the water, on fire, and listing heavily. Fires aboard the "Shining Moon" would burn throughout the night, finally reaching the depth charges stored on her afterdeck, resulting in a devastating secondary explosion that finished her destruction.

"The loss of my flagship, our newest and best destroyer, to such inferior enemy strength was a serious responsibility," Tanaka said later. "I have often thought that it would have been easier for me to have been killed in that first explosion."

Nine men aboard the *Teruzuki* were killed outright. The *Naganami* evacuated the dazed admiral along with 56 members of the crew, while the *Arashi* pulled 140 from the water. Lifeboats would carry another 156 men to the shores of Guadalcanal, where they would soon be sharing with their army comrades the same deprivations they had been sent to alleviate. The PT sailors could now rightly claim to have sunk a Japanese destroyer, and the flagship of the Tokyo Express at that.

In the meantime, PTs *44* and *61* were rapidly closing in from the northwest, their two young skippers anxious to join the fray. Aboard Frank Freeland's *PT-44* was a third officer, Lieutenant (jg) Charles Melhorn, who had come along on the mission as an observer after his regularly assigned boat was laid up for repairs. Melhorn would later dictate a vivid account of what happened that night to Sam Savage, intelligence officer for MTBRON 3.

"It was now close to 0030 the morning of December 12. The weather was clear and starry, visibility exceptionally good," Melhorn described. "We continued on a course due east without slackening speed. . . . We were throwing up quite a wake and with the Jap ship on our starboard quarter lighting up the whole area, I thought we would soon be easy pickings and I told the skipper so. Before he could reply, Crowe, the quartermaster, who was at the wheel, pointed and yelled out: 'Destroyer on starboard bow. There's your target, captain.'"

Melhorn peered through his binoculars as the *PT-44* veered to starboard and began her torpedo run. Scanning from right to left, he immediately spotted two more destroyers, *Kawakaze* and *Suzukaze*, just 4,000 yards off the port bow and headed due west at high speed.

"The skipper and I both saw at once that continuing our present course would pin us against the beach and lay us wide open to broadsides from at least three Jap cans," Melhorn said. Freeland then ordered Crowe to steer to port, intending to target the two destroyers on his left. Then a fourth Japanese ship appeared out of the gloom, just astern of *Kawakaze* and *Suzukaze*. As Melhorn was pointing this out to Freeland, the *Kawakaze* turned her guns upon the *PT-44* and began firing.

"The skipper ordered hard right rudder, increased speed, and made smoke," Melhorn reported. "We turned at right angles to the course of the column, and held until we were directly ahead of the lead ship who was firing steadily but over and astern. As we crossed his bow, we swung left again 90° to the west and retired behind our smoke. A few shots landed behind us as we turned, but they broke off firing at once, as soon as they saw we had gotten behind smoke. We retired at full throttle intending to get well under Savo before we made our next run."

Melhorn left the cockpit and made his way to the fantail, keeping a wary eye on the four Japanese warships as the *44* boat zigzagged her way toward Savo Island. Suddenly a great burst of flame erupted from the leading destroyer as she fired a full salvo from her main battery.

"That's for us!" Melhorn shouted, his words drowned by the frightening crescendo of incoming shells. Scrambling forward, Melhorn threw himself to the deck beside the charthouse. A split second later came a stunning flash and explosion, followed by a blast of superheated smoke and flying debris sweeping over the boat's main deck.

"We were hit aft in the engine room," Melhorn said. "I don't remember much. For a few seconds, nothing registered at all. I looked back and saw a gaping hole in what was once the engine room canopy. The perimeter of the hole in the canopy was ringed by little tongues of flame."

The young officer managed to rise to his feet, still somehow unharmed. The *PT-44* had completely lost way, the helm dead in Willard Crowe's hands. Freeland gave the order to abandon ship, and men began jumping overboard as the skipper, his XO, and the quartermaster hastened to deploy the boat's life raft. Hearing another enemy salvo screaming down upon them, Melhorn quickly dove over the port side and plunged head first into the dark water. A second direct hit landed just forward of the first, where the tanks of highly volatile aviation gas were located, and blew the *PT-44* to splinters.

"There was a tremendous explosion, paralyzing me from the waist down. The water around me went red," Melhorn remembered. "The life jacket took control and pulled me to the surface. I came up in a sea of fire, the flaming embers of the boat cascading all about me. I tried to get free of the life jacket, but couldn't. I started swimming feebly. I thought the game was up but the water, which had shot sky high in the explosion, rained down and put out the fires around me. From the first hit to this point took less than 15 seconds.

"I took a few strokes away from the gasoline fire which was raging about 15 yards behind me and as I turned back, I saw two heads, one still helmeted, between me and the flames," Melhorn continued. "I heard a cry which came from behind the flames. I called to the two men, told them that I expected the Japs to be over in short order to machine gun us, and to get their life jackets ready to slip. I told them to get clear of the reflection of the fire as quickly as possible and proceeded to do so myself."

Melhorn began swimming for Savo Island, "whose skyline ridge I could see dimly, and gradually made headway towards shore. Every two or three minutes I stopped to look back for other survivors, or an approaching destroyer, but saw nothing save the boat which was burning steadily, and beyond it—slightly to the west—the Jap ship which burned and exploded all night long. Sometime shortly before dawn a PT boat cruised up and down Savo, came out and passed about 25 yards ahead of me. I was all set to hail him when I looked over my shoulder and saw a Jap can bearing down on his starboard quarter. I didn't know whether the PT was maneuvering to get a shot at him or not, so I kept my mouth shut, let him go by, slipped my life jacket and waited for the fireworks.

The Jap can lay motionless for some minutes, and I finally made it out as nothing more than a destroyer-shaped shadow formed by the fires and smoke which etched the outline against Cape Esperance."

Melhorn decided to resume swimming for the distant island. "I was being set down rapidly to the east and finally made Savo by swimming due west," he recalled. "The PT circled and came back behind me. I yelled, but he swung off toward the wrecked boat. Although I heard both him and the SOC droning around most of the night, they never came close."

A search for survivors was commenced as soon as the Tokyo Express departed the area. Jack Searles and the men of *PT-109* found Lyle Downing paddling weakly amid the scattered wreckage and pulled him aboard. The nineteen-year-old striker from Detroit was utterly exhausted and numb with shock, but alive. Later in the morning the crew of *PT-40* spotted Charlie Melhorn standing on the beach at Savo and launched their rubber boat to retrieve him.

"Those poor guys," Melhorn told Stilly Taylor, "they never had a chance."

Melhorn and Dowling would be the only survivors of the *PT-44*. The bodies of Radioman Walter Moore of New York City and Ship's Cook George Saliba of Los Angeles would be recovered and buried in the military cemetery on Tulagi. Frank Freeland, John Chester, Will Crowe, Roy Giddens, Lewis Hubbard, Fred Bartell, and Burnell Rihn were listed as missing in action, never to be found. The loss of *PT-44* would hammer home the importance of making a slow, muffled approach when attacking Japanese destroyers equipped with excellent night optics. According to Bryant Larson, executive officer of the *PT-109*, the *44* boat's high speed had stirred "a tremendous phosphorescent wake that was like a searchlight pointing to the boat."

"From the *44* we learned two lessons," Larson wrote. "Don't make a high speed night attack, and if you are hit, under fire, and dead in the water, get all hands off the boat before another salvo blows everyone to hell—the sea-going equivalent of bailing out of a plane."

The Tulagi PT squadrons had lost their first boat to enemy fire and sustained their first combat deaths. Their sorrow was at least partially assuaged by the knowledge that they had consigned a 2,500-ton destroyer to the deep. They would also have the satisfaction of sinking 980 drifting supply barrels with machine gun fire as they motored through Ironbottom Sound in broad daylight, in full view of the Japanese on Starvation Island.

"Twelve-hundred cases of provisions are said to have been landed on shore, but I wonder how many cases were actually landed," Rear Admiral Matome Ugaki wrote in his diary on December 12, 1942. "All but destroyer *Terutsuki* returned to Shortland. Now we can hope that our forces on the island will be supported for some time. How hard it was! We must think of some ways to take revenge on those troublesome PT boats."

CHAPTER NINE

# The Hooligan Navy

BY DECEMBER 1942, MANY SENIOR STAFF OFFICERS OF THE IMPERIAL Japanese Army and Navy were asking themselves the very same question faced by American military and civilian leaders just eight weeks before: *Can we hold Guadalcanal?* Despite the remarkable courage and tenacity of its destroyermen, it had become obvious that the IJN wasn't capable of keeping the army forces on Guadalcanal adequately provisioned, much less reinforced. For the Japanese, the island had become "desperate ground," as the warrior-philosopher Sun Tzu would have described it. The initiative—the military profession's term for positive control of the battlespace and the forward momentum of operations—had been lost.

By default, the focus of the supply effort had now become the delivery of enough food and medical supplies for Hyakutake's soldiers to maintain an effective resistance, rather than building up sufficient forces to retake the island. At the headquarters of 8th Fleet and the 8th Area Army at Rabaul, aboard the Combined Fleet flagship *Yamato* in Truk Lagoon, and in the halls of Imperial General Headquarters in Tokyo, a few brave souls were beginning to express the opinion that Guadalcanal should be evacuated.

The fact that Japan's South Pacific forces were suffering intolerable losses in terms of ships, aircraft, and personnel in their vain, face-saving effort to hold Guadalcanal was only part of the problem. In early December, the Imperial General Staff was informed that the Japanese merchant marine did not possess enough shipping tonnage to keep the protracted campaigns on mainland China, Guadalcanal, and New

Guinea adequately supplied, while at the same time maintaining the flow of oil and other critically important strategic materials from conquered territories in Southeast Asia to mainland Japan. When Premier Hideki Tojo argued for more transports and cargo vessels to be made available for military operations in the South Pacific, one of his top advisors, Major General Kenryo Sato, stated quite boldly that the Guadalcanal campaign should be abandoned and the troops there withdrawn.

"We have no choice," Sato dared to say. "Even now may be too late. If we go on like this, we have no chance of winning the war."

On December 19, the head of the Operations Section at Imperial General Headquarters, Major General Joichiro Sanada, led a delegation of senior officers to Rabaul to discuss plans for renewing the offensive against Allied forces in the eastern Solomons. Sanada found an intense level of pessimism pervading both the army and navy headquarters at Rabaul, and was appalled by reports of just how few reinforcements and supplies were actually making it through to Hyakutake's troops.

Sanada spoke to several officers with firsthand knowledge of the situation on the ground, and many were unsparing in their graphic detail. Many soldiers on Guadalcanal, the general was told, were too weak to rise from their foxholes even to bury their dead. Those who still had their wits about them were praying for a final attack to come so they might die an honorable death, rather than succumb to disease or starvation. The situation had become so dire that one Japanese officer even developed a matrix for determining how long each of his emaciated soldiers would live: "He who can rise to his feet: 30 days. He who can sit up: 20 days. He who must urinate while lying down: 3 days. He who can no longer blink: dead at dawn."

Not a single one of the men interviewed believed that the island could be held. General Imamura himself did not say as much, but to Sanada he expressed a closely held fear: Should Japanese soldiers on Guadalcanal learn that an evacuation was being contemplated, they might commit mass suicide rather than face the dishonor of having been defeated in battle.

On December 29, General Sanada presented his findings to the Imperial General Staff in Tokyo. The 17th Army on Guadalcanal would prevail "only by a miracle," Sanada told the assembled general and flag officers. "Future operations must not, out of eagerness to regain Guadalcanal, be jeopardized by following previous plans and by continuing a campaign in which neither the area command nor the front line commanders have any confidence."

***

On the morning of December 15, 1942, a motor whaleboat was lowered from the *Gridley*-class destroyer USS *Craven* into the placid azure waters of Tulagi Harbor and got underway for the PT docks at Sesapi. Aboard the boat was Commander Allen Philip Calvert, who had been relieved as commanding officer of the *Craven* earlier that morning and was headed to his new assignment. At forty-one years of age, Calvert was physically unremarkable in almost every way—tall, spare, and round-shouldered, with a plain, oblong face and a pair of deep-set eyes that often held an impassive, deadpan expression.

Originally from Battle Creek, Michigan, Calvert studied engineering at the Carnegie Institute in Pittsburgh before entering the US Naval Academy and graduating with the Class of 1924. Most of Calvert's career had been spent in destroyers, and during his rotations of shore duty he obtained a master's degree in mechanical engineering from Columbia University and served at the Naval Engineering Experiment Station at Annapolis. The *Craven* had been Calvert's first command, and was at sea serving as part of the *Enterprise* destroyer screen when the Japanese attacked Pearl Harbor. Calvert and his crew joined Halsey's task force for the early hit-and-run carrier raids before returning to the West Coast to perform patrol and escort duty, an assignment that allowed the destroyer skipper to make brief visits to his wife and two teenaged children at the family home near San Diego. In November, the *Craven* was reassigned to Halsey's South Pacific Forces and set sail at once for Tulagi, where Calvert himself received new orders from COMSOPAC.

Commander Calvert was being sent to Sesapi to establish Motor Torpedo Boat Flotilla One, which would oversee the operations, administration, maintenance, and logistics of all PT squadrons in the Solomon Islands. He was to report directly to Captain Thomas Shock, who on

December 1 had relieved William Greenman as Commander Advanced Naval Base Cactus-Ringbolt. Having never served in PT boats, Calvert's learning curve was sure to be steep and the task before him, especially with regard to logistics, quite daunting. While his lack of experience in PTs undoubtedly caused some eyebrows to be raised among the boat crews, the navy was sending Calvert to Sesapi to employ his organizational talents, rather than his technical or tactical skills.

Destined for flag rank, Allen Calvert had been identified early on as a diligent taskmaster, and possessed the logical, detail-oriented, and analytical mind of a highly trained engineer. Though a bit rigid and by-the-book, traits that may have inhibited his ability to mesh with the free-wheeling, high-spirited young officers and men of his new command, Calvert was quite adept at project management and problem-solving. He was also smart enough to take his time in seeking out the most experienced, knowledgeable, and competent officers in the PT squadrons and appoint them to key positions within the new command organization.

Another period of relative calm settled over the waters of the eastern Solomons during these last three weeks of 1942. The Tulagi-based PT boats continued performing their nightly patrols, but without encountering the Tokyo Express or engaging in any major firefights. Only two noteworthy actions occurred during this period, both of which were frightening cases of near fratricide.

On December 14, four Bird-class corvettes of the Royal New Zealand Navy took up residence in Tulagi Harbor and began conducting antisubmarine patrols in the waters surrounding Guadalcanal. One of them, the 600-ton *Kiwi* commanded by thirty-three-year-old Lieutenant Commander Gordon Bridson of Auckland, was returning from one such mission when she was spotted by lookouts aboard Les Gamble's *PT-45* on a security patrol outside the harbor entrance. Mistaking the *Kiwi* for a Japanese destroyer, Gamble fired two torpedoes, which whined past either side of the New Zealander's slim hull.

"Crikey! Are you little bastards trying to sink *me*?" Bridson called over the tactical channel.

"Um . . . yes sir, I'm afraid we were," Gamble responded sheepishly.

"I'll expect an explanation when you report back in," Bridson said flatly, "and the bar aboard His Majesty's New Zealand Ship *Kiwi* is closed to you for the duration."

Bridson was waiting on the *Kiwi*'s quarterdeck when Gamble stepped aboard, his hands planted firmly on his hips and a deep scowl etched on his bearded face. He was an imposing figure, well over six feet tall and broad-shouldered. A competitive swimmer in his younger years, Bridson had since added a hundred pounds to his already considerable frame.

"Follow me, Mr. Gamble," Bridson growled after returning the American's stiff salute. Retiring below to the officer's wardroom, the captain listened as the mortified PT skipper poured out a sincere apology for nearly blowing his corvette out of the water. When Gamble was finished, Bridson rose from his chair and retrieved a bottle of Scotch and two whiskey glasses from the *Kiwi*'s well-stocked bar.

"All is forgiven," Bridson told Gamble. The two polished off the bottle in short order, and afterward became lifelong friends.

While on patrol in Ironbottom Sound on the night of December 24, *PT-40* and *PT-45* were mistakenly attacked by three American dive bombers. After dropping flares, two SBDs dove on the PT boats and released their bombs, all of which were near misses. The third plane then attempted a strafing run on the *PT-40*, which inflicted no damage. No one aboard either boat was killed, but two sailors on the *PT-45* were wounded.

"Boy, what a nice Christmas present that was," someone said over the radio. The Christmas Eve incident would be among the first, but unfortunately not the last, episodes of "friendly fire" between American aircraft and PT boats in the Pacific War.

According to Rear Admiral Raizo Tanaka, the mid-December pause was due in part to a directive from 8th Fleet Headquarters, which temporarily suspended destroyer runs to Guadalcanal during the moonlit period of December 15–29. Tanaka was instead ordered to shuttle army personnel from Rabaul to Munda Point on the island of New Georgia, 150 miles northwest of Guadalcanal, where a new airfield was being completed. Despite the desperate plight of Japanese troops on Guadalcanal, the Imperial Navy was now unwilling to run the gauntlet of American PT boats in Ironbottom Sound under the bright light of a waxing moon.

On New Year's Eve, six more 80-foot Elco PT boats arrived from Espiritu Santo. Two of these, PTs *111* and *112*, were from Westholm's MTBRON 2. The *115*, *118*, *123*, and *124* constituted the first echelon of MTBRON 6, led by Lieutenant Clark Faulkner, who had seen action with MTBRON 1 at Pearl Harbor and Midway. As the boats rumbled into Tulagi Harbor beneath a gloomy, overcast sky, their crews were greeted by a large, hand-painted billboard posted prominently on a hillside:

*ADMIRAL HALSEY SAYS "KILL JAPS, KILL JAPS, KILL MORE JAPS!"*

*YOU WILL HELP KILL THE YELLOW BASTARDS IF YOU DO YOUR JOB WELL.*

For these newcomers the sight of their old friends and new digs on Tulagi came as something of a shock. It was the middle of summer in the southern hemisphere and the peak of the rainy season in the Solomons. They would find the days uncomfortably hot and stifling, with a pungent, fecund stink emanating from the surrounding mangroves. Rains were frequent and intense, the mud deep and ubiquitous. Base facilities, such as they were, were even more crude and spartan than imagined. The enlisted living quarters, situated on a bluff overlooking the waterfront and given the name "Snob Hill" by its inhabitants, consisted of an odd collection of tightly arranged bamboo shacks, tarpaulin shelters, and pyramidal tents that more closely resembled a Depression-era Hooverville than a military camp.

One look at the salty PT veterans of Tulagi explained why many of their contemporaries in the fleet had begun referring to them as the "Hooligan Navy." As is often the case in front-line units, the rigid adherence to uniform regulations and grooming standards was considered impractical or superfluous. Both officers and enlisted alike were dressed in a motley array of items, with each individual ensemble tailored more toward functionality than uniformity. Strange pieces of headgear like pith helmets and Marine Corps utility caps worn at a rakish angle had become the fashion, as had shorts made from cut-off khaki or dungaree trousers. The shorts were worn without underwear—impossible to keep dry and horribly uncomfortable in the tropical heat—and often secured by a belt with a large sheath knife attached, lending further to the wearer's swashbuckling appearance.

Many were walking about the base shirtless, revealing the protruding ribs and collarbones that resulted from a meager and vitamin-less diet of baked beans, Vienna sausages, dehydrated potatoes, and Spam. Rather than being sun-bronzed as one might expect, their skin had a sickly yellow hue, a side effect of the daily doses of Atabrine taken to combat malaria. Their hair was long and unkempt, and several were sporting full beards, including both Searles brothers. The most noticeable difference—and to the new arrivals, the most disconcerting—was the look in their eyes. Their gaze was faraway and listless, reflective of the long, tense nights of patrolling, the many hours of exhausting work in port, and the strength-sapping routine of jungle living. They were, in the parlance of the day, "Tulagi Groggy."

Like the men who sailed them, the Ringbolt PT boats were also war weary, especially the older 77-footers of 'RON 3. Hulls, decks, and upper works were scuffed, streaked, splintered, and grimy from heavy use. All had become home to jungle rats and cockroaches, despite the best efforts of their crews to keep them clean, and had suffered varying degrees of damage from bullets, shrapnel, collisions, or running aground.

However, the intense pride that each veteran crew felt for their boat was quite evident. It is not unusual for a sailor to bond closely with his ship, but that bond seemed especially intimate among the PT sailors of Tulagi. The boats had been trusted to carry their crews into a harrowingly up-close and personal form of naval combat and then swiftly deliver them to safety. Great care and attention was therefore lavished over every component, especially the engines and guns. It seemed that some form of cleaning, maintenance, repair, modification, or tinkering was always taking place. The worst of the battle damage, noticeable due to the presence of freshly applied paint, had been carefully and lovingly patched.

Their affections were further reflected in the unofficial names many crews bestowed upon their craft, which were emblazoned on planks and mounted to the charthouse. Much like the clever "nose art" seen on bombers of the Army Air Forces, the names given to PT boats in World War II trended toward the pithy, the cartoonish, or the self-deprecating, and were often laced with fatalist sentiment or sexual innuendo. *Sea Gypsy, Lack-a-nookie, Coughing Coffin, Galloping Ghost, Miss Malaria, Green Banana, Dinah Might, Snafu, Hirohito's Headache, Plywood Bastard,* and *Eager Beaver* are but a few examples.

The island of Tulagi itself offered little in the way of recreation or amusement, the new men would soon realize. In their rare off-duty hours, sailors caught up on their sleep, wrote letters, fished the pilings of Government Wharf, or sat in on one of the marathon poker tournaments that always seemed to be going on in the tent camps. Pickup baseball games were played on the English cricket pitch—when it wasn't raining. Movie nights were hosted by Commander Beasley on the mess deck of the *Jamestown*, but first-run films were difficult to come by. Some remember watching Charlie Chaplin's *The Great Dictator* a dozen or more times.

Liquor was also scarce, but being American sailors, they called upon their powers of improvisation and managed to produce their own spirits. From the infantry they learned to make "Raisin Jack," adding handfuls of sugar to canned fruit and allowing it to ferment in the sun beneath a protective layer of cheesecloth. A more field-expedient method of making booze was devised by cutting the 180-grain alcohol that propelled their torpedoes with powdered GI fruit juice—a pernicious concoction that came to be know as "Torpedo Juice."

"It tasted awful," claimed one marine who sampled it, "but it sure did get you drunk."

The fresh crews and their brand-new boats, two of which had been completed by the Elco boatworks *after* the marines landed on Guadalcanal, could not have arrived at a better time. Their addition to the Tulagi PT fleet meant increased periods of rest between patrols for all hands, and if necessary the boats could now sortie from the advanced base at or near squadron strength. The new boat crews would have a little over forty-eight hours to settle into their new environment, before they too found themselves sailing into harm's way. The moon had begun to wane, and after a two-week hiatus the Tokyo Express was once again on the move.

***

In the final week of 1942, Raizo Tanaka was relieved as commanding officer of Destroyer Squadron Two and ordered to report to Tokyo to serve on the Navy General Staff. The relentless strain and sleepless nights of the previous five months had taken its toll on the admiral, who was still suffering from the effects of a concussion received when his flagship was torpedoed by the *PT-45* on the night of December 12.

"There were sad farewells to my staff and friends who had for so long shared, fought, and suffered the fates of war with me," Tanaka wrote. "In the late afternoon of that day, pained and weary, I boarded a plane and left Rabaul for the homeland."

Tanaka's replacement was forty-nine-year-old Rear Admiral Tomiji Koyanagi, who immediately set to work planning the next supply run to Tassafaronga. Another 1,200 drums of supplies and provisions were loaded aboard five destroyers with another five ships assigned to provide the screen, led by Koyanagi flying his flag from *Naganami*. In order to repel the fearsome devil boats, Koyanagi ordered additional 12.7-millimeter machine guns installed aboard each of the escort destroyers, and also arranged for close air support—a first for the Tokyo Express. Three "Pete" float planes from the "R" Area Naval Air Force were assigned to fly cover for the destroyer squadron, which departed from the Shortlands on January 2, 1943.

Allied signals intelligence, coastwatchers, and search aircraft once again sniffed out Japanese intentions, and in the late afternoon the destroyers were attacked by Flying Fortresses and SBDs. Five of the army's new and deadly Lockheed P-38 Lightning fighters accompanied the marine dive bombers, causing Koyanagi's three float planes to maintain a respectful distance. Damaged by near misses, the *Suzukaze* was forced to return to the Shortlands under the protection of *Inazuma*, while the remaining eight ships of Koyanagi's force continued for Tassafaronga.

Commander Calvert ordered nine PT boats to intercept the Tokyo Express, led by Rollin Westholm in the *PT-109*. Arriving off the coast of

Guadalcanal just before midnight, the boats attacked individually as they acquired targets, firing their torpedoes and withdrawing behind a smoke screen. As they did, the crews were forced to contend with not only the bright searchlights and heavy gunfire of the destroyers, but with swooping, strafing, and bombing float planes as well. Masked by darkness, the Japanese pilots employed the tactic of gliding silently along the glowing blue wake of a PT boat and releasing their bombs when directly overhead. The pilots would later report that they were able to spot the wake of a PT boat from as far away as 4 miles.

"The phosphorescence from the action of our propellers was like a neon light on Broadway," Jack Searles described. Another PT skipper would liken the wake of his boat to "a bright shining arrow pointing right up my ass." Other than a few jangled nerves, however, no significant damage or casualties were suffered during this first encounter with the night-flying Petes. No American torpedoes had found their mark either, and Koyanagi's destroyers were able to jettison 1,200 supply drums before making good their escape. Fewer than half were successfully recovered by Japanese troops on Guadalcanal; the remainder were sunk by the .50-caliber fire of American PT boats after dawn.

\*\*\*

On January 4, 1943, Major General Kijutsu Ayabe arrived in Rabaul from Tokyo, there to hand-deliver copies of a top secret order to Lieutenant General Hitoshi Imamura of the 8th Area Army and Vice Admiral Jinichi Kusaka, commander of the newly established Southeast Area Fleet. The order had been issued by Imperial General Headquarters and bore the seal of Emperor Hirohito himself. Operation *Ke-go*, the evacuation of all Japanese forces remaining on the island of Guadalcanal, was to commence in ten days' time.

What happened later that same evening would serve as further evidence that the tide of the Pacific War in general and the Solomons campaign in particular had turned irreversibly against Japan. At Admiral Halsey's direction, Rear Admiral Walden "Pug" Ainsworth's Task Force 67, consisting of the cruisers *Helena*, *St. Louis*, *Nashville*, *Louisville*,

*Honolulu, Columbia, Achilles,* and five destroyers, entered the Slot and steamed northwest for the New Georgia island group.

The Slot had now become a two-way street, and this time an Allied naval force would stand brazenly offshore and bombard a Japanese airfield with impunity. To the Japanese airmen and ground crews stationed at the new airstrip on Munda Point, Ainsworth's ships dealt the same sort of punishment Tanaka's destroyers had previously delivered to the marines at Henderson Field, sending 3,000 rounds of high explosives hurtling into their runways, parked aircraft, and encampments, destroying ten structures and killing or wounding thirty-two men.

After this little was heard from the Japanese until the late afternoon of January 10, when New Georgia–based coastwatcher Donald Kennedy broadcast over the Ferdinand emergency frequency that a column of eight Japanese destroyers was headed southeast down the Slot. Poor weather would allow the Tokyo Express to continue on their journey unmolested by the planes of the Cactus Air Force, but also prevented their own seaplanes from providing air cover.

Two scouting teams of PT boats were sent to patrol the strait between Cape Esperance and Savo Island, each pairing an experienced skipper with one of the new arrivals. The first was made up of Les Gamble's *PT-45* and Lieutenant (jg) Ralph Amstead's *PT-39*. The second scouting force was composed of *PT-48*, skippered by Bob Searles, along with *PT-115* under the command of Ensign Bartholomew Connolly. Ranging the waters of Ironbottom Sound were two striking forces of three boats each. One was led by Jack Searles in the *59* boat, along with PTs *36* and *46*. The other included the *40* and *43* boats and was commanded by Rollin Westholm aboard *PT-112*, with Bryant Larson at the helm.

"Our assigned patrol area was Tassafaronga Beach, the expected landing area for the Express," Larson recalled. "As we headed for the hot spot, our torpedoman—Claude Dollar—came to the bridge and handed me what he said was a 'lucky bean,' given to him that day by some native. He asked me to hold on to it, as we might need some special luck that night. How right he was!"

Gusty winds, rain squalls, and poor visibility may have denied Koyanagi his air cover, but the foul weather also allowed the Tokyo Express to slip past the two groups of scouting PT boats undetected. It wasn't until 1:00 a.m. that Westholm's striking force sighted four Japanese destroyers off Cape Esperance, steaming southeastward at 28 knots. As the three PT boats maneuvered to achieve a firing point for their torpedoes, one of the ships made an abrupt 180-degree turn and headed northwest, presumably after having dropped her load of supply barrels into the sea. Rollin Westholm then made the prudent but nevertheless fateful decision for his three boats to attack the remaining three destroyers.

"Deploy to the right and make them good," the squadron commander directed.

In command of the easternmost *PT-43* was Charles Tilden, a twenty-four-year-old Californian who had majored in zoology at the University of Redlands and graduated from the same V-7 class as Bob Wark and the Searles brothers. The young lieutenant had borne witness to the violent destruction of the *PT-44* at close range on the morning of December 12, and had since mourned the death of his friend Frank Freeland, whose fatal mistakes he did not intend to emulate. Selecting the leading destroyer *Tokitsukaze* as his target, Tilden closed in slowly with his engine mufflers engaged, maneuvering stealthily to achieve the proper angle of attack.

Rather than an inexperienced skipper's carelessness, it would be yet another flaw in the design of the Bliss–Leavitt Mark 8 torpedo and its tube-launching system that would spell tragedy for the crew of *PT-43*. Closing to within just 400 yards, Tilden triggered two fish, one of which flared brightly as it shot from the tube. Whether the result of a faulty powder charge or the ignition of lubricating grease in the tube, the flash served to mark the location of the *PT-43* for alert lookouts aboard the *Tokitsukaze*.

Quickly trapping the slow-moving PT boat in the beams of her searchlights, the destroyer let loose with all six of her 5-inch guns. Immediately Quartermaster Leo Elman firewalled the throttles while Tilden gave the order to make smoke and cranked the wheel hard right. Seconds later came the howling sound of the inbound salvo, followed by a stunning, shuddering crash and a searing blast of heat. A 5-inch shell had ripped through the engine room, disabling the motors and leaving the *43* boat suddenly dead in the water. Having been thrown to the deck by the explosion, Tilden rose to his feet in time to see the Japanese destroyer bearing down upon the disabled *PT-43* at flank speed.

"Abandon ship!" Tilden shouted. The young skipper and his crew dove overboard and breaststroked for depth as quickly as they could.

The Pacific War—in the air, on the land, and on the sea—had thus far been a savage conflict. Tilden and his men knew they could expect the Japanese to machine-gun any PT sailors they found in the water. Along with the churning of her twin screws and the sound of seawater rushing along the steel hull of the *Tokitsukaze*, the men could hear the distinctive *zip* of bullets striking the water above their heads. When they could take it no longer, the survivors returned to the surface to gulp the warm night air. The destroyer had thankfully passed by the blazing hulk of their boat and was continuing north. In that curious way that sound waves are amplified as they travel across calm water, the survivors of *PT-43* could hear clearly the voices of Japanese sailors on the fantail of the *Tokitsukaze* as she receded into the darkness.

In the meantime Clark Faulkner's *PT-40* was stalking the *Hatsukaze*, the second ship in the column of three. Faulkner had fought off enemy planes at Pearl Harbor and Midway but was engaging Japanese surface ships for the first time, and would execute a nocturnal torpedo attack straight out of the Melville textbook. Making a muffled approach and creeping to within 500 yards, Faulkner let go with all four fish before turning the *PT-40* to the east and roaring down the coast of Guadalcanal at full throttle behind a stream of white smoke. Seconds later came a fierce *crack*, a bright flash of yellow light, and a tall column of water sprouting from the sea alongside the destroyer's hull. Whether the result of steely nerves and skill or simply beginner's luck, Faulkner's portside aft torpedo had run true, blasting completely through the bow of the *Hatsukaze*.

The through-and-through shot struck the *Kagero*-class destroyer on the port side and exploded beneath the officer's wardroom, killing eight men and wounding twenty-three more. While the *Hatsukaze* was "certainly in bad shape," as her captain later described, her propulsion and steering were still intact. The explosion had also somehow failed to breach her wing tanks or touch off the forward powder magazine, which would have ensured her demise. Once the flooding was under control, *Hatsukaze* got underway for the Shortlands at a steady 18 knots. After receiving temporary repairs, *Hatsukaze* steamed for Truk Atoll and then on to mainland Japan, where she would be laid up in the Kure Navy Yard for the next eight months. *Hatsukaze* would finally meet her fate in November, at the hands of Captain Arleigh Burke during the Battle of Empress Augusta Bay.

The third Japanese ship, *Kawakaze*, became the target of the *PT-112*.

"Westy gave the command to close in and fire," Bryant Larson recounted. "I took the *112* to point-blank range—perhaps too close, for a torpedo needed 300 yards to arm itself—and fired all four torpedoes, as did the other two boats . . . I pushed the engines to full speed and tried to run between two of the destroyers, the only possible escape route."

Suddenly two Japanese shells smashed into the *112* boat almost simultaneously. The first punched a jagged hole in her mahogany hull just below the waterline amidships, while the second tore through and set fire to the engine room. As he scrambled topside, Motor Machinist's Mate Second Class Clayton Craig activated the boat's $CO_2$ fire extinguishing system, smothering the flames that were rolling across the engine compartment's forward bulkhead. It soon became apparent that the *PT-112* had been mortally wounded. With the lessons of the *PT-44* also fresh in his mind, Rollin Westholm immediately ordered the boat abandoned. Miraculously, no one had been killed by the two direct hits, and only Torpedoman Dollar received minor shrapnel wounds to one leg. All managed to climb aboard the boat's life raft after going over the side.

"By some miracle, or stroke of 'sea bean luck,' the Japs never fired again," Larson recalled. "As we were in the water, the Japs turned a searchlight on the boat and surrounding water, saw the boat was dead in the water and down at the stern, held their fire and left the scene."

Westholm and his crew paddled a fair distance away from the drifting *PT-112*, lest she attract the attention of another passing Japanese destroyer. After a half hour's time, Westholm decided that—quite literally—the coast was clear. The Tokyo Express had obviously retired for the night, and the *PT-112* was still afloat and adrift nearby. The order was given to return to the boat, but as the men in the raft drew near, the *112* was rocked by a sudden internal explosion and began to sink.

Having lost radio contact with their commander, the remaining boats initiated a hasty search for the *PT-112*. Westholm and his entire crew were rescued without further harm. The *112* continued to settle, finally going down as dawn broke over the eastern horizon. The searching PTs also picked up Charlie Tilden and all but two men from the *PT-43*. Torpedoman's Mate Second Class George Hartz of Denver and Motor Machinist's Mate Second Class Lawrence Mercer of Seattle were both listed as missing in action. Their bodies were never recovered. Motor Machinist's Mate Second Class Ray Lindberg of Des Moines, Iowa, would subsequently die from his wounds and be buried in the military cemetery overlooking Tulagi's White Beach.

The following morning while on a mission to sink the 250 supply drums still floating among the swells of Ironbottom Sound, Bart Connolly and the crew of *PT-115* spotted the wreck of *PT-43* washed up on the northwestern shore of Guadalcanal near the village of Aruligo, well behind enemy lines. When Connolly brought the *PT-115* close-in to check for survivors, Japanese machine guns on the beach opened fire. A brisk firefight ensued at close range, with Connolly withdrawing to Tulagi after Motor Machinist's Mate Charles Jump was felled by a bullet to the abdomen. Later that day, the *Kiwi* appeared off Aruligo and destroyed the *PT-43* with gunfire to prevent her from falling into enemy hands.

\*\*\*

"Guadalcanal is now hopeless," Rear Admiral Matome Ugaki confessed to the pages of his diary. "The 8th Area Army was said to have asked the reason for its receiving the directive to withdraw our positions at Guadalcanal in order to get ready for the next operation. What a slow perception they had!"

On January 9, 1943, the final plans for what would be the Japanese Dunkirk were finalized by the staffs of the Combined Fleet and the 8th Area Army. Operation *Ke-go*—the evacuation of all Japanese forces from Guadalcanal—would begin on the night of January 14–15, with destroyers landing a battalion of light infantry under the command of Major Keiji Yano on the shores of Cape Esperance. Yano's force was to be in position to act as rear guard by January 25, when Harukichi Hyakutake's 17th Army began their withdrawal from defensive positions in the island's interior to Cape Esperance. Any man too weak to make the long trek through the jungle to the evacuation point would be ordered to commit suicide "to uphold the honor of the Imperial Army."

The sick and starving remnants of the Guadalcanal garrison were to be taken off the island in three separate destroyer lifts, conducted over the first ten days of February. Twenty-one destroyers were assigned to the evacuation effort, escorted by two heavy cruisers and one light cruiser under Vice Admiral Gunichi Mikawa. A task force of two aircraft carriers, two battleships, four heavy cruisers, and numerous destroyers, under the command of Vice Admiral Nobutake Kondo, was to provide distant cover for the evacuation and, if possible, serve to distract Admiral Halsey's South Pacific Forces. Over 400 aircraft from the Imperial Army and Navy based at Rabaul and Bougainville would also take part, hoping to mount at least a temporary challenge to American air superiority in the region.

Despite the strength of its supporting forces, confidence in Operation *Ke-go* was not running high, even among those who framed the plan and endorsed its final form. Admiral Yamamoto predicted that half of Mikawa's destroyers would be lost and that a significant bite would be taken from the supporting air squadrons. Lieutenant Colonel Kumao Imoto, the officer charged with the unhappy task of delivering the evacuation order to 17th Army Headquarters on Guadalcanal, was met with fiercely stubborn resistance, even from officers surrounded by the decomposing bodies of their own soldiers.

In response to Imoto's pleas, General Hyakutake said reluctantly, "It is a very difficult task for the army to withdraw under existing circumstances. However, the orders of the Area Army, based upon orders of the Emperor, must be carried out at any cost. I cannot guarantee that it can be completely carried out."

# CHAPTER TEN

# 20,000 Souls

MAJOR KEIJI YANO'S BATTALION WAS BY NO MEANS AN ELITE FORMA-
tion of battle-hardened, professional soldiers. The provisional unit had
been activated on December 11, 1942, after 750 unassigned men were
drawn from the roster of the 230th Infantry Replacement Center in
Rabaul. Except for one of the three company commanders and a very
small number of noncommissioned officers—only two of whom would
be assigned to each rifle company—most had recently arrived in Rabaul
from mainland Japan and had no previous combat experience.

The *Yano Butai*, according to the diary of Petty Officer Sankichi
Kaneda of the Imperial Japanese Navy, "consisted of draftees averaging
32 years of age, poorly trained, lightly armed and in brand new uniforms."
Even Colonel Imoto, a former aide to Hideki Tojo who had super-
vised the experimental use of biological warfare agents against Chinese
civilians, struggled to hold back tears as he watched the newly formed
battalion of conscripts fall in for inspection prior to their departure. On
General Imamura's orders, these men were to be ruthlessly sacrificed,
forced to fight a delaying action against the advancing Americans on
Guadalcanal while the emaciated remnants of the once-proud 17th
Army were being evacuated.

On January 12, 1943, the Yano Battalion boarded the destroyers
*Urakaze*, *Tanikaze*, *Arashi*, *Akikumo*, and *Hamakaze* in Rabaul's Simpson Harbor and set sail for the Shortlands, arriving at Faisi Roads
on the morning of January 13. Despite their being hampered by bad
weather, Allied reconnaissance planes quickly discovered the newly

arrived destroyers at the Shortlands base. The following afternoon the five troop-laden destroyers departed for Guadalcanal, escorted by the *Kuroshio, Tokitsukaze,* and *Maikaze.* Rear Admiral Satsuma Kimura was in command.

American naval intelligence correctly deduced that "a Tokyo Express of eight DDs" was headed for Guadalcanal, but a dense band of rain squalls prevented air strikes on Kimura's destroyers and shielded them from the view of coastwatchers stationed on the islands flanking the Slot. Foul weather notwithstanding, Allen Calvert ordered all available PT boats to put to sea after sundown on January 14. A total of thirteen PTs were organized into two scouting groups and three striking forces under the tactical command of Rollin Westholm aboard *PT-109*. SOC Seagulls and PBY Black Cats were also sent aloft to aid in the search for the Tokyo Express. By the time the boats reached their assigned patrol sectors, Ironbottom Sound was completely socked in by violent thunderstorms producing heavy winds and pouring rain that reduced visibility at sea level to near zero.

At around midnight, Westholm decided to strike off to the northwest and search Sandfly Passage for the inbound Japanese column. A few minutes later a Pete float plane, whose pilot had decided to brave the dangerous gusts and low visibility, descended upon the darkened shape of the *PT-109* and released a bomb that dropped harmlessly into the sea off the boat's starboard quarter. Westholm broadcast a warning to all boats that Japanese float planes were in the area, and shortly afterward another Pete attacked Lieutenant John Clagett's *PT-37* and Les Gamble's *PT-45* southwest of Savo Island.

After missing with both of the 130-pound bombs it carried, the Pete dove on the *PT-37* with its two fixed 7.7-millimeter machine guns chattering. Sailors in the *PT-45*'s gun turrets returned fire with their much heavier .50-caliber Brownings and drove off the offending seaplane. The two boats then resumed their patrol, pitching and plunging in the heavy chop while a sustained wind of 22 knots sang through the halyards of their signal masts, the whipping rain and spray so intense that visibility was cut down to a few scant yards. Both boat captains made sure to keep a healthy distance from each other, not wanting to risk what would surely have been a disastrous collision. Suddenly the tempestuous seascape was brightened by the blue-white flash of a lightning bolt accompanied by the instantaneous crack of thunder, revealing the shadowy forms of five Japanese destroyers steaming eastward through the Savo-Esperance channel.

Amid the driving rain, brilliant flashes of lightning, sweeping search-lights, and blasting Japanese guns, both PTs closed with the enemy column and let fly with torpedoes. Johnny Clagett launched three toward the lead destroyer before wheeling the *PT-37* about and racing for Tulagi, the fourth fish still in its tube and rattling away on a hot run. While still firing upon the fleeing *37* boat, the destroyer executed a sharp high-speed turn and neatly combed the tracks of all three torpedoes.

A searchlight beam then fixated upon the *PT-45* just as Les Gamble began his torpedo run but was quickly extinguished by well-aimed bursts of machine gun fire. Gamble let go with two fish, both of which missed, before speeding northwest to make a clockwise sweep around Savo Island. Lightning soon revealed another Japanese destroyer steaming westward through the Sandfly Passage and blocking Gamble's path. That destroyer spotted the *PT-45* in turn and began firing her 5-inch main guns, forcing Gamble to turn south and attempt a counterclockwise run around the island. Suddenly there came a terrific jolt and a horrifying *crunch* as the *PT-45* ran aground. A few members of the crew were knocked about and bruised by the abrupt stop, and the boat's hull suffered significant damage, but the flooding was contained behind watertight doors. The following afternoon the *Bobolink* would haul the *45* boat off the reef.

The striking force made up of Stilly Taylor's *PT-46*, Hugh Robinson's *PT-47*, and Ensign Ralph Richards's *PT-123* also spotted the Japanese ships amid bursts of lightning and attacked with a total of six torpedoes. All of them missed, and the striking force was forced to retire in the face of heavy enemy fire. Bart Connolly's *PT-115* and the *PT-40*, skippered by Lieutenant Allen Harris, each attacked Kimura's destroyers independently with no result. Seeking to avoid the heavy fire of one pursuing destroyer, Clark Faulkner would also run the *PT-39* aground near the southern tip of Savo Island, but was able to back her clear and escape with only minor damage.

Despite the Ringbolt PT boats pressing home their attacks in the middle of a raging thunderstorm, Kimura's ships were able to successfully land Major Yano's entire battalion of 750 men onto the shores of Cape Esperance. The first phase of Operation *Ke-go* was complete. The evacuation of Japanese troops from Guadalcanal could now begin.

\*\*\*

Major General Alexander M. "Sandy" Patch had been in or around the US Army his entire life. He had been born at Fort Huachuca, a hot and dusty cavalry outpost in the Arizona Territory, tucked into the foothills along the Mexican border. Twenty years later, he followed in his father's footsteps to enter the US Military Academy at West Point. Graduating in 1913 and commissioned a second lieutenant of infantry, Patch was soon back in the deserts of the American Southwest, serving with the expeditionary force sent into Mexico to pursue the bandit Pancho Villa. When the United States entered the First World War, Patch sailed for France with the First Infantry Division and fought with distinction at the Marne, Saint-Mihiel, and the Meuse-Argonne.

Promoted to brigadier general shortly before the Japanese attack on Pearl Harbor, Patch was sent to Nouméa in March 1942. There he would organize the loose collection of army units defending New Caledonia into the 23rd Infantry Division, better known as the Americal Division, the name derived from a combination of "America" and "Caledonia." By the time the full complement of the Americal Division arrived on Guadalcanal, Patch was suffering badly from a case of viral pneumonia soon complicated by tropical dysentery and malaria, a combination of ailments that he would battle for the rest of his life.

Sandy Patch nevertheless soldiered on, ignoring all but the worst of the fever and weariness to lead his troops through one of the most grueling jungle campaigns in the US Army's history. Unlike some of his contemporaries, Patch was known as a modest, unselfish, and compassionate leader, a quiet and unassuming professional who avoided rough language and shunned publicity.

"Place the care and the protection of the men first; share their hardships without complaint and when the real test comes you will find that they possess genuine respect and admiration for you," Patch once wrote. "To do otherwise means failure at the crucial moment when the support of your men is essential to the success of battle, or maybe to the preservation of your own life."

Patch's relief of Vandegrift as commanding general of the Guadalcanal operation left him at the head of the US XIV Corps, which consisted of the Americal Division, the 25th "Tropic Lightning" Division from Hawaii, and the Second Marine Division. His objective, as Allied naval and air forces sought to seal off the island, was the final extermination of the Japanese 17th Army. On December 18, a series of infantry assaults was launched against a line of Japanese pillboxes and entrenchments on Mount Austen, a 1,500-foot rocky ridge 5 miles to the southwest of Lunga Point that dominated the Matanikau River basin. The attackers would encounter surprisingly stiff resistance and gain little ground, despite the severely debilitated condition of the defending Japanese.

After a brief tactical pause, Patch renewed the offensive on January 12, 1943, with the 25th Division attacking Japanese positions on Mount Austen and two adjoining ridges the GIs had nicknamed "The Seahorse" and "The Galloping Horse," due to the shape of their contours as seen on aerial reconnaissance photos. At the same time, the Second Marine Division mounted a westward drive along the coast of Guadalcanal toward the village of Kokumbona. Both prongs of the ground assault were supported by heavily concentrated artillery fire and air strikes from the Cactus Air Force.

Like all previous battles in the Guadalcanal campaign, the combat was ferocious and bloody, with isolated pockets of Japanese preferring to fight to the death rather than surrender. Mount Austen and environs were finally captured after eleven days of hard fighting that killed 175 Americans and between 1,100 and 1,500 Japanese. On January 28, the drive along the northern coast was unexpectedly slowed by the untried troops of the Yano Battalion, whom even the US Marines admitted were putting up a spirited defense.

\*\*\*

Admiral Bill Halsey and his staff did not expect the Japanese to evacuate Guadalcanal. Quite to the contrary, they were interpreting the recent uptick in enemy naval activity, including the concentration of shipping at Rabaul and the deployment of Kondo's carrier task force southward from Truk, as a signal that another all-out effort by the Japanese to reconquer Guadalcanal was in the offing.

"The enemy's obstinacy, the desperate plight of his troops on Guadalcanal, and the long lull since his last assault—long enough to replenish his carrier groups and task forces—all had led me to anticipate a final, supreme effort," Halsey wrote in his memoirs.

Intelligence analysts at Pacific Fleet Headquarters in Pearl Harbor agreed. "It is believed that a major attack on Guadalcanal is materializing," a staff officer recorded in the CINCPAC Running Estimate and Summary on January 31. "It may well be that enemy strength will surpass anything previously seen in this area."

Halsey ordered nearly all the naval forces at his disposal, which included the *Enterprise* and *Saratoga* carrier groups as well as two battleship task forces, to get underway from their bases in the New Hebrides and New Caledonia and take up station in the eastern Solomons to "await developments." The admiral also ordered explosive mines to be sown in the waters off the northwestern coast of Guadalcanal, in the spots most likely to serve as landing points for enemy reinforcements. Beginning at 8:00 a.m. on February 1, 1943, the destroyer-minelayers *Preble*, *Montgomery*, and *Tracy* deployed a total of 255 Mark 6 mines parallel to the shore between Doma Reef and the mouth of the Tenambo River near Cape Esperance.

Just after 2:00 p.m. that day, Cactus Control transmitted a high-priority radio message to all air and sea commands in the Guadalcanal-Tulagi area:

```
Coastwatcher reports 20 possible Dog Dogs 5 miles
north of Vella Lavella course east-southeast at
1320 local time.
```

As further intelligence was received, Commander Advanced Naval Base Cactus-Ringbolt issued a second alert at 5:30 p.m.:

```
Sixteen DD bearing 300 degrees true, distance
210, course 110, speed 25 at 1515 Love.
```

The original sighting report relayed by the Ferdinand coastwatcher was the more accurate in terms of the number of enemy ships. There were, in fact, twenty Japanese destroyers bearing down on Guadalcanal in two separate formations, led by Rear Admiral Shintaro Hashimoto flying his flag from the *Makinami*. One detachment of thirteen destroyers was destined for Cape Esperance, with the remaining seven bound for Kamimbo Bay. While Major Yano's green conscripts were busy fighting their brave rear guard action, 5,400 of General Hyakutake's depleted troops were leapfrogging westward to assemble at these two locations and await evacuation. It was the largest Tokyo Express run to date, and its arrival would trigger the bloodiest encounter with American PT boats in the Guadalcanal campaign.

The Cactus Air Force launched a total of ninety-two aircraft to attack the inbound Tokyo Express, including Dauntlesses, Avengers, Wildcats, Airacobras, Warhawks, and Lightnings—basically anything at Henderson Field that was capable of getting airborne and carrying ordnance. The destroyers *Fletcher*, *Radford*, and *Nichols* of Task Group 67.5, which had spent the day covering a shore-to-shore amphibious landing operation and fending off Japanese air attacks along Guadalcanal's northern coast, were ordered to proceed west and take up station between Savo and the Russells, where they would be in a position to launch torpedo attacks on the inbound Japanese columns.

The American planes hit the Tokyo Express in two waves, the first arriving at 6:20 p.m. as the Japanese ships passed to the south of New Georgia. While their fighter escort tangled with Hashimoto's combat air patrol of thirty Zeroes, dive bombers and torpedo planes bore down upon the writhing destroyers. The flagship *Makinami* was left badly damaged, her steering gear demolished by a bomb that exploded just off her fantail. Hashimoto instructed the *Fumizuki* to remain behind to assist, then shifted his flag to the *Shirayuki* before continuing east for the objective.

After dark, the destroyers of Task Group 67.5 were repeatedly buzzed by Japanese seaplane pilots hoping to draw the fire of their antiaircraft guns. The trick worked.

"Planes repeated harrassing tactics for the purpose of preventing an undetected approach on flanks of Tokyo Express DDs," read an entry in the *Fletcher*'s war diary. With their position now known to a much larger enemy force, the three destroyers could do little else but loiter to the south of the Savo-Russells line, reduced to spectators of the coming battle.

It would be up to the eleven seaworthy PT boats of Motor Torpedo Boat Flotilla One to face down the remaining eighteen destroyers of Hashimoto's eastbound Tokyo Express. At 7:00 p.m. Les Gamble's *PT-48* and Johnny Clagett's *PT-111* got underway for their patrol station 2 miles southwest of Savo Island. Bob Searles in the *PT-47* and Stilly Taylor's *PT-39* followed shortly thereafter, bound for their designated position 2 miles to the southeast of Savo in Ironbottom Sound. A striking force of three boats, led by Jack Searles in the *PT-59* followed by Bart Connolly's *PT-115* and Ensign Jim Kelly's *PT-37*, was instructed to lie in wait 3 miles northwest of Visale Point, a promontory on the extreme northwestern tip of Guadalcanal that formed Kamimbo Bay. The four remaining boats, Rollin Westholm's *PT-109*, Clark Faulkner's *PT-124*, Ralph Richards's *PT-123*, and Charlie Tilden's *PT-36*, were to form a skirmish line across the 9-mile-wide Savo-Esperance channel.

Japanese float planes were quick to discover the two PT boats skippered by Clagett and Gamble as they passed through Sandfly Passage. After dropping parachute flares to lighten the scene below, an Aichi E13A "Jake" attempted to strafe the *PT-48* and was fired upon by her machine gunners, their fiery red tracers curving through the night sky and just missing the tail section of the seaplane as it climbed away. Almost two hours later, at 9:50 p.m., another seaplane glided down the length of the *PT-111*'s neon-blue wake and released a bomb—probably one of the 500-pound variety—which missed by some 200 yards but produced a shock wave that tossed the two PT boats like toys in a bathtub.

Ten minutes after this nerve-wracking episode, Gamble and Clagett reached their assigned patrol sector and cut back to a slow cruising speed. Although a few scattered rain squalls were passing through, visibility was generally good, and just before 11:00 p.m. three Japanese destroyers were spotted in the distance. One was steering a southeasterly course 3 miles to the east of Cape Esperance; the other two were west of Savo Island and headed in the opposite direction. Gamble and Clagett decided to split up, with the *PT-111* going after the single destroyer while the *PT-48* attacked the homeward-bound pair.

Making a slow, methodical approach, Les Gamble closed to 900 yards before launching two torpedoes, both of which ran hot and straight but passed between the two Japanese ships. Gamble fired his remaining two fish, but before the results could be observed one of the destroyers opened fire and bracketed the *PT-48* with two rapid salvos from her main battery. As seawater rained down from the near misses, Gamble called for the smoke generator to be opened and turned the *PT-48* hard astarboard to reverse course.

"A steady rain of fire on his starboard bow from automatic weapons forced him to turn left towards Savo in order to avoid being trapped," read the MTB Flotilla One after-action report. "(Gamble) nosed in to the beach at Savo and gave the order to abandon ship, expecting the Japs to pick up the boat in searchlights and destroy it. The Japs failed to discover it and the boat was pulled off the beach and returned to base in the morning. No personnel casualties are reported."

In the meantime Johnny Clagett brought the *PT-111* to within 500 yards of the target and triggered two fish, then pressed on for another hundred yards before launching the remaining two. The destroyer, *Kawakaze*, suddenly veered hard to port, switching on her powerful searchlights and opening fire with every gun that could be brought to bear. A salvo of 5-inch shells ripped through the air, slamming into the little wooden boat like a giant sledgehammer and stopping her dead in her tracks. The *PT-111* was instantly wreathed in flames. Clagett found himself sprawled on the deck with his face and hands badly burned, but somehow managed to drag himself to the side and drop into the churning sea.

Several of the *111* crew were already in the water, having been hurled overboard by the tremendous impact and explosion. Torpedoman's Mate Merle Elsass and the boat's cook, Walter Long, grabbed onto the helpless Lieutenant Clagett and struck out for Savo Island. As they swam clear of the blazing PT boat, Ensign A. E. White and Fireman Second Class Lamar Loggins came across Russell Wackler, the boat's twenty-four-year-old radioman from New York City, floating helplessly in his kapok jacket with both legs mangled by compound fractures.

Blood flowing from Wackler's grievous wounds soon attracted the attention of the man-eating sharks that inhabited Ironbottom Sound. That might have been terrifying enough to cause any man to abandon a dying shipmate, but White and Loggins did not. For over two hours they stayed by Wackler's side, kicking and punching at the hard, blunt nose of every curious predator that drew near. Wackler eventually lost consciousness, and by the time White and Loggins were able to get him onto the beach at Savo Island, the young sailor was dead.

The three-boat element led by Jack Searles arrived off Visale Point at 9:40 p.m. and spent the next hour fighting off a series of bombing and strafing attacks by low-swooping Japanese float planes. The tactics employed were the same used against the destroyers of Task Group 67.5, with returned gunfire and floating flares revealing the position of the PT striking force to the Tokyo Express. The attacks also caused the three boats to scatter, and they were no longer in visual contact with one another. From the bridge of the *PT-59*, Jack Searles saw the silhouette of a *Yugumo*-class destroyer appear against the backdrop of stars on the western horizon. It was quickly followed by another . . . and then another. Searles told his XO, Al Snowball, that he could see at least a dozen enemy ships.

Snowball, who would later admit to Searles that he had memorized the standardized eye chart in order to pass his commissioning physical, scanned the surrounding sea with binoculars.

"There aren't any Jap cans out there," the XO told Searles. "You must be getting jumpy."

"Hell, skipper," snapped Quartermaster Harold Johnson. "I count the same dozen you do without the binoculars."

The Japanese ships were arrayed in a great arch, hemming the three PTs against the coast of Guadalcanal. Searles was able to escape the trap by steering the *PT-59* undetected into a fast-moving rain squall, while Connolly was forced to fight his way out. The young ensign ran the *PT-115* eastward through a torrent of enemy fire, launching two torpedoes at a destroyer before reversing course under a smoke screen. As the boat sped along the coast of Savo Island, another Japanese ship materialized out of the darkness 2,000 yards ahead.

Connolly fired his two remaining fish at this new target, then swung the *115* boat into another 180-degree turn and cut back the throttles to reduce the boat's wake. The Japanese gunfire grew increasingly sporadic and inaccurate. Connolly considered abandoning the boat and having the crew swim for Savo Island, but then detected a freshening breeze.

"Hold on," Connolly told his men, "I think there's a squall coming. We're going to make for the squall for cover."

Connolly steered the *PT-115* slowly west along the coast of Savo, the misty rain effectively masking the boat from passing enemy destroyers. After carefully inching the *PT-115* onto the beach, Connolly and his crew waited for the dawn of February 2 to arrive before heading back to Tulagi.

Little is known of the final actions of Jim Kelly and the crew of *PT-37*. While attempting to run the gaunlet of Japanese destroyers, the *37* boat received a direct hit, most likely in the compartment housing the three 1,000-gallon tanks of aviation gasoline. According to the after-action report, "The brilliant, blinding flash of the explosion lit up the whole sky in the vicinity of Cape Esperance." The drifting hulk of the *PT-37* would burn to the waterline before sinking 2 miles southeast of Savo Island. Motor Machinist's Mate First Class Eldon Jenter of Minneapolis would be the sole survivor of the crew, later rescued from the water suffering from severe burns and shrapnel wounds.

At 10:49 p.m., Clark Faulkner aboard *PT-124* spotted a Japanese destroyer heading east through the Savo-Esperance channel. Signaling for Ralph Richards to follow with the *PT-123*, Faulkner made a slow approach and from a distance of 1,000 yards sent three torpedoes streaking for the target. Lookouts aboard the *Makigumo* quickly spotted the bubbling wakes of the inbound torpedoes. Her captain, Commander Isamu Fujita, rang up flank speed and called for the helm to be put hard over. The *Makigumo* managed to avoid all three of Faulkner's torpedoes, but ran headlong into one of the sea mines deployed that very morning by the three American minelayers.

The resulting explosion killed three men aboard the *Makigumo* and wounded seven; two more were tossed into the sea and never seen again. Seawater poured through the gaping hole left in the *Makigumo*'s hull, and the destroyer quickly took on a heavy list. A tow line was passed over from the *Yugumo*, but the effort was aborted when it became obvious that *Makigumo* was destined for the floor of Ironbottom Sound. *Yugumo* would later scuttle her sister ship with a torpedo after taking off 237 survivors.

Faulkner was quite unaware of it at the time, but his causing the *Makigumo* to steer into a mine and eventually sink had served to at least partially avenge a war crime. The destroyer had been present at the Battle of Midway, where on the afternoon of June 4, 1942, she recovered the crew of a downed *Enterprise* SBD. After a tortuous interrogation, Ensign Frank O'Flaherty and Aircraft Machinist's Mate First Class Bruno Gaido were tied to heavy weights and thrown overboard. Had he not been killed later in the war, Fujita would have surely been tried for the murder of the two American prisoners and met his fate at the end of a rope.

While Faulkner was stalking the *Makigumo*, Ralph Richards had been likewise setting his sights upon the *Yugumo* when a Pete swooped out of the darkened sky and planted a bomb squarely onto the fantail of the *PT-123*. Motor Machinist's Mate Second Class Leonard Sileo was killed instantly, and the *123* boat immediately burst into flames and began to settle by the stern. Richards then ordered his men over the side, a quick head count revealing that three members of the crew besides Sileo were missing. Three more had been seriously wounded.

The remaining four boats in the Savo-Esperance channel were unable to engage the enemy ships or fire their torpedoes. "At dawn they assisted in recovering survivors and personnel," the after-action report concluded. "Taylor recovered three enemy landing scows with outboard motors attached. The scows appeared to have been hurredly abandoned and contained Jap rifles, knapsacks and personal effects. Documents were forwarded to Commanding General Cactus on 2 February, 1943."

\*\*\*

The furious and costly battle between American PT boats and the Imperial Japanese Navy on the night of February 1, 1943, would be the last of the Guadalcanal campaign. Three PT boats had been sunk and two moderately damaged. Six men had been killed and another six seriously wounded. Nine would be listed as missing in action and later declared dead.

On their first evacuation run, which cost them a destroyer, the Tokyo Express succeeded in rescuing 4,935 Japanese soldiers from Guadalcanal. "They wore only the remains of clothes," said Admiral Koyanagi, describing the wasted men that were brought aboard his flagship. "Their physical deterioration was extreme. Probably they were happy but they showed no expression. All had dengue or malaria, and their diarrhea sent them to the heads. Their digestive organs were so completely destroyed, we couldn't give them good food, only porridge."

The PT boats would remain in Tulagi over the night of February 5, when Japanese destroyers embarked another 3,921 men at Cape Esperance. A final evacuation lift was conducted just after midnight on February 8.

"With the help of 20,000 souls, the recovery of 1,972 men from Guadalcanal is reported complete," was the message broadcast to Rabaul by Colonel Iwao Matsuda of the 17th Army, referring to the total number of Japanese soldiers that had perished since the campaign began. Of the nearly 11,000 evacuees, 600 would die before reaching definitive medical care and another 3,000 were so ravaged by the lasting effects of disease and malnutrition that they would never fight again.

"Guadalcanal is no longer merely a name of an island in Japanese military history," General Kiyotake Kawaguchi of the 35th Infantry Brigade would remark. "It is the name of the graveyard of the Japanese Army."

On the morning of February 9, American troops pushed as far west as the coastal village of Tenaro. No resistance was encountered along the way, and only a few shockingly emaciated Japanese were found, left to die among the countless corpses that lay beside the beaten footpaths.

Numerous pillboxes and foxholes were manned only by the dead. Strewn about the jungle, in the clearings and on the beaches, were discarded rifles, helmets, packs, uniforms, bandages, ration bags, makeshift litters, and a myriad of personal gear—the scattered detritus of a beaten army.

That afternoon, General Patch had a message transmitted to Admiral Halsey:

```
Total and complete defeat of Japanese forces
on Guadalcanal effected 1625 today. The Tokyo
Express no longer has a terminus on Guadalcanal.
```

# Epilogue

## CARTWHEEL AND JACK KENNEDY

In the wake of the Allied victory at Guadalcanal, General Douglas MacArthur submitted to the Joint Chiefs of Staff his plan for the continued prosecution of the war against Japan. Codenamed Operation Cartwheel, the plan called for his Southwest Pacific Forces to conduct a series of leapfrogging assaults to rout the Japanese from their lodgments on the northern coast of New Guinea, establish a beachhead at Cape Gloucester on New Britain to secure the Dampier Strait, and seize the Admiralty Islands.

Cartwheel also called for Admiral Halsey's South Pacific Forces to make a simultaneous thrust into the heart of the Solomon Islands to capture the New Georgia archipelago and eventually the big island of Bougainville. The ultimate objective of Operation Cartwheel, which was approved by the Joint Chiefs on March 28, 1943, was to isolate the Japanese bastion of Rabaul and secure advanced bases to support a northward advance toward the Philippines.

Halsey had already taken the step of occupying the Russells, 25 miles up the Slot to the west of Guadalcanal, where the Third Marine Raider Battalion and the army's 43rd Infantry Division landed unopposed on February 21. That operation yielded sites for another airfield and naval base on the island of Mbanika, which would include a forward operating point for PT boats. Having proven their ability to disrupt naval bombardment missions and harrass enemy supply lines during the fight for Guadalcanal, PT boats would be an integral part of the planning for future offensive operations in the Central Solomons.

The invasion of New Georgia, the key objective of which was the seizure of the Japanese airfield at Munda Point, was set for June 30, 1943. In addition to landings on the main island, the lightly defended Rendova would also be taken. Rendova was positioned to the south of Munda across the 7-mile-wide Blanche Channel, and would serve as a base for artillery in support of the assault on the airfield. A string of barrier islets along Rendova's northern coast was also being eyed as a potential spot for another PT base.

While preparations for the New Georgia operation were underway, Sesapi was being transformed into a more permanent rear echelon naval base. Steel marston matting was laid down over the muddy avenues, and the Seabees were hard at work building warehouses, an engine overhaul facility, a torpedo shop, an infirmary, and last but certainly not least, an officer's club. A more elaborate base housing area, which the PT sailors quickly dubbed "Calvertville," was established just across the narrow channel on Florida Island. A concrete dock on the nearby islet of Macambo that had once served as home to the interisland steamer *Mamutu* was taken over, providing additional berthing space for PTs. That February, another four-boat division from MTBRON 6 arrived in Tulagi Harbor, along with five boats and their crews recently detached from MTBRON 8 and assigned to MTBRON 2.

The MTB command structure was also undergoing a significant expansion. In late January, Captain Marcy Dupre Jr. was detached from his billet as XO of the battleship *Indiana* and appointed Commander Motor Torpedo Boat Squadrons South Pacific Force. Dupre immediately set about clearing the logistical logjam that had been plaguing the PT squadrons ever since their arrival in the combat theater, and started badly needed supplies, equipment, spare parts, and base force personnel flowing to Tulagi. Commander Allen Calvert, in the meantime, was taking advantage of the lull in the fighting to finally build a headquarters staff for MTB Flotilla One. Calvert named Hugh Robinson as his material officer in charge of repairs and modifications to the boats, and placed Rollin Westholm in charge of operations. Jack Searles was subsequently made commanding officer of MTBRON 3, with his brother Bob as his XO, while Allen Harris took over command of MTBRON 2.

With Westholm's appointment as the Flotilla operations officer, full-time command of the *PT-109* was passed on to Bryant Larson, a billet he would occupy until April 26, 1943, when he was relieved by a twenty-five-year-old lieutenant junior grade from Massachusetts named John Fitzgerald Kennedy.

***

Like the elder of the two Searles brothers, he was known as "Jack" to his family and friends. Kennedy was born into an affluent Irish-Catholic family in the Boston suburb of Brookline in 1917, the second of nine children. His father, Joseph P. Kennedy Sr., had been general manager of the Bethlehem Steel shipyard in Weymouth Fore River during the First

World War, during which time he made the acquaintance of then–Assistant Secretary of the Navy Franklin D. Roosevelt.

After gaining the White House, Roosevelt appointed Joseph Sr. to lead the fledgling Securities and Exchange Commission and then the US Maritime Commission before naming him ambassador to Great Britain in 1938. An outspoken supporter of Nelville Chamberlain's appeasement of Nazi Germany, Joseph Sr. would soon develop a contentious relationship with Chamberlain's successor, Winston Churchill. His fervent isolationism and public criticism of the Churchill government would also cause him to fall out of favor with Roosevelt, who recalled the elder Kennedy in the fall of 1940.

Since 1928, the Kennedy family maintained a summer home at Hyannis Port on the shores of Cape Cod, where young Jack and his siblings learned the sport of sailing. Upon entering Harvard in 1936, Jack joined the day sailing team and that same year won the Nantucket Sound Star Championship. After graduating *cum laude* from Harvard in 1940, and with America's entry into the war appearing imminent, Kennedy applied for the US Army Officer Candidate School. He was rejected due to a long history of health issues, which included scarlet fever, asthma, gastrointestinal ailments, and a lingering back injury suffered while playing football at Harvard. With the help of his father's former naval attaché, Captain Allan Kirk, Kennedy was accepted by the Naval Reserve after being certified to be in good health by a private physician. Commissioned an ensign in October 1941, Kennedy was assigned to the Office of Naval Intelligence (ONI) at Main Navy in Washington.

The following January, Kennedy was suddenly transferred to the 6th Naval District in Charleston, South Carolina, after it was discovered that he had been having a romantic affair with the Danish American screenwriter and Hollywood gossip columnist Inga Arvad. A personal guest of Adolf Hitler at the 1936 Summer Games in Munich, the fetching blonde Arvad was being investigated by the FBI as a possible Nazi spy. The allegation was later deemed false, but the scandal irreparably damaged Kennedy's standing within the ONI. Joseph Sr. once again intervened on his son's behalf, arranging a meeting at his New York City offices with

Commander John Bulkeley, who by then had become a national hero and was serving as a recruiting officer for the Mosquito Fleet.

Impressed by the young ensign's carriage, intelligence, and extensive experience in handling small craft, Bulkeley arranged for Kennedy to be transferred to the Motor Torpedo Boat Training Center in Melville. Kennedy achieved high marks during the training course, after which he was promoted to lieutenant (jg) in command of the Huckins-built *PT-101* and retained in Melville for a short time as an instructor assigned to MTBRON 4. In January 1943, the *PT-101* along with her captain and crew was reassigned to the Panama Canal Zone. A month later Jack Kennedy would bargain for and manage to receive—against the express wishes of his father—a combat assignment.

Once at Tulagi, Lieutenant Kennedy would find the well-worn *PT-109* in need of a great deal of care and attention after having endured the worst of the Guadalcanal campaign. Along with Bryant Larson, most of the original crew of the *109* was being rotated back to the States. Their replacements were a mix of seasoned PT sailors transferred from other boats and a number of inexperienced rookies fresh from the training school in Melville. The next month would be spent restoring the *PT-109* to shipshape and getting the newly formed crew working together as a cohesive and disciplined team. During this period the *109* participated in a few night security patrols in Ironbottom Sound and the Savo-Esperance area, all of which were uneventful.

On May 30, the boats of 'RON 2 were moved to the new staging base in the Russells located on the shores of Sunlight Channel, which separates the two main islands of Mbanika and Pavuvu. There the PT officers were comfortably quartered in an abandoned Lever Brothers plantation house and continued performing routine security patrols, most of which were tedious but for the occasional close encounter with a prowling Japanese float plane. In late June the *109* was assigned to the new PT base at Lumbaria Island, a tiny spit of jungle-covered coral on the northern coast of Rendova, and began conducting combat patrols in support of the New Georgia landings.

In addition to intercepting the Japanese destroyers that ventured into New Georgian waters at night, the PT boats were soon taking on a new role—that of barge hunter. With command of the sea now in Allied hands, the Japanese were growing increasingly reluctant to use their steadily dwindling number of destroyers for supply missions. In order to deliver food, ammunition, and other badly needed supplies to their embattled troops on New Georgia, the Japanese were making extensive use of motorized Daihatsu barges.

Being easy targets for Allied aircraft, the slow-moving barges operated only by night and hid beneath the jungle canopy of coastal estuaries and inlets during the day. Heavily armored, they were for the most part impervious to the standard weapons carried by PT boats, and their draft was much shallower than the minimum depth setting of a torpedo. The barges were themselves armed with a dangerous array of automatic weapons and anti-boat cannon, and more than one crew of an attacking PT had been appalled to find themselves outgunned by a lumbering Daihatsu scow.

In response, the US Navy began upgrading the armament of their PTs. Several boats, including the *PT-109*, had their stern-mounted 20-millimeter Oerlikon autocannon replaced with a heavier Swedish-designed 40-millimeter Bofors, loaded with armor-piercing ammunition capable of punching through the reinforced steel hull of a Japanese barge. Kennedy's crew also managed to obtain an army 37-millimeter anti-tank gun, which they lashed to the *PT-109*'s foredeck.

On the afternoon of August 1, 1943, a column of four destroyers, *Arashi, Shigure, Hagikaze, and Amagiri*, were spotted to the north of Bougainville on a course for the New Georgias. Embarked on the four destroyers was a battalion of infantry along with 70 tons of supplies bound for the island of Kolombangara. From there the soldiers would be ferried by barge to New Georgia, then marched overland into the front lines at Munda. Kolombangara is an almost perfectly round island, 19 miles in diameter and dominated by an extinct 5,800-foot stratovolcano, lying 10 miles to the northwest of New Georgia across the Kula Gulf. Separating Kolombangara from its neighbor to the south, Kohinggo, is a narrow channel known as the Blackett Strait, 17 miles long and averaging less than a mile wide.

A "Condition Red" message was flashed to the PT base at Lumbaria from the flagship of Vice Admiral Theodore Wilkinson, Commander Task Force 31, ordering "all available Peter Tares" to get underway. Before that could happen, a formation of eighteen Japanese bombers struck Lumbaria, sinking PTs *117* and *164* at their berth and killing two sailors. Despite this setback, by the time the sun set at 6:45 p.m. a total of fifteen PTs were at sea, dispersed throughout the waters of Blackett Strait to await the arrival of the Tokyo Express. The boats deployed in four separate divisions, one of which consisted of PTs *159, 157, 162,* and John F. Kennedy's *PT-109*.

\*\*\*

At 2:30 a.m. on August 2, the *PT-109* was idling slowly on one engine in the middle of Blackett Strait just to the northwest of Ferguson Passage, a narrow channel between two sprawling coral reefs that led to the open Solomon Sea. Jack Kennedy was at the wheel. Beside him in the cockpit were his XO, Ensign Leonard Thom, Quartermaster Ed Mauer, and Radioman John Maguire. On the forecastle was Ensign George "Barney" Ross, whose *PT-166* had been sunk two weeks earlier in a friendly fire incident involving a pair of army B-25s. Not wanting to miss out on what would be one of the largest PT actions of the Pacific War, Ross had asked Kennedy if he could accompany the crew of the *109* on the mission. The remaining crew were either taking their turn standing watch or sprawled on the warm wooden deck, trying to snatch a few moments of sleep.

Several miles off to port was the ink-black cone of Kolombangara's Mount Veve, and somewhere out in the gloom nearby were PTs *162* and *169*, their softly gurgling motors barely audible across the dark water. It was the beginning of the new moon phase, and an unbroken ceiling of clouds completely blotted out the light of the stars. The intense blackness of the tropical night was so heavy and oppressive that it seemed to border on the supernatural, broken only by occasional flashes of distant lightning.

Captain Kaju Sugiure, the officer in tactical command of the Tokyo Express reinforcement mission, had already led his destroyers down the western side of Kolombangara and into Blackett Strait, bound for Vila

Plantation on the southeastern tip of the island. At around midnight the SO-type radar of the *PT-159*, skippered by Lieutenant Henry Brantingham, detected the four vessels as they skirted south along the coastline. Guessing that the targets were Daihatsu barges, Brantingham began closing the distance and told his gunners to prepare to open fire. Following closely behind Brantingham's boat was the *PT-157*. The barge theory was quickly dispelled after the destroyers turned on their searchlights and unlimbered their main batteries. The two PT boats hurriedly launched half a dozen torpedoes at the Japanese ships before running south behind a smokescreen. All the torpedoes missed.

As the destroyers proceeded east by northeast through the Blackett Strait at high speed, they were attacked in turn by six individual PTs that fired a total of two dozen torpedoes without scoring a single hit. For the PT boats on this particular night, the only thing lacking more than their marksmanship was their communications. Kennedy and the crew of the *PT-109* were able to hear a few fragmented radio exchanges between boats as they pressed home their attacks, but no one had bothered to broadcast a proper contact report describing the type, position, course, or speed of the Japanese ships. In the confusion the PT divisions had become widely scattered, with the stray *169* joining up with the *162* and Kennedy's *109*. Brantingham's *PT-159*, the only one of the original four-boat section equipped with radar, was returning to base after expending her torpedoes.

The Tokyo Express arrived at the mouth of Vila's Disappointment Cove at 12:30 a.m., where the *Arashi*, *Shigure*, and *Hagikaze* slowed to a creeping pace and lowered their cargo nets. Soon 900 soldiers were scrambling down the nets and into the landing barges that swarmed alongside the three destroyers, while crates of supplies were being lowered over the side. The escort destroyer *Amagiri* kept station a short distance away, ready to fend off any further attacks by American torpedo boats. A tense hour passed before the job was finally finished. Captain Sugiure, not wanting to run the risk of encountering American cruisers in the open waters of Kula Gulf, signaled for his destroyers to double-back through Blackett Strait. Forming another loose column, they steamed westward through the narrow channel at flank speed, with *Amagiri* in the van.

***

"Ship at two'oclock!" shouted Harold Marney, one of the *109*'s machinists manning the forward gun turret. Shooting a glance off to starboard, Kennedy could just make out the ghostly black form of a surface vessel, which he believed at first to be another PT boat wandering about in the dark. In the space of only a few seconds, it became horrifyingly clear that it was not. Out on the forecastle, Barney Ross grabbed a 37-millimeter shell and tried to load the anti-tank gun.

"Lenny," Kennedy said to Thom, dozing beside him in a cockpit chair. "Lenny, look at this!"

It was the *Amagiri*, bearing down on the *PT-109* with a blue phosphorescent wave cresting alongside her towering steel hull. The *109* was still running on only one muffled engine at a dead-slow speed. Kennedy's reflexes told him to crank the wheel hard right in order to bring the boat's torpedo tubes to bear, but the range was already too close for the fish to arm themselves. The *PT-109* responded to the helm slowly, haltingly, as if reluctant to face the violent end that she knew was coming.

"General Quarters," Kennedy ordered at the last moment, the words repeated in a shout by Maguire, which jolted the sleeping crew members awake. Gazing up at the onrushing bow of the destroyer, the twenty-seven-year-old radioman clutched the Catholic talisman suspended on a chain around his neck.

"O Mary, conceived without sin . . . "

The *Amagiri* rammed the *PT-109* in the starboard side amidships at over 30 knots, cleaving the little wooden boat in two. Harold Marney was killed instantly, as was Torpedoman's Mate Second Class Andrew Kirksey, standing at his battle station beside the starboard aft torpedo tube. Everyone else was either thrown overboard or onto the pitching deck, including Kennedy, who watched the monstrous steel hull of the destroyer slide past just a few feet from his head. Gasoline spilled from the boat's ruptured fuel tanks and onto the surrounding water, where it readily ignited with a bright flash. As the *Amagiri* steamed indifferently on and vanished into the night, her roiling wake carried away the burning gasoline, a strange quirk of fate that undoubtedly saved many of the *109* crew from a gruesome death.

The severed stern section of the *PT-109* quickly took on water and sank, dragged down by the tremendous weight of the three Packard engines. The larger bow portion still remained afloat, with its internal watertight compartments grossly intact. Kennedy tried to shake off the effects of the collision and regain his bearings, then set to work accounting for his crew. Three men were still with him on the bow section, and they could hear the voices of others calling out from the surrounding water.

"Mr. Kennedy! Mr. Kennedy!" Gunner's Mate Charles "Bucky" Harris shouted from across the water. "McMahon is burned bad!"

Kennedy slid into the water and swam in the direction of Harris's voice. Motor Machinist's Mate First Class Patrick "Pappy" McMahon, who at the age of thirty-seven was the oldest man on the crew, had been at his station in the engine room when the collision occurred. After being engulfed by a flash fire, McMahon was suffering from second and third degree burns on his face and all four limbs—over 60 percent of his body. Kennedy grasped the straps of McMahon's life jacket and towed him to the floating portion of the boat. Then he returned for Harris, who had injured his leg after being hurled against a torpedo tube.

"Skipper, I can't swim," gasped the struggling Harris.

"You've got to try," Kennedy told him.

"I can't!" Harris replied.

"You know what, Harris?" Kennedy said in a stern voice. "For a guy from Boston, you're sure putting up a great exhibition out here."

The harsh rebuke from his skipper seemed to snap the young sailor from his panic, and Harris managed to dog-paddle the rest of the way to the floating wreckage. It would take over three hours, but Kennedy was finally able to gather his scattered crew and get them aboard the still-buoyant bow section by sunrise. Three officers and eight men had survived the collision with the Japanese destroyer. Many were nursing painful injuries or retching violently after nearly drowning in gasoline-tinged seawater.

The shattered remains of the *PT-109* continued to drift steadily southward with the current in Blackett Strait, in the direction of the enemy-occupied islands of Kolombangara and Ghizo. Kennedy was puzzled as to why the other PTs did not move in to rescue the *109*'s survivors, unaware that the sound of the collision and the dramatic explosion that followed had led them to believe there weren't any. Around 1:00 p.m., with no rescue in sight, Kennedy made the decision to abandon the hulk and swim for land before darkness fell and the waterlogged bow section finally sank.

Kennedy was an exceptionally strong swimmer, having lettered in swimming at Harvard (one of his varsity teammates, incidentally, had been future war correspondent Richard Tregaskis). Using the breast-stroke, and with the straps of McMahon's life jacket clenched in his teeth, Kennedy began towing the badly burned sailor toward Plum Pudding Island, a tiny speck of land about three and a half miles away on the western side of the Ferguson Passage. The rest of the crew followed, grasping onto one of the timbers that had once supported the boat's 37-millimeter gun. Four hours later, the shipwrecked crew of the *PT-109* finally crawled over the jagged coral reef and onto the narrow beach, then gained the cover of trees where they collapsed in utter exhaustion.

That night Kennedy swam another 2 miles into the Ferguson Passage with the boat's salvaged battle lantern wrapped in a life jacket. Kennedy had hoped to signal a patrolling PT boat but none passed near him, and after several hours of treading water he returned to the island. On the night of August 3 Barney Ross gave it a try, with similar results.

There was no food or fresh water to be had on Plum Pudding Island. On August 4, Kennedy and Thom decided to make another swim for Olasana Island, another 3.5 miles farther south. Once again Kennedy towed the helpless McMahon through the water, while Thom and the crew held onto the timber and followed in their wake. On Olasana they found coconuts, their first nourishment in three days, and that night the men were able to capture rainwater using the broad leaves of jungle bushes.

The following afternoon, Kennedy and Ross decided to reconnoiter nearby Nauru Island, half a mile closer to the Ferguson Passage, in the hope of signaling a passing PT boat from its shores. On the reef at Nauru they found a wrecked and abandoned Japanese barge, along with a box containing biscuits and hard candy, a cask of drinking water, and a small one-man dugout canoe. While exploring the barge, they spotted two Melanesian natives in their own dugout canoe at a fair distance out to sea. The natives quickly paddled away, fearing that the sunburnt, ragged men on the beach might be Japanese soldiers.

As it turned out, the two Melanesians were Biuku Gasa and Eroni Kumana, native scouts in the employ of Lieutenant Reg Evans, an Australian coastwatcher stationed on Kolombangara. In the early morning of August 2, Evans witnessed the fireball that signaled the destruction of the PT boat from his mountaintop hideout and later that day observed the hulk through field glasses as it drifted southward through the Blackett Strait. Receiving a radio message confirming that the *PT-109* had been lost, Evans dispatched his scouts to comb the islets along the Ferguson Passage for possible survivors.

After observing Kennedy and Ross on the beach at Nauru, the two scouts made their way to the shores of Olasana, where Lenny Thom managed to convince them that the shipwrecked party was, in fact, made up of Americans. Later that day Kennedy returned to Olasana in the one-man canoe with a cache of food and drinking water for his men, and was properly introduced to Gasa and Kumana. In a bit of duplicated effort, Thom composed a note for Gasa to carry to Allied forces, using a blank message form and pencil stub that Maguire had found in one of his pockets. Kennedy used a sheath knife to carve a similar message on the husk of a coconut:

*NAURU ISL COMMANDER NATIVE KNOWS POSIT HE CAN PILOT 11 ALIVE NEED SMALL BOAT KENNEDY*

The following day Gasa and Kumana struck out for the island of Vona Vona, 12 miles to the east across the Ferguson Passage, where they informed Sergeant Benjamin Kevu of their discovery. The senior scout directed them to proceed to Rendova with Kennedy's message and sent another scout to Evans's new station on the island of Gomu to deliver the news. On August 7, the stranded crew of *PT-109* awoke to the sight of two canoes bearing Kevu and six other men, along with drinking water, yams, rice, cooked fish, canned hash, and cigarettes. The smiling Kevu handed a message to Lieutenant Kennedy:

*On His Majesty's Service*

*To Senior Officer, Nauru Island*

*Friday 11 PM Have just learnt of your presence on Nauru Is. and also that two natives have taken news to Rendova. I strongly advise your return to here in this canoe and by the time you arrive here I will be in radio communication with authorities at Rendova and we can finalize plans to collect balance your party.*

*A.R. Evans Lt.*

Following the coastwatcher's advice, Jack Kennedy traveled to Gomu in a canoe paddled by native scouts. Because the route was heavily trafficked by Japanese planes, Kennedy spent the entire voyage lying on the bottom of the canoe covered by palm fronds. At his Gomu hideout, Evans poured Kennedy a cup of tea and together they devised a plan for the rescue mission, which Evans then radioed to Rendova. At 10:00 p.m. on August 8, the *PT-157* retrieved Jack Kennedy, who was waiting aboard a native canoe just off the beach at Gomu, then proceeded for Olasana.

A half hour later, the executive officer of the *PT-109* heard a voice with a distinct Boston accent calling to him over the rumbling of the surf. "Hey, Lenny! Lenny! Where are you?"

Emerging from their makeshift jungle shelter, the castaways saw their skipper approaching the beach in a rubber boat. Standing just offshore were PTs *157* and *171*. After seven long days, their harrowing ordeal was finally over.

\*\*\*

Jack Kennedy emerged from the hospital on Tulagi two weeks later, after receiving treatment for dehydration, malnutrition, and infected lacerations to both feet. Kennedy had always been slender, but now looked painfully gaunt and weary. His fragile digestive tract had once again decided to revolt, and the jarring collision with the Japanese destroyer had aggravated his old back injury.

Despite all that he had been through, Kennedy declined the standard navy "survivor's leave" and decided to stay on at Tulagi to await another command. His new squadron commander, Lieutenant Commander Alvin Cluster, agreed to make Kennedy the skipper of *PT-59* once he regained his health. The boat that Jack Searles had used to sink the *I-3* was to be stripped of her torpedo tubes and converted into a floating gun platform for sinking Japanese barges.

Cluster also recommended Kennedy for the Silver Star in recognition of his bravery and leadership after the sinking of *PT-109*. The story had already appeared in the headlines of major newspapers across the United States, hailing the former ambassador's son as a hero. A stirring account of the *PT-109* incident by the celebrated author John Hersey was also published in the *New Yorker*.

"We were kind of ashamed of our performance," admitted Barney Ross. "I had always thought it was a disaster, but Hersey made it sound pretty heroic, like Dunkirk."

Kennedy was eventually decorated for his role in the incident, but the award was downgraded by the navy brass from the Silver Star to the Navy and Marine Corps Medal. For many of Kennedy's fellow officers, the story of the *PT-109* sinking left more questions than answers. A few wondered aloud why Kennedy had been running on only one engine in the middle of the channel, and why his crew had not been fully on the alert. Even General MacArthur chimed in, expressing the opinion that Kennedy should be court-martialed rather than cited for bravery.

"What I really want to know," wrote Jack's older brother Joseph Jr. in a scathing letter, "is where the hell were you when the destroyer hove into sight, and exactly what were your moves?"

After being discharged from the hospital on Tulagi, Jack Kennedy shared a tent with Lieutenant Ted Robinson, who had been aboard the

*PT-157* on the night Kennedy and his crew were rescued. The two had become good friends, and one evening Kennedy expressed to Robinson his frustration over such intense criticism.

"Robbie, I'm a nobody," Kennedy said. "But my father was ambassador to the Court of St. James in England and I have a lot of experience with reporters. They're going to say 'How in the hell could this happen?' They're going to say it years after the war, in a nice well-lit room back in Miami Beach, writing a book, wanting to make $100,000."

"But what am I going to do?" Kennedy went on. "I'm going to put them in a perfectly dark room, just like it was in the Blackett Strait. Then I am going to take their camera and their flash bulbs and flash them in the face, just like we were blinded with lighting and gunfire. Then I am going to twist them around, like how we maneuvered in position so we were all confused, and then I am going to pick up a chair and hit them with it and then say 'Now you figure it out, you son of a bitch.'"

A board of inquiry was convened—standard protocol after the loss of a naval vessel—which failed to find sufficient evidence of negligence or misconduct to bring charges against Lieutenant Kennedy. He would go on to command the *PT-59* and serve with distinction until November 18, 1943, when he was readmitted to the hospital on Tulagi. His health had deteriorated once again, and soon the tired young officer was headed home to Boston.

To say that the popular version of the *PT-109* story served Jack Kennedy well as he transitioned into civilian life and pursued a career in politics would, of course, be a gross understatement. On January 20, 1961, John F. Kennedy became the thirty-fifth president of the United States. During his all-too-brief time in the White House, someone once asked how he had become a war hero.

"It was involuntary," Kennedy responded. "They sank my boat."

\*\*\*

American PT boats would continue to serve throughout the remainder of the Solomons campaign and operate in the littoral environments of New Guinea, the Philippines, and in many other hot spots of the Pacific War. PT crews destroyed Japanese supply barges, attacked surface ships, strafed enemy bases, rescued downed aviators, conducted scouting and security patrols, and even performed what would eventually be known as special operations missions.

PT boats inserted teams of Marine Raiders and Army Rangers onto Japanese-held islands to conduct reconnaissance and direct action raids, and often extracted them under enemy fire. For this reason today's Special Warfare Combatant-Craft Crewmen, operating their small and heavily armed speedboats in support of the US Navy's SEAL teams, trace their unit lineage directly to the daring PT crews of World War II. On a few occasions even the PT sailors themselves served as naval commandoes, going ashore in armed landing parties to destroy Japanese outposts. Along with the exploits of men like John Bulkeley, Robert Kelly, Alan Montgomery, Hugh Robinson, Charlie Tufts, Stilly Taylor, John Legg, Les Gamble, and the Searles brothers, these daring actions would add to the lore and legend of the Mosquito Fleet.

The final American victory in the bitter and desperate six-month-long fight for Guadalcanal, when the sailors of the Tulagi-based PT boats made their brave stand against the Imperial Japanese Navy and its brazen destroyer squadrons, was a historic watershed that altered the course of the Pacific War. The Japanese Navy had been dealt a stunning blow at the Battle of Midway, but afterward still exerted a great deal of control over the Pacific Basin. After Guadalcanal, Japan's command of the sea had been irretrievably lost and Allied victory in the Pacific War all but assured. Guadalcanal had been the true test of the American fighting sailor, proving at last that he possessed the courage, skill, and perseverance to defeat his vaunted Japanese adversary.

\*\*\*

In March 1943, the intelligence officer for Motor Torpedo Boat Flotilla One, Lieutenant Sam Savage, composed a twenty-three-page summary of combat actions involving the Tulagi PT crews between the dates of October 13, 1942, and February 2, 1943. The classified report was sent to COMSOPAC Headquarters in Nouméa, where it was reviewed by Admiral Bill Halsey's deputy commander, Vice Admiral Theodore "Ping" Wilkinson.

"It is a report of hard-fought and courageous action," Wilkinson commented. "Those involved merit the highest praise for the part they played in the destruction of enemy forces, and for their equally important success in often preventing the enemy from carrying out his mission."

The report was sent on to Pacific Fleet Headquarters in Pearl Harbor, where it was stamped with a serial number and duly logged, with mimeographed copies placed into the local CINCPAC files. A yeoman then typed a cover letter indicating the endorsement of Admiral Chester W. Nimitz and placed it along with the original report into the queue of documents requiring the admiral's signature. Once endorsed, the report would be forwarded to Washington and eventually delivered into the hands of the Chief of Naval Operations, Admiral Ernest J. King.

"Operated by courageous officers and men, they demonstrated themselves to be an important striking force," read the cover letter's closing paragraph. "Commander-in-Chief US Pacific Fleet is pleased with the performance of Motor Torpedo Boat Flotilla One and the part it played in the reduction of Guadalcanal."

Before affixing his signature in blue-black ink, Admiral Nimitz drew an arrow into the space before the word "pleased" and in his own hand inserted the word "highly."

# ACKNOWLEDGMENTS

Thank you once again to Tom McCarthy and Lee Barnes for your continued encouragement and advice. I am also indebted to Gene Brissie and the staff of Lyons Press for being so easy to work with and willing to listen to my ideas. Thanks to Cheryl, Martin, and Wendy for helping me find that one elusive word, and to Mom, Dad, Juan, Paul, Maz, and everyone in Queen Creek for always being in my corner and cheering me on. As always I must say thank you to Kathleen, not only for being the most patient and supportive of wives, but for her assistance in dealing with that most exasperating but necessary facet of the writing business: marketing.

Thank you to the staff of the National Archives and Records Administration in College Park, Maryland, for safeguarding the documents and photographs that made researching this book possible. Yours is not an easy task.

Hard-to-find photographs of PT crew members and the Tulagi PT base were obtained from PT Boats Inc. of Germantown, Tennessee, founded by James M. "Boats" Newberry. I owe thanks to the late Alyce Guthrie for her assistance.

Special thanks to Chris Nardi and the staff of the National PT Boat Museum at Battleship Cove in Fall River, Massachusetts, for being so accommodating and helpful.

# Sources

## BOOKS

Andruss, Frank J., Sr. *Building the PT Boats*. Ann Arbor, MI: Nimble Books LLC, 2009.

Boomhower, Ray E. *Richard Tregaskis: Reporting under Fire from Guadalcanal to Vietnam*. Alberquerque, NM: High Road Books, 2021.

Bulkley, Robert J., Jr. *At Close Quarters: PT Boats in the United States Navy*. Washington DC: Naval History Division, 1962.

Cave, Hugh B. *Long Were the Nights: The Story of a PT Boat Squadron in World War II*. New York: Dodd, Mead and Company, 1943.

Chun, Victor. *American PT Boats in World War II*. Atglen, PA: Schiffler Publishing Ltd., 1997.

Churchill, Winston S. *The Hinge of Fate*. Boston: Houghton Mifflin Company, 1950.

Clemens, Martin. *Alone on Guadalcanal: A Coastwatcher's Story*. Annapolis, MD: Naval Institute Press, 1998.

Dyer, George C. *The Amphibians Came to Conquer: The Story of Admiral Richmond Kelly Turner*. Washington DC: US Government Printing Office Naval History Division, 1969.

Donovan, Robert J. *PT-109: John F. Kennedy in World War II*. New York: McGraw-Hill Book Company, 1961.

Feldt, Eric A. *The Coast Watchers*. Oxford: Oxford University Press, 1979.

Frank, Richard B. *Guadalcanal: The Definitive Account of the Landmark Battle*. New York: Random House, 1990.

Griffith, Samuel B. II. *The Battle for Guadalcanal*. Philadelphia and New York: J.B. Lippincott Company, 1963.

Halsey, William Frederick. *Admiral Halsey's Story*. New York: Whittlesea House, 1947.

Heinl, Robert Debs, Jr. *Soldiers of the Sea: The US Marine Corps, 1775–1962*. Annapolis, MD: Naval Institute Press, 1962.

Herman, Arthur. *Freedom's Forge: How American Business Produced Victory in World War II*. New York: Random House, 2012.

Hornfischer, James D. *Neptune's Inferno: The US Navy at Guadalcanal*. New York: Bantam Books, 2011.

Jersey, Stanley Coleman. *Hell's Islands: The Untold Story of Guadalcanal*. College Station: Texas A&M University Press, 2008.

Johnston, Stanley. *Queen of the Flat-Tops: The USS Lexington and the Coral Sea Battle*. New York: E.P. Dutton and Company, 1942.

Jones, James. *WWII*. New York: Grosset and Dunlap, 1975.

Keresey, Dick. *PT-105*. Annapolis, MD: Naval Institute Press, 1996.

Layton, Edwin T. *And I Was There: Pearl Harbor and Midway—Breaking the Secrets*. Annapolis, MD: Naval Institute Press, 1985.

Leckie, Robert. *Helmet for My Pillow—From Parris Island to the Pacific*. New York: Random House, 1957.

London, Jack. *South Sea Tales*. New York: Macmillan Publishers, 1911.

Lord, Walter. *Lonely Vigil: Coastwatchers of the Solomons*. New York: The Viking Press, 1977.

MacArthur, Douglas. *Reminiscences of General of the Army Douglas MacArthur*. New York: McGraw-Hill, 1964.

Manchester, William. *American Caesar: Douglas MacArthur 1880–1964*. New York: Little, Brown and Company, 1978.

Morison, Samuel Eliot. *History of United States Naval Operations in World War II, Volume 3: The Rising Sun in the Pacific 1931–April 1942*. Boston: Little, Brown and Company, 1948.

———. *History of United States Naval Operations in World War II, Volume 4: Coral Sea, Midway and Submarine Actions May 1942–August 1942*. Boston: Little, Brown and Company, 1949.

———. *History of United States Naval Operations in World War II, Volume 5: The Struggle for Guadalcanal August 1942–February 1943*. Boston: Little, Brown and Company, 1949.

———. *History of United States Naval Operations in World War II, Volume 6: Breaking the Bismarcks Barrier July 1942–May 1944*. Boston: Little, Brown and Company, 1950.

———. *The Two Ocean War: A Short History of the United States Navy in the Second World War*. Boston: Little, Brown and Company, 1963.

Nelson, Curtis L. *Hunters in the Shallows: A History of the PT Boat*. Washington, DC: Brassey's, 1998.

Potter, E. B. *Nimitz*. Annapolis, MD: Naval Institute Press, 1976.

Rottman, Gordon L. *US Patrol Torpedo Boats, World War II*. Oxford: Osprey Publishing, 2008.

Searles, John M. *Tales of Tulagi: Memoirs of World War II*. New York: Vantage Press, 1992.

Simmons, Walter. *Joe Foss, Flying Marine*. New York: E.P. Dutton & Co., 1943.

Smith, George W. *MacArthur's Escape: John "Wild Man" Bulkeley and the Rescue of an American Hero*. St Paul, MN: Zenith Press, 2005.

Stillwell, Paul. *Battleship Commander: The Life of Vice Admiral Willis A. Lee Jr.* Annapolis, MD: Naval Institute Press, 2021.

Taussig, Betty Carney. *A Warrior for Freedom*. Manhattan, KS: Sunflower University Press, 1995.

Toland, John. *But Not in Shame: The Six Months After Pearl Harbor*. New York: Random House, 1961.

———. *The Rising Sun: The Decline and Fall of the Japanese Empire 1936–1945.* New York: Random House, 1970.

Toll, Ian W. *The Conquering Tide: War in the Pacific Islands 1942–1944.* New York: W.W. Norton and Company, 2015.

Tregaskis, Richard. *Guadalcanal Diary.* Garden City, NY: Blue Ribbon Books, 1943.

———. *John F. Kennedy and PT-109.* New York: Random House, 1962.

Ugaki, Matome, Donald Goldstein, Katherine V. Dillon, Masataka Chihaya. *Fading Victory: The Diary of Admiral Matome Ugaki 1941–1945.* Pittsburgh, PA: University of Pittsburgh Press, 1991.

Vandegrift, A. A., and Robert B. Asprey. *Once a Marine: The Memoirs of General A.A. Vandegrift, USMC.* New York: W.W. Norton and Company, 1964.

White, Robb. *Torpedo Run.* New York: Doubleday, 1962.

# PERIODICALS

"Bart J. Connolly, Earned Navy Cross As Skipper." *Boston Globe*, September 10, 1997.

Domalgalski, John J. "Disaster at Cavite." *Naval History Magazine*, United States Naval Institute, December 2018, Vol. 32/6.

Hersey, John. "PT Squadron in the South Pacific." *Life Magazine*, May 10, 1943, 74–87.

Jepson, George D. "Clark Faulkner: Recollections of a Pearl Harbor Survivor." *Quarterdeck Maritime Literature and Art Review*, Autumn 2021, 15–21.

Lilly, Michael A. "How Nimitz Coped." *Naval History Magazine*, United States Naval Institute, February 2022, Vol. 36/1.

McGrath, Jamie. "Peacetime Naval Rearmament 1933–1939." *Naval War College Review*, Spring 2019, Vol 72/2.

O'Donnell, John, and Doris Fleeson. "Navy Asks Help of Speedboat Designers." *New York Daily News*, June 9, 1938.

Pedroncelli, Rich. "JFK—A PT Skipper Remembers." *Naval History Magazine*, United States Naval Institute, December 1999, Vol. 13/6.

Shribman, David. "Recalling Another Voice on What the US Fights For." *Boston Globe*, January 28, 2003, 28.

Tanaka, Raizo. "Japan's Losing Struggle for Guadalcanal." *Proceedings*, United States Naval Institute, July 1956 Vol. 8/7/641.

Toler, John T. "Our Hero of the South Pacific: PT Boat Commanders Faced Extreme Odds during WWII." *Fauquier Times*, May 29, 2017.

Wukovits, John. "Dear Admiral Halsey." *Naval History Magazine*, United States Naval Institute, April 2016, Vol. 30/2.

# WEBSITES

"Admiral Ernest J. King—Chief of Naval Operations, 1942." Naval History and Heritage Command. https://www.history.navy.mil/about-us/leadership/director/directors-corner/h-grams/h-gram-008/h-008-5.html. Accessed March 30, 2022.

"Combined Fleet Operations Order Number 1." Pearl Harbor History Associates. http://ibiblio.org/pha/monos/152/152app01.html. Accessed March 23, 2022.

Fleming, Thomas. "The Truth about JFK and His PT Boat's Collision with a Japanese Destroyer in WWII." Historynet. https://www.historynet.com/john-f-kennedys-pt-109-disaster/. Accessed November 20, 2022.

"IJN Submarine I-3 Tabular Record of Movement." Imperial Japanese Navy Page. http://www.combinedfleet.com/I-3.htm. Accessed October 7, 2022.

"Japanese Monograph No. 98 (Navy)," Southeast Area Naval Operations Part I, May 42–February 43. Prepared by Second Demobilization Bureau 1947–1949." http://www.ibiblio.org/hyperwar/Japan/Monos/pdfs/JM-98_SEAreaNavalOps/JM-98.pdf. Accessed July 26, 2022.

"Japanese Naval and Merchant Shipping Losses During World War II by All Causes. Joint Army-Navy Assessment Committee (JANAC), February 1947." https://www.ibiblio.org/hyperwar/Japan/IJN/JANAC-Losses/index.html#fwd. Accessed July 26, 2022.

"Memories of My PT Boat Duty," Save the PT Boat Inc. https://www.savetheptboatinc.com/pdf-doc/BryantLarsonrecalls.pdf. Accessed October 16, 2022.

"NavSource Online, Motor Torpedo Boat Photo Archive." http://www.navsource.org/archives/12/05idx.htm. Accessed March–December 2022.

"Night Combat." The Pacific War Online Encyclopedia. http://pwencycl.kgbudge.com/N/i/Night_Combat.htm. Accessed July 21, 2022.

"Nimitz Gray Book: War Plans and Files of the Commander-in-Chief, Pacific Fleet." American Naval Records Society. http://www.ibiblio.org/anrs/graybook.html. Accessed March–December 2022.

"Pacific Wrecks." https://pacificwrecks.com. Accessed March–December 2022.

"Tulagi Club, Tulagi British Solomon Islands, Rules 1939." National Library of Australia. https://nla.gov.au/nla.obj-52870653/view?partId=nla.obj-105758363#page/n0/mode/1up. Accessed March 23, 2022.

"United States Navy Casualties—World War 2, United States Navy at War." Navy History. https://www.naval-history.net/WW2UScasaaDB-USNbyNameH.htm. Accessed November 12, 2022.

"US Navy Personnel Strength, 1775 to Present." Naval History and Heritage Command. https://www.history.navy.mil/research/library/online-reading-room/title-list-alphabetically/u/usn-personnel-strength.html. Accessed May 10, 2022.

"US Ship Force Levels, 1886 to Present." Naval History and Heritage Command. https://www.history.navy.mil/research/histories/ship-histories/us-ship-force-levels.html#1938. Accessed May 10, 2022.

# VIDEO

*Giant Killers: Story of the Elco PT Boats.* Electric Boat Company, Elco Naval Division, Periscope Films, 1945. Accessed August 2, 2022.

*Great Ships: The PT Boats.* The History Channel, A&E Television Networks, 2008. Accessed August 1, 2022.

# ORAL HISTORIES
Keresey, Richard (MTBRON 2) interviewed May 3, 1993, Admiral Nimitz Museum and University of North Texas Oral History Collection.

Land, Emory Scott (VADM USN) interviewed January 30, 1963, by John T. Mason, Oral History Research Office, Columbia University.

O'Keefe, John (MTBRON 5) interviewed August 10, 2006, by Edward Metzler, Admiral Nimitz Historic Site, Center for Pacific War Studies, National Museum of the Pacific War.

Robinson, Hugh M. (CAPT USN) interviewed February 21, 1997, by William J. Alexander, Admiral Nimitz Museum and University of North Texas Oral History Collection.

Sackett, Albert M. (RADM USN) interviewed October 3, 1997, by William J. Alexander, Admiral Nimitz Museum and University of North Texas Oral History Collection.

Stockdale, Alphonsis (MTRBON 1) interviewed December 8, 2001, by Jerry Wens, Admiral Nimitz Historic Site, Center for Pacific War Studies, National Museum of the Pacific War.

# OTHER SOURCES

*Building the Navy's Bases in World War II: History of the Bureau of Yards and Docks and the Civil Engineer Corps, 1940–1946.* Washington, DC: US Government Printing Office, 1947.

"Command History, US Naval Advanced Base Guadalcanal, 1942 August–1945 August." Naval Historical Collection Archives, US Naval War College, Newport, Rhode Island, 1945.

FMFRP 12–46. *Advanced Base Operations in Micronesia*, Marine Corps Combat Development Command, Quantico, Virginia, 1992.

"Hearings before the Committee on Appropritations, House of Representatives, Seventy-Fifth Congress, Third Session on the Second Deficiency Bill for 1938." Washington, DC: US Government Printing Office, 1938.

Miller, John Jr. *United States Army in World War Two, The War in the Pacific, Guadalcanal: The First Offensive.* Center of Military History, US Army. Washington, DC: US Government Printing Office, 1949.

"Miscellaneous Actions in the South Pacific, August 8, 1942–January 22, 1943." Office of Naval Intelligence Combat Narrative Series, 1943. Department of the Navy, Naval History and Heritage Command.

*Motor Torpedo Boat Manual, February 1943, US Navy.* Washington, DC: US Government Printing Office, 1943.

National Archives Record Group 24: *Records of the Bureau of Naval Personnel 1798–2007, Log Books of US Navy Ships ca. 1801–1947.*

National Archives Record Group 38: *Records of the Office of Chief of Naval Operations 1875–2006, World War II War Diaries, Other Operational Records and Histories, ca. 1/1/1942 - ca. 6/1/1946, Personal Interviews*, 1638–54.

———. *Records of the Office of Chief of Naval Operations, Records Relating to Naval Activity During World War II, WWII Action and Operational Reports MTB Flotilla to MTBRON 7, 10/24/44.*

———. *World War II War Diaries, Other Operational Records and Histories,* compiled 01/01/1942—06/01/1946, documenting the period 09/01/1939—05/30/1946. United States Naval Administration in World War II, Commander-in-Chief Pacific Fleet, Motor Torpedo Boat Squadrons.

———. *World War II War Diaries, Other Operational Records and Histories,* compiled 01/01/1942—06/01/1946, documenting the period 09/01/1939—05/30/1946. Report of Night Action, TF-64–11/14–15/42–3rd Battle of Savo Island.

———. *World War II War Diaries, Other Operational Records and Histories,* compiled 01/01/1942—06/01/1946, documenting the period 09/01/1939—05/30/1946. War Diary, USS Washington 11/1–30/42.

NAVSHIPS 250-222-1. *Know Your PT Boat.* Technical Publication No. 9, July 1945. Department of the Navy, Bureau of Ships, 1945.

Parker, Frederick D. *A Priceless Advantage: U.S. Navy Communication Intelligence and the Battles of Coral Sea, Midway and the Aleutians. Series IV: World War II, Volume 5.* Center for Cryptologic History, National Security Agency, Fort Meade, MD, 2017.

Photographic Archive, WWII PT Boats Museum and Archives, Germantown, Tennessee.

"Researching Japanese War Crimes Records—Introductory Essays." National Archives and Records Administration for the Nazi War Crimes and Japanese Imperial Government Records Interagency Working Group, Washington, DC, 2006.

"The Attack on Lae and Salamaua March 10, 1942." *Early Raids in the Pacific Ocean.* Office of Naval Intelligence Combat Narrative Series, 1943. Department of the Navy, Naval History and Heritage Command.

"The Raids on the Marshall and Gilbert Islands February 1, 1942." *Early Raids in the Pacific Ocean.* Office of Naval Intelligence Combat Narrative Series, 1943. Department of the Navy, Naval History and Heritage Command.

"USS *Estes* AGC-12 Cruise 1959." *US Navy Cruise Books 1918–2009.* Department of the Navy, Naval History and Heritage Command.

# INDEX